HIGH SPEED DIETS

HIGH SPEED DIETS

British Library Cataloguing in Publication Data

Slimming Magazine's High Speed Diets
1. Reducing diets – Recipes
641.5'635   RM222.2
ISBN 0 7278 2027 3

First published in Great Britain in 1983 by Severn House Publishers
Ltd, 4 Brook Street, London W1Y 1AA

© Slimming Magazine, S.M. Publications Limited 1983

Editor: Sybil Greatbatch

Writer: Gaynor Hagan

Diets: Joyce Hughes, Glynis McGuinness, Jenny Salmon
Illustrations: Josephine Martin
Photography: Martin Brigdale
Design: June Lancaster
Stylist: Gina Carminati
Props: One Major Meal: cutlery/Harvey Nicholls. The Metabolic:
tray/Casa Fina, Covent Garden; dishes and bowls/Habitat. Big Bowlful:
bowls/Habitat. Slim and Sin: dishes/Harvey Nicholls. Big Brother:
scales/Bush and Hall, 40 Theobalds Road, WC1. High Fibre: dishes
and plates/David Mellor, Covent Garden. Vegetarian: dishes and
plates/Casa Pupo.

Phototypeset by Tarmigan Publicity Ltd, London EC1.

Printed in Great Britain by Anchor Press Ltd, and bound by Wm.
Brendon & Son Ltd, both of Tiptree, Essex.

CONTENTS

INTRODUCTION

You want to lose weight and you want to lose it fast. This is the book that will help you do it. If you are the red-blooded slimmer we take you for, you will secretly be hoping that these pages contain the magic wand that will reduce your weight back to normal before you can say 'diet'. There isn't a diet in the world that can do that. This book does, however, offer the next best thing. Every diet in it guarantees that you *will* shed excess weight at the fastest possible rate that your body is capable of losing it. All the diets are based on an intake of 1,000 calories or less a day. Although this is a calorie allowance at which you cannot fail to lose weight, and lose it speedily, you are not in for a spell of deprivation and tears. Check through carefully and you are sure to find one or more diets that seem absolutely tailor-made for you and your lifestyle; that allow you to eat when and how you wish; even, in some cases, as much as you wish.

The secret? Calories. Most people think they know all about calories, but there is a surprising amount of confusion attached to this subject. Once you get your head clear on calories, you will understand why all successful dieting – and all successful diets! – depend on reducing the number of calories you consume. You will also grasp the cheering fact that reducing your calorie intake does not necessarily mean reducing the quantity of food you eat to penitential levels and that dieting does not spell punishment.

So what exactly is a calorie?

It is simply a unit of energy. Our bodies use energy all the time, whether we are sleeping or waking. Even if you never got out of bed, or never moved from the chair in which you were reading this, the quiet efficiency with which your body keeps your blood circulating, your lungs breathing and your heart beating would be burning up about one calorie a minute. (If you haven't already done the sum, that's 1,440 calories in each 24 hours). The rate at which our bodies burn calories in basic self-maintenance is known as the basal metabolic rate or BMR. Some people have a high BMR and burn up calories a little faster; others have a slower BMR and use slightly fewer calories in staying alive. Add to this the number of additional calories used in activities and it is estimated that the average man burns up from 2,500 to 3,500 calories a day; and the average woman burns up from 1,750 to 2,500 calories a day. Now, the body cannot manufacture its own energy. The calories needed to stay alive and fuel all activity come from food and drink. All food – whether nutritious or 'junk' – and nearly all drinks contain calories. In other words, whether it's bursting with vitamins and nutrients, or absolutely valueless from a nutritional point of view, every mouthful of food you eat and nearly every sip you drink is also providing energy fuel for the body to burn up *or* – and this is the bad news – *to store as fat.*

People who get the ratio right and consume no more calories than their bodies burn up every day are the ones who stay at their correct weight. But, as most of us know, it is extraordinarily easy to eat *more* calories than we burn up. No way has yet been found of changing the prime physical law that if you eat more calories than your body needs, it will store them as fat.

There is a widely held theory that this ability of the body to store energy reserves in the form of fat deposits was an essential part of primitive man's survival kit. In easy-hunting good times, our ancestors ate a lot so as deliberately to have some nice fat deposits handy for lean times. When hunting became difficult and food scarce, the fat deposits got used up to give him energy to keep going. Though most of us wish this particular part of our human heritage had not been handed down so freely, there is no doubt that it still works both ways. If you are overweight, and start eating fewer calories than you burn up every day, your body will call on its own fat reserves to make up the energy difference and keep the energy balance right. *And you will get slim.*

How many calories is 'fewer' calories?

The majority of men and most women will lose weight automatically if calorie intake is fixed at 1,500 a day; but weight loss will be relatively slow for anyone who is burning up just 2,000 calories daily. It takes 3,500 calories to make or lose one pound of body fat. By reducing her intake to 1,500 calories the average woman creates a situation where her body will be calling on 500 calories' worth of fat per day to make up the difference. This amounts to a total of 3,500 calories a week – and a weight loss of just one pound. Though this is better than nothing, few people would consider such a relatively small loss very encouraging! If, however, you are heavily overweight, very active, or one of the lucky people who have a high basal metabolic rate, then you may well burn up more than 2,000 calories a day.

Intensive research and direct experience working with slimmers over the years has shown *Slimming Magazine* experts that the ideal calorie figure at which a diet should be set for maximum weight loss over the long term is that of 1,000 calories a day. This is the calorie allowance that allows all the factors that should be integral to a successful diet: a full complement of all the nutrients needed for health; variety and flexibility. You may safely follow any one of the 1,000 calories a day diets in this book for as long as you wish. However, to get you going and cheer you on with super-fast results, we have also included a number of very-low-calorie diets: the Superfast Starters. These offer a strict 850 to 950 calories a day and will get any diet off to a flying start. They are also an excellent way to lose those few obstinate pounds that settle around the waistline of an otherwise normal figure; and the bulges that collect after a good holiday. These Superfast Starters are intended to be followed for no longer than two weeks. For a longer-term weight loss programme, you should choose one of the 1,000 calorie diets which we have called Fast Followers. Should you wish to increase your daily calorie allowance up to 1,500 calories "Extras for Big Losers" on page 20 tells you how you may safely do so without wrecking your diet plans!

Which diet to choose?

Daily calorie allowance is not the only factor that governs successful dieting. There is also the very important Human Factor! If dieting were only a question of cutting down on calories, the world would be full of slim people – but also there is the question of what many people call willpower.

We believe that the amount of actual willpower that is necessary in a dieting programme is a debatable point. There is no doubt that many slimmers make it extra difficult for themselves by trying to make too drastic a change in all their eating habits and become saints overnight, and that this can place far too great a strain on the will to win. For example, if you are a person who likes to eat little and often instead of having three well-spaced meals, it is wishful thinking to suppose that willpower alone will get you through those long empty mornings and afternoons without so much as a nibble; or maybe you are one of those many people who can get by on very little food all day so long as you can eat well in the evening. A diet that forces you to eat a large breakfast and a simple little supper could become unendurably hard. Research has shown that nowadays there are almost as many eating patterns as there are people who want to slim down. There are nibblers and three-meals-a-dayers; breakfast eaters and breakfast loathers; slimmers who prefer to be told exactly what to eat and when to eat it, and those who can't bear not to have some choice. So that is why there are so many different diets in this book. It makes super slimming sense to choose the diet that slips effortlessly into your own way of eating, and your own way of living. The diet you keep is the one that you find *easy* to keep to. You will certainly find yours here.

DIETING AND NUTRITION

What exactly is good nutrition? This question is of the greatest importance to anyone who is planning to shed weight by cutting down on food quantities. Naturally, it is vital to ensure that although you are eating less, you are still getting all the protein, vitamins and minerals your body requires for good health. This is neither as difficult nor as complicated as you may think. All foods supply us with calories. Some foods, like fats and sugar, contain a great many. Others, such as fruit and vegetables, contain relatively few. Nearly all foods contain at least some of the nutrients that are essential for the repair and restoration of body tissue and functioning and are necessary for good health. It just so happens that on the whole – with just a few exceptions – the very high-calorie foods are precisely those which contain least nutrients; whereas low and medium-calorie foods tend to be rich in the nutrients required for body health and maintenance. Let us repeat, since all foods contain calories you can shed weight simply by cutting your calorie intake to 1,500 calories or under daily. Theoretically, you could still lose weight even if you chose to take all your calories in the form of sugar. Thirty heaped teaspoons of sugar would supply you with 1,000 calories; and you would certainly lose weight. You would not, however, remain in good health for very long; since sugar is a food which contains no nutrients at all. In the same way, you could lose weight merely by counting the calories carefully, and eating nothing but 'junk' foods – foods rich in fat and sugar but very little else; but again, your good health would be at risk after a while. Naturally, nobody who is seriously concerned with successful weight loss is going to try to do anything of the kind; but those who believe that dieting necessarily means that you are depriving your body of essential nutrients, and therefore imagine it necessary to take large doses of vitamin supplements are – in the opinion of modern nutritionists – almost as confused as those who think it doesn't in the least matter *what* you eat.

The secret of good nutrition lies in variety. Indeed, nutritional deficiencies are virtually unknown in the West simply because we select our daily menus from such an immense variety of foods. What one food lacks in the way of vitamins and minerals, another supplies. Nutritional requirements are usually given in daily terms because this happens to be the most convenient way of expressing them; but this does not mean that you have to take daily doses of every vitamin and mineral there is in order to remain healthy. It is now known that the body can, and does, store all nutrients for a greater or lesser amount of time, so that no single one is needed on a daily basis – not even Vitamin C, for example. Although this vitamin is not stored by the body for a very long period, nutritionists consider that it would take weeks or even months for your body to show any sign of deficiency, even if you never ate a single fruit or vegetable. And it takes only one orange every other day or normal amounts of vegetables to ensure that you get your full Vitamin C requirement. Other vitamins, like Vitamins A and D for instance, are stored for quite lengthy periods of time. Vitamin A, essential for correct functioning of eyes and necessary to help protect the body – particularly the mucous membranes – from infection, is found in eggs, milk, butter, cheese and liver. Just 4oz liver a week would give your body its full requirement, even if you ate none of the other foods containing it. Vitamin D is synthesised by the action of sunlight on the skin and it also occurs in eggs, milk, cheese and butter. The B vitamins occur in wholegrain cereals, liver, fish, nuts and many other everyday foods. Provided your diet is based on a wide selection of different foods, it is almost impossible to go short of any essential nutrient.

Protein is undoubtedly an essential. It is the major component of the human body and we need a constant supply to build and repair body cells. However, the relatively huge amounts of protein once thought necessary are now known to have been over-estimated. Advanced nutritional research indicates that a daily protein intake of 40 grams is sufficient and you may need even less. As a general rule, 275ml/ ½ pint of milk and a portion of fish, meat or cheese will supply this minimum protein requirement.

You need have no fear in following any of the diets in this book that you are going to go short of any nutrient essential for good health. Each and every one has been nutritionally designed to supply all the vitamins, minerals and protein you need. Even the very low-calorie Superfast Starters are well-balanced nutritionally. The main reason we do not recommend they be followed for more than two weeks is simply that a calorie intake of under 1,000 a day is quite difficult to stick to for long; and if you are leading a normally active life, over the long term there is no great advantage in dieting at below 1,000 calories a day.

You may safely follow a 1,000 calories a day diet for as long as you wish. If, however, you find such a diet too strict, there is a chart of extra foods that may safely be incorporated into your weight-loss diet programme up to a maximum of 1,500 calories a day. In selecting extra foods (and this applies whether you are strictly following the directions in this book, or for one reason or another 'breaking' your diet), follow the basic nutritionally sound rule of variety in foods. Vary your meals each day, and include some fresh fruit and vegetables, protein-containing foods such as lean meat, poultry, fish, eggs, cottage or curd cheese and skimmed milk in your overall weekly diet. Wholegrain cereals and brown rice will provide the fibre needed to prevent constipation and ensure good digestion. If you are vegetarian, include pulses such as peas, beans and lentils in your menus. These are all good protein-containing foods.

Finally a word about 'junk' foods. As we have said, 'junk' foods tend to be high in calories and low in nutrients; but this is not to say that they will hurt you or poison you (as some fanatics have claimed!) if you eat them occasionally. But don't use up too many of your calorie allowance on foods that give you little *but* calories. If you think you'll go mad without that packet of crisps or bar of sugary goo, by all means have them from time to time if they are included in your calorie count. It is best not to allow strong desires for these foods to build up into an enormous binge. You will probably find, though, that once you've embarked on a healthy eating plan, your longings for some foods will gradually diminish.

YOU AND YOUR WEIGHT
How much should you weigh?
All 'ideal weight' charts are based on the statistical weight averages of healthy people. This means that you must allow yourself a certain latitude in estimating your own ideal weight against that given for your height and frame size. The chart given here is a useful guide to what you should weigh; but it is only a *guide* and the figures give the average weight for medium-framed people. Your own individual weight could be up to 7lb more if you have a big-boned large frame; or up to 7lb less if you have a fine-boned, small frame.

Though bone structure and size is important (people with big bones *do* weigh more, and take more flesh/fat and muscle to cover them nicely), for practical purposes it is best to forget about the size of your bones. Look instead at your skeleton's *spread*. Neat and narrow body structures call for less covering than rangy bones; but if you aim for a body that looks good and feels firm without any excess flab, you can't go wrong whatever your bone structure.

If you are heavily overweight, be prepared for a surprise once you are halfway towards your ideal weight. Many a formerly fat person who truly believed that big bones were half the trouble has been amazed to discover quite a small-boned structure emerging as excess poundage is shed! And some – though less often – find they appear a bit bony if they achieve the weight given for a medium-frame figure; and look better with four or five pounds more.

While we're on the subject of 'ideal' weight, let's dispose of another myth: the one that believes that middle-age spread is inevitable, and that people – particularly women – are bound to put on weight as they grow older. Middle-age spread comes from exactly the same cause as any other form of excess fat: that is, eating more calories than your body can burn up in energy. Many people tend to become less active and more sedentary as they grow older. The best remedy for a thickening waistline and bulges below is a sensible low-calorie diet, together with some active daily exercise like a brisk walk. Specific exercises to tone up muscles can be of great benefit, too.

When should you weigh yourself?
Many people following a strict diet are understandably tempted to weigh themselves every day. Please don't – because you may disappointedly find that the scales don't register a loss. The reason is that (in slim and overweight people) body weight fluctuates all the time. Most people, for example, are 3 or 4lb heavier at night than they were in the morning; and unless you have starved all day (not advisable!) you will probably find this is true of you. The heavier evening weight is partly because of food eaten earlier; and partly because after you have absorbed this food into your body cells – especially the carbohydrate part of it – you retain some additional water. During the night, your body will continue burning up that food and getting rid of it. Some will evaporate as carbon dioxide and

water in your breath; and some as water in your urine the following morning. This is only one example of the many minor fluctuations in weight that each individual body undergoes – but it illustrates why it can be so disheartening to the slimmer who steps on the scales too often. The most accurate way to check how the fight against fat is progressing is to weigh yourself once a week at exactly the same time of the day. However, one word of warning: many women retain more water in the body cells just before a period, so the scales can very temporarily 'lie' at this time.

If you know you have been following a strict diet without 'cheating' and the scales show that weight has unaccountably not gone down, or – worse – shows an increase of a few pounds, it is more than possible that pre-menstrual water retention is the reason. This is nothing to worry about. The actual *fat* you have lost from your body cells will show up a few days later.

How to weigh yourself

1 Make sure that your bathroom scales stand evenly. A slightly sloping surface literally tips the scales – sometimes in your favour, sometimes against it. They also need to stand on a hard surface; so if your bathroom is carpeted, put a piece of wood under your scales.
2 If you are not absolutely sure your scales are accurate, weigh yourself on a balance scale at the chemist. Then make a careful note of the difference so that you can make allowances. For example, if you find your scales add 2lb to your correct weight, take this into every calculation in future.
3 Stand on the scales, with your weight evenly balanced on both feet and as close to the centre of the scale as possible.
4 It is best to weigh yourself unclothed; but if you do wear any garments, make sure you wear similar ones each time. Do not wear shoes.

HOW MUCH WEIGHT WILL YOU LOSE?

Despite the exaggerated promises made by many get-slim-quick diets, there simply isn't a diet in the world that can promise you a *specific* amount of weight loss. On any of the diets in this book you will lose weight as fast as it is possible for you to lose it. That *is* a promise! But exactly how *much* weight you will lose each week depends on several factors.

Many people, particularly those with a considerable amount of weight to lose, report quite dramatic weight losses in the first week or two of following a strict diet. This can happen because along with the fat you are losing a store of excess water. However, this rate of weight shedding will probably slow down to a far more usual 2-3lb a week later on. Heavily overweight people can also lose weight faster initially simply because, being so heavy, they burn up more calories in moving their bodies about from place to place – just as you burn more calories if you walk back from the shops carrying heavy baskets

WHAT A WOMAN SHOULD WEIGH
without shoes, allowing 2 to 3lb (or about 1kg) for light indoor clothing

Height		Medium Frame	
4-ft-10	1.47m	7-st-8	48kg
4-ft-11	1.50m	7-st-11	49.5kg
5-ft-0	1.52m	8-st-0	51kg
5-ft-1	1.55m	8-st-3	52.5kg
5-ft-2	1.57m	8-st-7	54kg
5-ft-3	1.60m	8-st-9	55kg
5-ft-4	1.63m	8-st-12	56.5kg
5-ft-5	1.65m	9-st-1	57.5kg
5-ft-6	1.68m	9-st-8	61kg
5-ft-7	1.70m	9-st-9	61.5kg
5-ft-8	1.73m	9-st-12	62.5kg
5-ft-9	1.75m	10-st-2	64.5kg
5-ft-10	1.78m	10-st-5	66kg
5-ft-11	1.80m	10-st-10	68kg
6-ft-0	1.83m	11-st-0	70kg

WHAT A MAN SHOULD WEIGH
without shoes, allowing 2 to 3lb (or about 1kg) for light indoor clothing

Height		Medium Frame	
5-ft-1	1.55m	8-st-11	56kg
5-ft-2	1.57m	9-st-1	57.5kg
5-ft-3	1.60m	9-st-4	59kg
5-ft-4	1.63m	9-st-7	60.5kg
5-ft-5	1.65m	9-st-10	62kg
5-ft-6	1.68m	10-st-1	64kg
5-ft-7	1.70m	10-st-5	66kg
5-ft-8	1.73m	10-st-9	67.5kg
5-ft-9	1.75m	10-st-13	69.5kg
5-ft-10	1.78m	11-st-4	72kg
5-ft-11	1.80m	11-st-8	73.5kg
6-ft-0	1.83m	11-st-12	75.5kg
6-ft-1	1.85m	12-st-3	77.5kg
6-ft-2	1.88m	12-st-8	80kg
6-ft-3	1.90m	13-st-0	82.5kg

full of goods than you would if you walked back empty handed (see the section on exercise). The amount of weight you lose also depends on how active you are. Physically active people burn more calories and lose weight faster than those who are relatively inactive.

As a general rule, the more overweight you are, the more rapidly you shed weight when you start dieting. During a prolonged period of dieting, however, the body gradually adjusts itself to its lowered calorie intake. Most dieters who have lost considerable amounts of weight tend to find the last stone difficult to shift. Similarly, people who have only a few pounds of excess weight to lose often find these extraordinarily stubborn. A week or two on one of the Superfast Starter diets will prove invaluable in such cases.

Finally, no matter how much or how little weight you wish to lose, there is one factor which cannot be ignored. This is the human genius for self-deception! Not only is it fatally easy to forget all about that extra chocolate bar (around 300 calories!) or the couple of biscuits eaten at elevenses (about 150 calories!) – it is also too easy to start getting careless about exact weights and measurements of the foods your diet allows. One of the reasons that so many diets appear to work so well to begin with and then get written off as 'no good after all' is that slimmers who embark on a long-term diet invariably weigh and measure carefully and follow the diet with strict accuracy to start with. However, as time goes by, the initial enthusiasm very often wanes, and a little bit of slapdash guesswork comes in here and there. Unfortunately guesswork is seldom if ever accurate, and errors are invariably on the generous side. To give you an example: in a recent test, several slimmers who had been following a diet for many weeks were asked to measure by eye alone and cut an ounce of cheese. Their guesswork 'ounces' weighed up to twice as much – two ounces – on the scales. Had they eaten their pieces of cheese, they would unknowingly have doubled their calorie count and consumed not the estimated 120 calories for one ounce of cheese but up to 240 calories! Mistakes like this are easy to make; and even two or three of them in a day can add up to a very great number of extra, unsuspected calories. If you are serious about shedding weight on a regular and satisfactory basis, it cannot be emphasised enough that *every* calorie counts.

SPEED UP TACTICS
What works and what doesn't
Slimming is a subject around which myths, fads and fancies gather like so many bees around honey. In this chapter, we discuss some popular theories and bring you the latest scientific and nutritional research findings.

'The less you eat, the faster you lose'
Although specialists in obesity clinics are known to put some heavily obese patients on minimal calories – 350 a day or so – this is only

ever done under the strictest medical supervision. For the ordinary person leading a normal life, it can be damaging to health to attempt to diet on near-starvation levels like these. Furthermore, very low calorie intake does *not* speed up weight loss. There comes a point of diminishing return in calorie reduction. The direct principle of 'the less you eat, the faster you lose' ceases to apply at levels much below 750 calories a day. When people restrict themselves to only a few hundred calories a day for prolonged periods there is a tendency for the basal metabolic rate to change and slow down. So it has been generally found that starvation or near-starvation does not produce appreciably faster weight-loss results than strict diets of from 750 to 1,000 calories daily. For practical purposes, 1,000 calories a day is the strictest allowance you need consider; though in the short term, a diet offering slightly less than this can be useful to give an initial boost to a weight loss programme or to get rid of a few obstinate pounds.

'Food is more fattening at some times of the day than it is at others'

There is just a tiny grain of truth here, but hardly enough for it to matter. Strictly speaking, the best way to eat your calorie allowance so as to speed up weight loss is in the form of about five little snacks, spread out at intervals through the day; and the *least* helpful way is to eat it in the form of one big meal just before you settle down to a sedentary evening.

The reason for this is that after a meal the body's metabolic rate speeds up and burns up calories at an appreciably faster rate. This effect lasts for an hour or two and tails off gradually over the next few hours. So if you have your first meal early in the morning and space your other meals out at two to three-hourly intervals during the rest of the day, your body will be burning calories at this slightly faster rate for most of your waking hours. This means, of course, that exercise or any other physical activity performed within these after-meal periods burns up more calories per minute than it would if performed several hours after a meal.

The key question is how much difference in real terms this makes? How much real advantage do you gain from eating little and often, and spreading your calorie allowance through the busy day? Correspondingly, how much advantage do you lose if you save most of your calories for one big meal in the evening? How 'fattening' are those after-dark calories?

The scientific indications are that both gains and disadvantages are modest. There is the factor of how much your metabolism speeds up after eating to be considered, and this depends on how much you eat. The larger the meal, the higher the speed-up rate, and vice versa. Research has not yet come up with cast-iron figures, but the indications are that after a really substantial meal, the metabolic rate might well speed up by as much as 20 per cent; but after a small meal, or snack (such as a dieter's meal of 200 calories) the rate is much lower – probably only around 5 per cent. It is a case of swings and roundabouts. Eating little and often gives a longer but relatively lower metabolic speed-up rate. Eating a large meal – no matter at what time of the day or evening – gives a shorter but relatively higher speed-up rate. It may well be that the 'over eater', the person who consumes *three* large meals a day, gains most advantage from this metabolic factor; but the gains are dubious! No dieter can afford to eat several substantial meals in a day; and whatever timing pattern you follow for your meals, you won't lose weight if you overstep your calorie allowance.

Nutritionist Derek Miller of London University, who has done a great deal of scientific research in this field, emphasises that science has not yet come up with a definitive answer to the question of exact difference in calorie expenditure; but his educated guess is that the dieter who eats little-and-often throughout the day probably burns up something in the region of 100 calories a day more than the evening eater. In terms of weight loss, this estimated increase in calorie expenditure would take about five weeks to produce the loss of one extra pound of body fat. This is cheering news if you happen to be a person who much prefers eating at the end of the day. Calories after dark do not make you fat! The only way to put on weight is to eat more calories than your body can burn. And the only way to lose weight is to eat fewer calories than your body burns; so once again the conclusion is that the *number* of calories you consume far outweighs any other factor in determining how quickly you shed weight. Provided you keep within your dieting calorie allowance, you cannot fail to lose weight, no matter at what time you eat your meals, whether they are individually large meals or small ones. On the other hand, if you find it easy and comfortable to switch from the big-meal-at-night habit to several smaller ones during the day, you will gain the additional advantage that any physical activity you engage in – like walking, for example – will burn up extra calories.

'Exercise helps you slim'

The short answer is yes, it does. But you don't have to rush off and book a session on the squash court or make dismal vows to do a regular keep-fit class or go jogging. Exercise does not necessarily mean sport. Indeed those 'experts' who do calorie sums that prove you have to run from London to Brighton to burn off the calories in a good meal have a lot to answer for. Confusing equations like this encourage the slothful to settle back in the armchair with a quiet sigh! Even the charts showing how many calories you can burn off in activities like playing squash or swimming a couple of lengths often tend to be discouraging rather than inspiring. It is easy to conclude that a depressingly large amount of exercise is needed to achieve a significant increase in overall calorie expenditure.

16

If you drop the word exercise from your vocabulary altogether for a moment and start thinking in terms of physical activity instead, the picture become much more optimistic. Physical activity is a term that embraces *all* bodily movement. Every single movement your body makes burns up *some* of the energy supplied by the calories in the foods you have eaten, or in the fat your body has stored. Slow movements that use relatively few muscles and little effort – like ironing, driving a car, or standing and shuffling forward in a queue for example – require minimal extra energy. Brisk and fast movements use considerably more and therefore burn up many more calories. If you are on a slimming diet, the more calories you use up in physical activity, the more your body will have to draw on its fat reserves to provide the energy fuel it needs. So obviously increasing your energy expenditure is an excellent way of speeding up your weight loss when you are on a diet. You still don't have to book that strenuous squash court session, though – unless you want to. Just speeding up the movements you *have* to perform in the course of your everyday activities can be far more effective in the long term than an occasional breathless hour chasing after a ball.

Scientists are beginning to recognise that it is the sum total of all the movements we make in the course of a day which has the most significant effect on calorie expenditure and therefore on weight. What are the best calorie-burning movements? There are some good rules of thumb which can be applied both to everyday activities and to formal 'exercise(s)'.

The first is that they all involve moving the whole body from one place to another, as you do when you walk or run. This means that any job or chore that requires you to stand fairly still will not be burning up many extra calories, no matter how tiring it is. It also means that exercises that keep you in the same spot while you just move your limbs and body-firming disciplines like yoga, while excellent for toning up the muscles, are not necessarily the best exercises for burning up extra fat. The second rule of thumb to determine even better calorie-burning is speed. The faster the body has to move itself from one place to another, the more calories it burns. So fast walking uses up more calories than slow pacing; and the faster you walk, the more calories you burn. Jogging and running will burn up almost twice as many calories as most speeds of walking.

There is one last factor. To reach the ultimate speed rate of calorie expenditure, you need to move your whole body quickly – *upward against the force of gravity*. Running upstairs is one of the best calorie-burning exercises of all, and that is something most of us can do every day (don't attempt this, though, if you are very overweight or suffer from high blood pressure – it's *very* strenuous).

There is no question that if you make a habit of moving about more and moving faster, you will be burning up a really useful number of extra calories. If you can bring yourself to indulge in some 'real' exercise – either a sport like swimming or tennis or badminton, for example – or a truly fast brisk walk every day, not only will you be burning extra calories, you will benefit from all the hidden assets that regular exercise brings. One special benefit to a dieter is that exercise doesn't only speed up your metabolic rate while you are doing it. It also continues to keep the metabolism working at a faster rate for some time afterwards. The longer and more energetic a session of exercise, the greater the calorie-burning aftermath.

Even more important than the calorie-burning effects of exercise are the psychological benefits to the slimmer. It is now almost universally recognised in the medical world that exercise can change moods; and that a reasonably vigorous session of exercise (such as a brisk walk, or even a session of on-off running on the spot) is one of the best methods of lifting a depressed mood. It is bored, listless or depressed states of mind that are most likely to induce diet-breaking. The dieter who makes a habit of speeded-up physical activity and who exercises regularly is less likely to cheat on a diet and is therefore more likely to shed weight at a good rate.

Don't discount the value of relatively static exercises like those of yoga and isometrics. Though they do not necessarily have any marked effect on calorie expenditure, they are useful to firm up muscles, tone up the system and make you feel good. In fact, there is one isometric exercise that actually does increase your metabolic rate without your having to move from your chair: just pressing your hands together at shoulder level as hard as you can. A human guinea pig who tested the value of this for London University's nutritional research department was asked to press his hands together really hard for ten minutes, relax for ten minutes and press again for ten minutes alternately for an hour. He was found to have doubled his metabolic rate during that time; and the metabolic boost achieved during each bout of hand pressing continued through the ten minutes following. Frankly, few people could keep this exercise up for a whole hour, or even be able to sustain it for as long as ten minutes at a time; but it might be worth considering for the times when you are either in the grip of a particularly obsessive mood when you feel determined to burn up every single fraction of an ounce you possibly can; or for those times (probably more frequent!) when you are tempted to down a few extra calories!

So try sitting in your TV chair and lift your arms to shoulder level. Press palms hard together, fingers pointed upwards, for two or three minutes and relax for the same number of minutes between each hand-pressing bout. You will probably increase your metabolic rate from its normal sedentary one calorie per minute to two calories per minute – and the minute's effort it takes to 'press away a calorie' should at least make you think twice when you are tempted to eat perhaps more than 100 surplus calories in one minute's brief indulgence.

Please note, however, that there is a health warning attached to this calorie-burning tactic. To achieve results, the hands must be pressed together with real force, and this is not advisable for anybody suffering from heart or blood pressure problems.

'Certain foods have special slimming properties'

Despite many years' intensive research, no scientist has yet discovered any food that has magical slimming powers. The popular idea that foods like grapefruit or hard-boiled eggs possess the power to dissolve surplus pounds is sheer fallacy. Any miracle diet based on a so-called wonder food works, if it works at all, for one reason and one reason only: it is low in calories! You should remain highly suspicious of over-the-counter pills which appear to claim this fat-dissolving virtue, too. None that can speed weight loss in this way is known to science.

However, research – notably that carried out by Derek Miller at London University – has shown that there are some 'thermogenic' substances present in certain foods and drinks that do have the effect of speeding up your metabolism, and which could have a certain effect in helping to speed up weight loss. The problem lies in locating these substances in forms which can be consumed in sufficient quantity to have a measurable effect on increased calorie-burning. Vitamin C is one such substance, but it would have to be consumed in massive quantities in the region of one gram a day (50 times the normal daily requirement) to have any effect on metabolism. Many medical experts believe such massive overdosing of this vitamin (or any vitamin) for prolonged periods could endanger health. The good news is that there is one relevant thermogenic substance which can easily be consumed in generous quantities and which appears to be reasonably safe. This is caffeine as it occurs in tea and coffee. Some experts argue against the advisability of consuming caffeine. Medical research, however, indicates no major health hazards associated with caffeine-containing drinks – only comparatively minor problems such as sleeplessness and irritability. Many people can drink vast amounts of tea and coffee without experiencing either; but obviously if you are a person who reacts to the caffeine in them in this way, then it is wiser to forego the possible advantages to be gained from their speed-up effect on your metabolic rate.

For most people, drinking plenty of coffee and tea presents an effortless and agreeable way of not only speeding weight loss while dieting, but also giving psychological benefits. A cuppa can often help to 'bridge that gap' between meals and rescue you from a need to have a little high-calorie something. How much caffeine is needed to speed metabolic rate? Experiments have shown that a daily intake of about one gram of caffeine is about right. You get this amount from drinking about eight cups of moderately strong tea or coffee throughout the day; or ten cups of instant coffee made with a well-heaped teaspoon. The effect is to speed up your metabolic rate by from 15 to 20 per cent. In terms of weight loss, this means that for those already on a diet of 1,000 calories, it could result in the loss of one extra pound every fortnight. Because plenty of tea or coffee involves no sacrifice – and indeed is often pleasurable – it seems well worthwhile indulging yourself and gaining this little extra boost to metabolism and weight loss. The one point to watch, of course, is what you put in your cuppas. Tea and coffee are only calorie-free if you take them with neither milk nor sugar. Saccharin is a perfectly acceptable calorie-free substitute for sugar; but if you can't drink lemon tea or black coffee, then make sure your milk is a low-fat dried variety, or skimmed. And since *every* calorie counts, it is essential to remember to subtract the milk calories from your daily allowance.

Extras for Big Losers

This chapter is primarily for anyone who has a lot of weight to lose, although other slimmers will benefit from the long-term habit changes we suggest. If you have followed one of the High Speed Diets in this book for two weeks and still find you have a way to go, then don't make life too difficult for yourself. Pick one of the 1,000-calorie Fast Followers and allow yourself some extra treats occasionally. If you have over three stone to lose you can probably eat 1,500 calories a day and lose weight at a steady rate. Most people find some days easier than others for sticking to a diet. You may be involved in an absorbing hobby, for example, and food seems the last thing on your mind. Take advantage of these days to keep your calories low. This will allow you to save some extra calories for those days when you are invited to dinner with friends, or feel prone to nibbling because of a depressing mood.

Choose your extra calories from the chart at the back of the book; or, if you prefer, choose calorie-counted meals and snacks from those listed in the diets. The **One-Major-Meal-a-Day Diet** includes 150-calorie snacks. The **Slim and Sin Diet** has treats which range from 50 to 200 calories and includes alcoholic drinks. All the meals in the **No-Need-To-Cook Diet** total 200 calories and all the meals in the **Metabolic Diet** 180 calories. The **Buy-it Diet** features 150-calorie and 200-calorie meals and snacks. If you are very over-weight, then it is likely that you are going to have to change some of your eating habits permanently if you want to get slim and stay that way. Here are some painless changes you should consider.

1 Don't be ruled by the clock

Breakfast . . . elevenses . . . lunch . . . afternoon tea . . . dinner . . . Has it ever occurred to you just how much of Western society's eating pattern is determined not by hunger, but by social convention insisting that, because the clock says it's time to eat, we must eat? But must we? If you have been brought up on the three-meals-a-day syndrome and still have an unquestioning belief that if you miss one of them it may have disastrous consequences, then it is time to think again. There is absolutely *no* medical evidence to suggest that skipping breakfast – or lunch – or dinner does harm of any kind. There is, however, considerable evidence to show that eating by the clock, whether you are hungry or not, leads to excessive calorie intake and overweight. Indeed, research has shown that one of the major differences between overweight and slim people is that the former tend to panic at the idea of missing a meal, whereas slim people think nothing of it and cheerfully go without any meal they don't feel hungry enough to want.

We are not saying that you must skip meals. If going without breakfast, for example, means that you fall on the elevenses trolley like a starving lion, you are better off with your calorie-controlled breakfast. Most slimmers find that if they try to go without food all day, the result is a disastrous binge in the evening! However, it certainly will do you no harm not to eat if you are not hungry. Before each clock-locked meal, ask yourself whether you really feel hungry enough to eat it – and if the answer is no, try going without. Have a cup of tea or coffee instead of food; and monitor just how long it is before real pangs of hunger overtake you. Most people are agreeably surprised to discover that missing meals you genuinely aren't hungry for leaves no disagreeable after-effects at all.

2 Eat more slowly

There are several physiological and psychological reasons why rapid eating frequently means over-eating. One of the most important is that it takes several minutes for your brain to register the food you have just eaten and declare that hunger is being satisfied. Quite a small amount of food will give the same satisfied-hunger feeling as a larger quantity; but if you are a fast eater, you can consume an awful lot of calories in those few minutes. Then again, since the pleasure of eating is frequently triggered by the sight of food, if you finish off what's on your plate or in your hand too fast, your eyes will unconsciously be looking around for more to satisfy your appetite. Eat more slowly is important advice. Concentrate on slowing down the rate at which you eat, especially during the first five minutes of a meal (which happens to be the time when everybody eats fastest, the normal eating pattern being to eat quickly at first and slow down as a meal progresses).

The best method of doing this is to leave longer gaps between bites. It is a good idea to put down your knife and fork quite deliberately between mouthfuls; and to leave a longer time interval between courses. Ideally, any meal should last at least 20 minutes. Another slow-down trick which gives extra pleasure, too, is to arrange your food attractively on a tray or table; and sit down to enjoy it. Eating standing up invariably means fast eating and very often mindless eating, when you are so busy doing or thinking about other things that you literally don't notice what's in your mouth or how much is going into it. This slow-down advice applies to everything you eat – even to snacks like a packet of crisps or a bar of chocolate. If (having decided that you want this treat, and are aware that you will be counting it as part of your total calorie intake for the week) you sit down and eat each piece of chocolate or crisp slowly, savouring the taste, you will enjoy it far more. You will also find that you are likely to be satisfied with a much smaller amount.

3 Don't be afraid to leave food

Maybe you were brought up to finish every scrap on your plate, but there is no reason on earth why you should continue to obey this old childhood rule now you are grown up. In fact, if you are not particularly hungry, there is every reason why you shouldn't obey it. There is really nothing particularly virtuous about a Jack Sprat and his wife's clean platter. You and your weight have a real advantage to gain if you can train yourself to ask the question: 'Do I need this?' before you finish everything in front of you.

4 Throw away the leftovers

Research among many thousands of slimmers has revealed that the little leftovers on the children's plates or the delicious morsels remaining after the guests are gone are great temptations to break a diet. First comes the virtuous feeling: I mustn't waste this – it would be really wicked to throw it away. Then the eye-appeal comes into play to give the message: How nice these leftovers look. And before you know it, the fingers and the spoons are doing their diet-wrecking work.

Throw your leftovers away. Waste? Who will benefit if you eat them? *You* certainly won't. Large leftovers, of course, are another matter. You won't be so tempted to eat them now – but if you put them in the fridge with a vague idea of using them up sometime, there's a strong chance that you will be the person who does the finishing-up because they will be there to tempt you whenever you open the fridge door. Your safest and most sensible move is to put them firmly into the freezer. This way, they will be there for another meal; and a meal that you have *planned*.

SUPERFAST STARTERS

You will probably find it easiest to be super-strict during the first two weeks of your dieting campaign. Your resolve is likely to be at its strongest then and there is nothing more encouraging than to see the bathroom scales rapidly pointing lower and lower. To get you off to a flying start we have devised eight diets which will keep your daily intake under 1,000 calories. Choose the diet that suits your own individual tastes and lifestyle. If you are quite happy to eat very little during the day so that you can have a big meal in the evening, choose the **One-Major-Meal-A-Day Diet.** Each day you have two attractive snack meals and a generous 500-calorie two-course main meal.

If you tend to eat irregularly, try the **Busy Person's Diet.** For three days out of your 14 you eat just fruit and vegetables, then for the rest of the fortnight you choose from the easy-to-prepare daily menus.

The **No-Need-To-Cook Diet** offers a whole variety of delicious and nutritious snacks and meals which add up to two weeks' worth of speedy weight loss; and all you need to do is select your choice of dishes for the day and boil an occasional kettle!

Meat and fish, although valuable sources of protein, minerals and vitamins, are not essential to health. In the **Vegetarian Diet** they have been replaced by cheese, eggs, yogurt, beans, cereals and nuts.

One of the most common ways in which dieters slow their weight loss is by making mistakes when they are weighing and measuring. We've organised the **Buy-it Diet** around convenience foods which come in individual portions so that all the weighing and measuring is done for you.

The **Metabolic Diet** will suit you if you like to eat little-and-often and it has the added advantage that it will encourage your metabolic rate to speed up.

Nothing could be simpler than the **Munching Diet.** Choose two items from the list of protein-containing foods and eat as much as you like from the list of fruit and vegetables.

Slimming experts have known for a long time that limiting food choice can be a most effective way for dieters to reduce their calorie consumption. In the **Big Bowlful Diet** you make up a big bowl of one recipe and eat it throughout the day.

These diets are all very strict and so we don't recommend that you continue them for more than two weeks. If you are not down to your target weight by that time, then switch to one of the Fast Followers. These allow you to be a little more self-indulgent and are easier to keep to for a longer period.

THE ONE -MAJOR - MEAL - A-DAY DIET 850-900 Calories

This diet is tailor-made for people who find they can be super-strict during the day if they know that they'll be eating a hearty meal in the evening.

For most of us the first hours of the day are the most shining hours of weight-control resolve. Well-rested after a good night's sleep, we are usually feeling strong enough to achieve our most ambitious goals. But later on, tired and fatigued after a day at the office or from running around after the children, our willpower weakens and our ability to control our behaviour is at its lowest ebb. If you find your diet usually crumbles after 5 o'clock, then try the One-Major-Meal-A-Day method.

This is also a good diet for anyone who tends to feel resentful and left out if she can't eat with the family in the evening. Many of the main meals can be cooked in larger quantities and served to other members of the family (make sure you carefully take out your own portion, though). Non-dieting eaters can be served additional vegetables.

Each day gives you a choice of two attractive meals at 150 calories each, together with a generous 500-calorie main meal. When you eat the meals is entirely up to you. If you prefer to miss breakfast you can save a snack for mid-morning or supper-time. If you wish to eat your main meal for Sunday lunch, then by all means do so. Plan your menus in advance so that you always have the ingredients you need available. Then you won't be tempted to eat something that is not included in your diet plan. You can repeat your favourite recipes; but to ensure a good supply of all the nutrients and vitamins you need, keep your menus as varied as possible.

This is a very strict diet, even though the main meal is a substantial one, so we recommend that you follow it for two weeks only. If after that time you are not down to your target weight, you may carry on with the diet if you increase your calories to 1,000 a day minimum. You can do this very easily by doubling your milk allowance to 275ml (½ pint) skimmed milk and having an additional two pieces of fresh fruit each day.

DIET RULES

1 Choose any *two* snacks you like from the list below each day. You may eat these at any time you wish.

2 Choose *one* main meal each day.

3 You are allowed 150ml (¼ pint) skimmed milk each day to use in drinks. If milk is given in a snack meal, this is extra to your allowance. Measure out your milk allowance at the beginning of the day and keep it in a separate jug so that you know just how much you are using.

4 Unsugared tea and coffee, taken black or with milk from your allowance, are unlimited. You may also drink as much as you like of the following: soft drinks, mixers and squashes labelled 'low-calorie'; PLJ; Oxo; Marmite; and bottled or tap water. Do not use sugar. Artificial sweeteners may be used instead.

5 All foods must be weighed and measured accurately. Don't be tempted to go by guesswork. The eye is usually more generous than the scale and you can easily add extra calories by mistake.

6 Vary main meals and snacks each day to give a balanced diet. Be sure to use at least seven different main meals during your two-week campaign.

150-CALORIE
CEREAL SNACKS

Weetabix
2 Weetabix with 125ml/4fl oz
skimmed milk.

All-Bran with Dried Fruit
25g/1oz Kellogg's All-Bran, with
30ml/2 level tablespoons raisins
or sultanas and 75ml/3fl oz
skimmed milk.

**Cornflakes, Rice Krispies or
Puffed Wheat**
25g/1oz Cornflakes, Rice
Krispies or Puffed Wheat, with
75ml/3fl oz skimmed milk and
5ml/1 level teaspoon sugar.

Shredded Wheat and Orange
1 Shredded Wheat, with 75ml/
3fl oz skimmed milk, followed by
1 medium orange.

Muesli and Yogurt
25g/1oz muesli and 1 small
carton Safeway or Raines natural
yogurt.

150-CALORIE
EGG SNACKS

Grapefruit and Boiled Egg
½ grapefruit (no sugar), followed
by 1 boiled egg, size 3, and 1
slice Slimcea bread with 5ml/
1 level teaspoon low-fat spread

Poached Egg on Toast
1 egg, size 3, poached and served
on 1 small slice white bread
(25g/1oz), toasted.

Scrambled Egg on Toast
1 egg, size 3, scrambled with
45ml/3 tablespoons skimmed
milk and seasoning in a non-stick
pan and served on 1 slice Nimble
Family bread, toasted.

Egg Salad
1 egg, size 3, hard-boiled and
served with a mixed salad of
lettuce, watercress, cucumber, a
few spring onions, 2 sticks celery,
chopped and 2 tomatoes, sliced,
with 15ml/1 level tablespoon
Waistline or Heinz low-calorie
salad dressing.

Savoury Egg and Watercress
1 St Michael Picnic Egg and
small bunch watercress.

150-CALORIE
SOUP SNACKS

Soup with Bread
295g/10.4oz can Heinz Low
Calorie Scotch Broth, Tomato or
Vegetable Soup, with 1 slice
wholemeal bread (40g/1½oz).

Soup, Crispbreads and Apple
295g/10.4oz can Boots Low
Calorie Chicken Soup, with 2
Energen crispbreads followed by
1 medium eating apple.

Savoury Snack and Soup
1 small packet KP Cheesey
Crunchies or Griddles or
Rancheros, with 295g/10.4oz can
Boots Low Calorie Oxtail or
Tomato Soup.

**Quick Soup with Bread and
Cheese**
1 sachet Batchelor's Slim-A-
Soup, any flavour, with 1 slice
wholemeal bread (25g/1oz),
spread with 1 triangle cheese
spread and topped with 1 sliced
tomato.

Soup and Griddles
295g/10.4oz can Boots Low
Calorie Mushroom Soup and 1
packet KP Griddles.

Soup with Celery
1 sachet Batchelor's Onion and
Beef Cup-a-Soup, with 25g/1oz
Edam cheese and 2 sticks celery.

Soup and Chicken Sandwich
1 sachet Borden's Chicken, Beef
or Tomato Soup Break and 2
small slices Slimcea, spread with
35g/1¼oz pot Sainsbury's
Minced Chicken in Jelly topped
with slices of cucumber or sprigs

of watercress.

150-CALORIE CHEESE SNACKS

Cottage Cheese Salad
113g/4oz carton Eden Vale or St Ivel cottage cheese (any flavour except 'Onion and Cheddar') with small bunch watercress, 1 stick celery, cucumber, 1 tomato and 1 Lyons Krispen.

Cottage Cheese Sandwich
2 slices Slimcea bread, spread with 7g/¼ oz low-fat spread and filled with 50g/2oz Eden Vale or St Ivel cottage cheese (any flavour except 'Onion and Cheddar') and a little mustard and cress.

Crispbreads and Cheese
2 Energen crispbreads topped with 25g/1oz Edam cheese, 1 tomato and 2 sticks celery.

Cheese on Toast
25g/1oz Edam cheese, grated, on 1 slice toasted Nimble Family bread, grilled until the cheese melts and served with 1 tomato or 15ml/1 level tablespoon tomato ketchup.

Krispen and Cottage Cheese
113g/4oz carton cottage cheese with onions and peppers and 2 Lyons Krispen with a few slices cucumber.

Crispbreads and Cheese spread
3 Energen crispbreads, spread with 2 triangles cheese spread and 1 tomato.

150-CALORIE BREAD AND CRISPBREAD SNACKS

Crispbreads with Mackerel Paste
4 Ryvita crispbreads, spread with 75g/2.65oz pot Princes Mackerel and Cucumber paste.

Bread with Fish Paste
1 large thin slice wholemeal bread (40g/1½ oz), spread with a 35g/1.23oz pot Shippams Salmon and Shrimp or Sardine and Tomato Paste.

Pineapple and Carrot Open Sandwich
1 small slice wholemeal bread (25g/1oz), spread with 15g/½ oz Rowntree Mackintosh Cheddar Spread, topped with 1 ring canned, drained pineapple and 1 medium carrot, grated.

Pizza Grill
1 small slice wholemeal bread (25g/1oz), topped with 1 Birds Eye Griller, grilled and served with 125g/4oz raw carrot sticks.

Crispbreads and Kipper Spread
2 Ryvita crispbreads, spread with 53g/1⅞ oz pot Princes Kipper Spread and 1 tomato.

Krispen and Beef Paste
2 Lyons Krispen, spread with 35g/1.23oz pot Shippams Country Pot Paste, Beef and Horseradish or Beef and Pickle, followed by 1 small (150g/5oz) banana.

Crispbreads and Ham
2 Energen crispbreads, topped with 50g/2oz Scot Honey Roast Ham, sliced, a little made mustard and 1 sliced tomato.

Tomato Juice and Salmon Sandwich
113ml/4fl oz Campbell's V8 and 1 slice (40g/1½ oz) wholemeal bread, spread with 35g/1.23oz pot Shippams Salmon and Shrimp or Anchovy Paste.

150-CALORIE SWEET SNACKS

Biscuits and Apple
2 medium digestive biscuits and a 150g/5oz eating apple.

Milk and Biscuits
150ml/¼ pint hot or cold Silver Top milk and 2 Marie or Morning Coffee biscuits.

Ice Cream
75g/3oz portion vanilla ice cream.

Yogurt with Honey and Orange
1 small carton Chambourcy or Sainsbury's natural yogurt, mixed with 1 medium orange, segmented, and 10ml/2 level teaspoons honey.

Mousse
1 small carton Findus Raspberry or Strawberry Ripple Mousse.

Flavoured Yogurt
1 small carton Sainsbury's Banana or Hazelnut Yogurt.

Fruit and Yogurt
220g/7.8oz can Boots Fruit Cocktail or Pears or Pineapple in Low Calorie Syrup with 1 small carton Safeway fruit yogurt, any flavour.

Fruity Yogurt
1 small carton St Ivel or Chambourcy natural yogurt, with 15ml/1 level tablespoon raisins and a 150g/5oz eating apple, cored and chopped.

Fruit and Ice Cream
227g/8oz can Koo Peach Slices or Pear Halves in Apple Juice, with 25g/1oz vanilla ice cream.

Dessert Bar and Fruit
1 Prewett's Date & Fig or Fruit & Bran Dessert Bar, with 1 medium orange or pear.

Fresh Fruit
1 small (150g/5oz) banana, 1 medium orange and 1 medium apple.

Pears and Tip Top
227g/8oz can Koo Pear Halves in Apple Juice, with 45ml/3 tablespoons Nestlé Tip Top.

150-CALORIE SAVOURY SNACKS

Baked Beans on Toast
150g/5.3oz can baked beans on 1 slice Nimble Family bread, toasted.

Chipolatas and Vegetables
2 beef chipolatas, well grilled, served with 150g/5oz Birds Eye Cauliflower, Peas and Carrots or Peas and Baby Carrots.

Fish Fingers with Mushrooms and Tomatoes
2 frozen fish fingers, grilled or baked without fat, served with 213g/7½oz can Chesswood Button or Small Whole Mushrooms in Brine, drained, and 227g/8oz can tomatoes.

Grilled Fish Cakes and Tomatoes
2 frozen fish cakes, grilled or baked without fat, served with 2 large tomatoes, halved and grilled without fat.

Crisps and Celery
1 small packet Chipmunk or Golden Wonder or KP Crisps, with 1 stick celery.

Crisps and Apple
1 packet Golden Wonder Crisps followed by 1 medium apple.

Beans and Bacon
150g/5.3oz can baked beans with 1 rasher streaky bacon, well grilled.

Sausage and Tomato
2 pork chipolatas, well grilled with 2 tomatoes, grilled without fat.

500-CALORIE MAIN MEALS

Grilled Lamb Chop with Vegetables / Rice Pudding

150g/5oz lamb chump chop.
15ml/1 tablespoon mint sauce.
125g/4oz carrots, boiled.

125g/4oz cabbage, boiled.
170g/6oz can Ambrosia Creamed
Rice.

Grill the lamb chump chop and serve with mint sauce, boiled carrots and cabbage. Follow with creamed rice, hot or cold.

Mixed Grill / Fresh Fruit

125g/4oz lamb's liver.
1 lamb's kidney.
2.5ml/½ teaspoon oil.
2 rashers back bacon.

1 tomato.
125g/4oz mushrooms.
1 medium orange or pear.

Brush liver and cored and halved kidney with oil, then grill until cooked on one side. Grill bacon at same time. Turn liver and kidney over and add halved tomato. Continue to grill until liver and kidney are cooked and bacon is crisp. Serve with mushrooms, poached in stock or water. Follow with the orange or pear.

Herby Cheese Omelet with Vegetables / Banana with Yogurt

2 eggs, size 3.
30ml/2 tablespoons water.
salt and pepper.
pinch dried mixed herbs.
7g/¼oz low-fat spread.
25g/1oz Edam cheese.

125g/4oz button mushrooms.
125g/4oz mixed vegetables,
frozen.
1 small banana (150g/5oz).
1 small carton natural yogurt.

Beat the eggs with water, add herbs and seasoning to taste. Grate the cheese. Grease a non-stick omelet pan or small frying pan with the low-fat spread, then heat. Pour in the egg mixture and cook over a moderate heat until just set. Sprinkle grated cheese over the omelet and fold in half. Turn out onto a warm dish and serve with mushrooms poached in stock or water and cooked mixed vegetables. Follow with sliced banana mixed with yogurt.

Cottage Pie with Vegetables / Ice Cream and Fruit

125g/4oz raw lean minced beef.
1 small onion.
25g/1oz mushrooms.
5ml/1 level teaspoon plain flour.
salt and freshly ground pepper.
70ml/2½ fl oz beef stock made
from ¼ beef stock cube.
15ml/1 tablespoon tomato purée.
½ medium packet Cadbury's

Smash.
7g/¼ oz low-fat spread.
125g/4oz cabbage, boiled.
75g/3oz carrots, boiled.
50g/2oz vanilla ice cream.
1 ring pineapple canned in
natural juice or 125g/4oz fresh
raspberries or strawberries.

Fry the minced beef in a non-stick pan until well browned, then drain off and discard the fat which has cooked out. Finely chop the onion, slice the mushrooms and add, with flour, to the meat in the pan. Season to taste. Blend stock with tomato purée and stir into the meat and vegetables. Heat to boiling point, stirring continuously, then cook for 5 minutes until mixture thickens. Spoon into a small ovenproof dish. Make up the Smash and stir in the low-fat spread. Season to taste. Spoon mashed potato on top of meat and fork the top. Bake at 200°C/400°F, gas mark 6, for 30 minutes or until top is browned. Serve cabbage and carrots with cottage pie. Follow with ice cream and fruit.

Curried Chicken and Banana Salad / Mousse *(pages 80-81)*

125g/4oz cooked chicken.
½ small carton natural yogurt.
15ml/1 level tablespoon mango
chutney.
1.25ml/¼ teaspoon curry paste.
salt and pepper.
paprika.
1 small banana (150g/5oz).
10ml/2 teaspoons lemon juice.

½ small green pepper.
50g/2oz cucumber.
15ml/1 level tablespoon raisins.
few lettuce leaves.
few sprigs watercress.
1 carton Findus Strawberry
Mousse or Zoo Surprise Mousse
or Sainsbury's Mousse.
3 raspberries (optional).

Remove and discard skin from chicken; cut the meat into bite-size pieces. Mix yogurt, mango chutney and curry paste together. Season to taste with salt, pepper and paprika. Stir the chicken, chopped green pepper, chopped cucumber and raisins into the yogurt dressing. Cover with clear food wrap and chill for at least 30 minutes to allow the flavours to blend. Peel and slice the banana and toss in lemon juice. Serve chicken with lettuce and banana, garnished with sprigs of watercress. Follow with the mousse decorated with raspberries.

Oven Baked Chicken and Chips / Banana and Ice Cream

225g/8oz chicken joint.
125g/4oz Findus Grill Chips.
lettuce.
watercress.
spring onions.

cucumber.
15ml/1 tablespoon oil-free French dressing.
50g/2oz vanilla ice cream.
1 medium banana (175g/6oz).

Season the chicken joint, wrap in foil and bake until tender (about 40 minutes). Bake the chips for the last 15 – 20 minutes. Remove and discard all skin from chicken and serve with dressed green salad and chips. Follow with the ice cream topped with sliced banana.

Baked Chicken and Jacket Potato

250g/9oz chicken joint.
200g/7oz potato.
30ml/2 tablespoons natural yogurt.
chives.
lettuce.

cucumber.
watercress.
green pepper.
spring onions.
15ml/1 tablespoon oil-free French dressing.

Bake chicken joint without added fat alongside the well scrubbed potato at 200°C/400°F, gas mark 6, for 45 minutes or until cooked. Split potato in half and top with natural yogurt and a pinch of chopped chives. Serve with a green salad and oil-free French dressing.

Corned Beef and Cheese Savoury / Orange

15g/½ oz low-fat spread.
1 small onion.
50g/2oz corned beef.
125g/4oz canned tomatoes.
salt and pepper.

pinch mixed herbs.
40g/1½ oz Cheddar cheese.
125g/4oz runner beans.
1 orange.

Melt the low-fat spread in a small pan and fry the chopped onion gently until soft. Add the diced corned beef, canned tomatoes, salt and pepper to taste and mixed herbs. Heat through. Transfer to a shallow ovenproof dish and sprinkle the top with grated cheese. Place under a hot grill until the cheese melts and begins to brown. Serve with boiled runner beans. Follow with the orange.

Beef Casserole / Stewed Apple and Custard

125g/4oz lean stewing steak.
5ml/1 level teaspoon plain flour.
1 medium carrot.
25g/1oz onion.
1 stick celery.
salt and pepper.
1 bay leaf.
pinch mixed herbs.

¼ beef stock cube.
200ml/7fl oz boiling water.
15ml/1 tablespoon tomato purée.
175g/6oz cauliflower florets.
125g/4oz cooking apple.
artificial sweetener.
150ml/¼ pint custard.

Trim off and discard any visible fat from meat; cut meat into cubes and toss in the flour. Place meat in a small ovenproof dish with sliced carrot and onion, chopped celery, salt and pepper, bay leaf and herbs. Dissolve stock cube in boiling water and stir in tomato purée. Pour over meat and vegetables. Cover dish and cook at 170°C/325°F gas mark 3, for 2 hours. Meanwhile, boil the cauliflower. Drain and arrange in a circle on a warm serving plate. Discard bay leaf and serve beef casserole in the centre of the cauliflower. Follow with the apple, stewed in a little water and sweetened after cooking with artificial sweetener. Top with custard.

Lemon and Parsley Herring / Fruit and Ice Cream

175g/6oz whole herring.
salt and pepper.
25g/1oz fresh breadcrumbs.
1 small onion.
1 lemon.
15ml/1 tablespoon fresh parsley
chopped

7g/¼oz low-fat spread.
125g/4oz mixed vegetables,
frozen.
1 Wall's Cornish Ice Cream Bar
or Lyons Maid Vanilla Kup.
75g/3oz raspberries or strawberries, fresh or frozen.

Remove the head, tail and fins of the herring, then clean thoroughly and remove the backbone (or ask your fishmonger to do this for you). Season the inside of the herring with salt and pepper. Mix together the breadcrumbs, finely chopped onion, parsley, grated lemon rind and lemon juice. Spoon stuffing into the herring and fold into its original shape. Grease one side of a piece of foil with a little of the low-fat spread and lay the fish on it. Place the thawed mixed vegetables alongside the fish and top with the remaining low-fat spread. Wrap the foil around the fish and vegetables and seal. Bake at 180°C/350°F, gas mark 4, for 30 minutes. Unwrap, lift onto a warm dish and serve. Follow with ice cream and raspberries or strawberries.

Baked Smoked Haddock and Macaroni / Biscuits and Cheese

25g/1oz macaroni.
170g/6oz packet Findus Buttered Scottish Smoked Haddock.
15ml/1 level tablespoon cornflour.
30ml/2 level tablespoons powdered skimmed milk.

salt and pepper.
1 tomato.
15g/½oz Edam cheese.
125g/4oz green beans.
2 Energen crispbreads.
1 triangle cheese spread.

Cook macaroni in boiling salted water. Drain. Cook smoked haddock as instructed on the packet. Make the liquid from the fish up to 150ml/¼ pint with water. Blend cornflour and skimmed milk powder with a little liquid to make a smooth paste and then add to the remaining liquid. Bring to the boil, stirring all the time and cook for 2 minutes. Discard skin from haddock and flake fish. Add fish and macaroni to the sauce. Season to taste with salt and pepper, and reheat gently. Turn into an ovenproof dish and arrange sliced tomato on top. Sprinkle with grated cheese and grill until melted. Serve with boiled green beans. Follow with crispbreads spread with cheese.

Seafood au Gratin

175g/6oz cod or coley fillet.
5ml/1 teaspoon lemon juice.
25g/1oz prawns, fresh peeled or frozen thawed.
½ small carton natural yogurt.
45ml/3 tablespoons Waistline Seafood Sauce.

salt and pepper.
125g/4oz spinach, fresh or frozen.
25g/1oz Cheddar cheese.
1 tomato.
150g/5oz runner beans.

Place fish on a plate and sprinkle with lemon juice. Cover with a second plate and cook over a pan of boiling water for 10-15 minutes until tender. Flake the fish, removing any bones and skin. Mix prawns with the fish. Blend yogurt and seafood sauce together and stir into the fish and prawns. Season to taste. Cook the fresh spinach or heat the frozen spinach, press out any liquid and spoon into the bottom of a small ovenproof dish. Spoon fish and prawn mixture over spinach. Cover with grated cheese and cook at 190°C/375°F, gas mark 5, until cheese is melted and beginning to brown. Garnish with sliced tomato and serve with boiled runner beans.

Fish Hawaian Style / Melon

half a 227g/8oz can pineapple in natural juice.
50g/2oz long grain rice.
1 tomato.
50g/2oz green pepper.
175g/6oz cod or coley fillet.
5ml/1 teaspoon lemon juice.
salt and pepper.
lettuce.
watercress.
cucumber.
spring onions or onion rings.
15ml/1 tablespoon oil-free French dressing.
200g/7oz slice melon, Cantaloupe, Ogen, Honeydew or Yellow.

Drain and chop pineapple and reserve juice. Make juice up to 150ml/¼ pint with water and put in a small pan with the rice. Cook the rice for 10 minutes, then add the pineapple, skinned and chopped tomato, chopped green pepper and a little more water, if necessary. Continue to cook for a further 5 minutes or until rice is tender. Meanwhile put the fish in a shallow pan with the lemon juice and sufficient water to cover. Cook for 10 to 15 minutes. Drain and flake the fish. Stir flaked fish into the rice mixture and season to taste. Serve hot with a dressed green salad. Follow with the melon.

Mackerel with Orange Salad / Cheese and Crispbread

225g/8oz whole mackerel.
salt and pepper.
15ml/1 tablespoon sweet mixed pickle.
1 medium orange.
1 small head chicory.
15ml/1 tablespoon lemon juice.
5ml/1 teaspoon soy sauce.
1 Energen crispbread.
15g/½oz Edam cheese.

Cut the head, tail and fins off the mackerel, clean thoroughly and remove backbone (or ask your fishmonger to do this for you). Sprinkle the inside with a little salt and pepper, then spread with sweet pickle. Fold mackerel into its original shape. Place on a sheet of foil, wrap the foil around the fish and seal. Bake at 180°C/350°F, gas mark 4, for 30 minutes. Meanwhile, prepare the orange salad. Peel and segment the orange, cutting the segments away from the membranes. Wash the chicory. Toss the orange segments and chicory in the lemon juice and soy sauce. Remove baked mackerel from foil and serve with the salad. Follow with crispbread and cheese.

Tuna and Green Bean Bake / Flanby Caramel

125g/4oz runner beans, fresh or frozen.
half a 275ml/½ pint packet mushroom sauce mix.
150ml/¼ pint skimmed milk.

100g/3½oz can tuna in brine.
1 tomato, sliced.
15g/½oz Lancashire cheese.
1 small carton Chambourcy Flanby Caramel.

Slice and cook fresh runner beans in lightly salted water until just tender, and drain; or cook the frozen beans as instructed and drain. Arrange beans in bottom of a shallow ovenproof dish. Make up mushroom sauce mix with skimmed milk as instructed. Drain the tuna, then flake and arrange over the beans. Pour the hot mushroom sauce over the fish and beans. Heat, uncovered, in a hot oven, 200°C/400°F, gas mark 6, for 5-10 minutes. Remove dish from the oven, arrange tomato slices over the top, then sprinkle over the cheese. Return to the oven until the cheese has melted and begun to brown. Serve hot. Follow with the Flanby Caramel.

Creamy Liver / Fresh Fruit

125g/4oz lamb's liver.
1 small onion.
50g/2oz button mushrooms.
7g/¼oz low-fat spread.
1.25ml/¼ level teaspoon dried sage.
salt and freshly ground black pepper.
5ml/1 level teaspoon flour.
30ml/2 tablespoons beef stock.

10ml/2 teaspoons lemon juice.
½ small carton natural yogurt.
25g/1oz ribbon noodles.
125g/4oz broccoli or Brussels sprouts.
1 slice lemon, optional.
sprig of parsley, optional.
125g/4oz grapes or 1 large eating apple.

Wash the liver, dry well and cut into bite-size pieces. Peel and chop onion finely; slice mushrooms. Heat low-fat spread in a non-stick pan. Add onion and cook over a low heat until transparent. Add liver, mushrooms, sage and seasoning. Stir well, then cover and cook for 5-10 minutes until tender, stirring occasionally. Sprinkle with flour, stir and continue to cook for 1 minute. Add the stock and lemon juice and bring to the boil. Turn the heat down very low and stir in the yogurt; heat briefly but do not allow to boil. Serve immediately with boiled noodles and broccoli or Brussels sprouts. Garnish with a lemon slice and a sprig of parsley. Follow with grapes or an apple.

Spaghetti with Seafood Sauce / Cheese Crispbreads

50g/2oz spaghetti.
227g/8oz can tomatoes.
1 Findus cod steak.
1 small onion, finely chopped.
pinch dried marjoram, oregano
or mixed herbs.

pepper.
garlic salt.
50g/2oz prawns, fresh peeled or
frozen thawed.
2 Energen crispbreads.
1 triangle cheese spread.

Cook spaghetti in plenty of boiling salted water for about 12 minutes until just tender. Meanwhile sieve or purée canned tomatoes and place in a pan with the cod steak, onion, herbs, pepper and garlic salt to taste. Cover and simmer for 15 minutes or until fish is cooked. Flake fish into the sauce, add prawns and heat through. Drain the spaghetti and serve with the sauce. Follow with the crispbreads spread with cheese.

Liver, Leek and Tomato Casserole / Grapefruit

200g/7oz potato.
125g/4oz lamb's liver.
1 leek.
227g/8oz can tomatoes.

salt and pepper.
pinch mixed herbs.
½ grapefruit.
artificial sweetener (optional).

Scrub potato well and bake at 200°C/400°F, gas mark 6, for ¾ – 1 hour or until soft when pinched. Wash and slice the liver. Trim most of the green part from the leek, wash thoroughly and slice. Put the liver, leek and canned tomatoes in a small ovenproof casserole. Season well with salt and pepper and sprinkle in the mixed herbs. Cover and cook in the oven with the potato for 40 minutes. Serve the baked potato (no butter) with the liver casserole. Start or complete the meal with ½ grapefruit, sweetened if liked, with artificial sweetener.

Roast Beef and Vegetables / Mousse

75g/3oz lean roast topside beef.
50ml/2fl oz gravy made with
gravy mix.
125g/4oz roast potato.

125g/4oz carrots.
125g/4oz Brussels sprouts.
1 individual frozen mousse.

Serve beef with gravy, roast potato, boiled carrots and sprouts. Follow with mousse.

Stir-Fried Chicken / Fruit and Ice Cream

125g/4oz raw chicken, without skin.
15ml/1 tablespoon oil.
1 small onion.
1 small leek or 4 spring onions.
125g/4oz button mushrooms.
125g/4oz bean sprouts.

15ml/1 tablespoon soy sauce.
15ml/1 tablespoon dry sherry (optional).
salt and pepper.
220g/7¾oz can Boots Fruit Cocktail in Low-Calorie Syrup.
25g/1oz vanilla ice cream.

Cut the chicken into bite-size pieces. Heat the oil in a non-stick frying pan. Add the finely chopped onion, sliced leek or spring onions and fry over a medium heat for 2 minutes, stirring continuously. Add the chicken and continue to stir-fry for about 5 minutes until chicken is tender. Add sliced mushrooms and stir-fry for a further 2 minutes. Add the bean sprouts, soy sauce and sherry and stir-fry briskly for 2 more minutes. Season with salt and pepper to taste and serve at once. Follow with fruit cocktail and ice cream.

Chicken Risotto / Mousse

50g/2oz long-grain rice.
25g/1oz onion.
50g/2oz mushrooms.
50g/2oz green pepper.
1 tomato.
½ chicken stock cube.
225ml/8floz boiling water.
pinch mixed herbs.

salt and pepper.
25g/1oz peas, frozen.
50g/2oz roast chicken, with skin removed.
5ml/1 teaspoon parsley, chopped.
1 individual Birds Eye Mousse or Super Mousse, any flavour.

Place the rice, finely chopped onion, sliced mushrooms, chopped pepper and tomato in a shallow pan. Dissolve stock cube in boiling water and pour into the pan. Bring to the boil, add the mixed herbs and seasoning to taste, then simmer about 15 minutes until the stock is absorbed and the rice is tender. Stir in the thawed peas and chopped chicken and heat through gently for 5 minutes. Serve hot, sprinkled with chopped parsley. Follow with the mousse.

Turkey with Mushroom Sauce / Strawberry Fool

175g/6oz raw turkey breast, without skin or bone.
150ml/¼ pint chicken stock made from ¼ chicken.
stock cube.
25g/1oz onion.
50g/2oz mushrooms.
7g/¼oz low-fat spread.

10ml/2 level teaspoons flour.
30ml/2 level tablespoons skimmed milk powder.
salt and pepper.
50g/2oz peas.
125g/4oz carrots.
1 St Ivel Strawberry Fool.

Place turkey breast in a small saucepan with the stock, chopped onion and sliced mushrooms. Bring to the boil, cover and simmer gently for 30 minutes. Remove the turkey and mushrooms and keep warm. Drain the stock into a measuring jug and make up to 150ml/¼ pint with water. Pour into a saucepan and add the low-fat spread, flour and milk powder. Bring to the boil, whisking all the time and cook for 2 – 3 minutes. Season to taste and stir in the mushrooms. Pour over the turkey breast and serve with boiled peas and carrots. Follow with Strawberry Fool.

Potato with Porky Stuffing / Baked Banana

200g/7oz potato.
30ml/2 tablespoons skimmed milk.
salt and pepper.
50g/2oz chopped pork and ham.
15ml/1 tablespoon mustard

pickle.
lettuce.
watercress.
cucumber.
1 small banana (150g/5oz).
15ml/1 tablespoon orange juice.

Scrub potato well and bake at 200°C/400°F, gas mark 6, for ¾ – 1 hour or until soft when pinched. Remove from the oven and split in two lengthwise. Scoop out the potato flesh and cream it with the skimmed milk and seasoning to taste. Dice the chopped pork and ham and stir into the creamed potato with the mustard pickle. Pile back into the potato shells and reheat in the oven. Serve with lettuce, watercress and cucumber. Follow with Baked Banana. Peel the banana, place in a piece of foil and sprinkle with orange juice. Fold up foil so no juice can escape. Place on a baking sheet and bake at 200°C/400°F, gas mark 6, for 15 – 20 minutes.

THE BUSY PERSON'S DIET

under 1,000 Calories

Busy people tend to eat irregularly. In the rush of trying to get everything done, there often seems to be no time to make a meal and the temptation is to grab a quick sandwich or a chocolate bar. Such foods can be very fattening and this haphazard way of eating can add untold calories without your realising it.

The first thing you must do is get out of the habit of mindless eating. Stop whatever you are doing and sit down at the table with your food. Concentrate on enjoying what you are eating and you will finish your meal feeling satisfied. Most people need to fill two food quotas during a day. There's the physical quota, requiring enough food to satisfy the stomach. There's a psychological quota, too – requiring sufficient food to provide pleasure and relaxation to satisfy the mind. When food is eaten while the mind is distracted, it fails to fulfil the second quota. Hence the temptation to eat more food. When you eat without thinking about what you are eating, it is almost as if you just haven't eaten at all.

The Busy Person's diet has been designed to fit neatly and painlessly into the busiest schedule. It is the ideal diet for anyone who works from Monday to Friday and spends weekends catching up with housework, laundry or home decorating. Over the fortnight that we recommend you do this diet, 11 days are planned to give three meals and 1,000 calories. Each day's menu includes a simple breakfast or supper meal, a satisfying but quick-to-prepare soup meal and a main meal. Some of the soup meals may be taken to work in a

41

vacuum flask, others can be prepared on the spot with hot water from a kettle. We have given you 17 menus to choose from. You don't have to follow them in any order; just pick out your favourites. You should, however, make sure you eat at least seven different menus during the fortnight to ensure a good nutritional balance.

What makes this diet a superfast starter is that for three days out of your fortnight you eat nothing but fruit and vegetables. These very low-calorie days will give you an overall calorie intake of less than 1,000 calories a day and you will be rewarded with a fast weight loss. When you do your three fruit and vegetable days is entirely up to you. Some people feel ''strongest'' right at the beginning of their diet; others find they don't want to think about preparing food when they are in the middle of an absorbing task. Space the days out if you can, and don't do more than three fruit and vegetable days in the two weeks.

If you find you like this method of dieting, then you can continue to use your 1,000 calorie daily menus if you need to lose more weight when your two weeks are finished. If you find you have a dinner date or want to meet a friend for lunch, you can cancel out any indiscretions by doing one or two fruit and vegetable days afterwards. It is wise to have all the foods you will eat each week bought in advance and, if necessary, stored in the fridge or freezer. This takes a bit of organisation to begin with, but it pays dividends in terms of time saved later on.

DIET RULES

1 On three of the 14 days you eat only fruit and vegetables from the list below. You may choose any fruits and vegetables you like and eat them cooked or raw whenever you wish, but no fat and no dressings are allowed with the vegetables and no sugar is allowed with the fruit. You may use artificial sweeteners with cooked fruits if necessary.

2 On the fruit and vegetable days you are also allowed 275ml/½ pint skimmed milk for use in unsugared tea and coffee. Black coffee and tea, soft drinks labelled 'low-calorie' and water may be taken freely.

3 Try to space out your low-calorie fruit and vegetable days and plan them for the times you know you will be busiest.

4 On the other eleven days of your diet, you choose one of the 1,000 calorie menus. These give three meals a day which may be eaten at any time that suits you. They have been carefully calorie-counted so do not swap individual meals from one menu to another. If one particular meal or menu does not suit you, repeat one of your favourites instead: but use at least seven different complete menus during your diet.

5 As well as the foods listed in the menus, you may have milk for use in tea and coffee. Choose from the following:
275ml/½ pint Silver Top milk *or*
575ml/1 pint skimmed milk *or*
378ml/⅔ pint semi-skimmed milk.

6 You may substitute drinks from those listed on pages 154 and 155 for some or all of your milk allowance. Your milk allowance is worth 200 calories a day.

BUSY DAYS

Three days out of each fortnight you should eat only raw or stewed/boiled fruit and vegetables. ADD NOTHING ELSE. You are allowed 275ml/½ pint skimmed milk for use in tea or coffee (add artificial sweetener if you wish). These are the fruit and vegetables which you may choose from:

Fruit
Raw or stewed without sugar or sweetened with artifical sweetener:

Apples	Greengages	Pears
Apricots, fresh	Gooseberries	Plums
Bananas	Kiwi fruit	Pineapple
Bilberries	Lemons	Pomegranates
Blackberries	Loganberries	Raspberries
Blackcurrants	Mango	Redcurrants
Cherries, fresh	Melon, all types	Satsumas
Cooking apples	Nectarines	Strawberries
Damsons	Oranges	Tangerines
Grapefruit	Passion fruit	
Grapes	Peaches	

Vegetables
Raw or boiled or cooked and served without added fat:

Asparagus	Cucumber	Radishes
Aubergine	Endive	Runner beans
Bean sprouts	French beans	Salsify
Beetroot	Gherkins	Seakale
Broad beans	Globe artichoke	Spinach
Broccoli	Jerusalem artichoke	Spring greens
Brussels sprouts	Leeks	Spring onions
Cabbage, all kinds	Lettuce	Swede
Carrots	Marrow	Sweetcorn
Cauliflower	Mushrooms	Tomatoes
Celery	Mustard and cress	Turnips
Chicory	Onions	Watercress
Chinese leaves	Peas	
Courgettes	Peppers, green or red	

1,000 CALORIE MENUS

Milk Allowance

Each day you are allowed 575ml/1 pint skimmed milk *or* 375ml/⅔ pint semi-skimmed milk *or* 275ml/½ pint Silver Top milk for use in tea and coffee. Where milk is given in breakfasts or recipes, this is in addition to your milk allowance.

MENU 1

Breakfast or Supper

3 rashers streaky bacon, well grilled.
2 tomatoes, grilled without fat.
1 slice Nimble Family bread.

Soup Meal

295g/10.4oz can Boots Low Calorie Chicken & Vegetable Soup.
1 slice Nimble Family bread.
1 medium apple or pear.

Main Meal
Chicken Curry with Rice / Orange

25g/1oz onion.
15ml/1 level tablespoon sultanas.
225g/8oz chicken joint.
½ packet Colman's Indian Curry Mix (any strength).
150ml/¼ pint water.
40g/1½oz long-grain rice.
1 medium orange.
Finely chop the onion and place in a small casserole with sultanas. Skin chicken joint and place on top. Blend Colman's Indian Curry Mix with the water and pour over. Cover the dish and bake at 180°C/350°F, gas mark 4, for an hour. Boil rice and serve with the chicken. Complete the meal with an orange.

MENU 2

Breakfast or Supper

2 Weetabix.
125ml/4fl oz skimmed milk.

Soup Meal

1 sachet Knorr Tomato & Bacon or Chicken Quick Soup.
2 slices Nimble Family bread.
7g/¼oz low-fat spread.

Main Meal
Cod Steak with Vegetables / Mousse

1 Birds Eye Cod Steak in Crisp Crunch Crumb, baked without added fat.
15ml/1 tablespoon Waistline Tartare Sauce.
2 tomatoes, baked without fat.
75g/3oz peas, boiled.
1 Birds Eye Super Mousse.

MENU 3

Breakfast or Supper

50g/2oz muesli.
150ml/¼ pint skimmed milk.

Soup Meal

295g/10.4oz can Heinz Low Calorie Scotch Broth, Tomato or Vegetable Soup.
2 Ryvita crispbreads.
1 medium orange.

Main Meal
Liver Casserole / Eclair

125g/4oz lamb's liver.
5ml/1 level teaspoon flour.
50g/2oz onion.
50g/2oz carrots.
227g/8oz can tomatoes.
salt and pepper.
pinch dried sage or mixed herbs.
½ medium packet Cadbury's Smash.
1 Birds Eye Eclair.
Slice liver and toss in flour. Place in small casserole with chopped onion, sliced carrots and tomatoes. Season with salt, pepper and herbs. Cover dish and cook at 170°C/325°F, gas mark 3, for 2 hours. Serve with Smash, made up without butter. Follow with Birds Eye Eclair.

MENU 4
Breakfast or Supper
2 Weetabix.
125ml/4fl oz skimmed milk.

Soup Meal
Home-made Cauliflower Soup
25g/1oz onion.
175g/6oz cauliflower.
275ml/½ pint chicken stock.
15ml/1 level tablespoon dried skimmed milk powder.
salt and pepper.
5ml/1 level teaspoon grated Parmesan cheese.
1 small slice wholemeal bread (25g/1oz).
5ml/1 level teaspoon low-fat spread.
Chop the onion and break cauliflower into florets. Cook in chicken stock until tender (about 15-20 minutes). Sieve or blend the soup and return to the saucepan. Beat in the dried skimmed milk powder and season to taste. Reheat gently. Serve topped with Parmesan cheese and bread with low-fat spread.

Main Meal
Sausage and Beans / Fruit
2 large pork sausages, well grilled.
225g/7.9oz can baked beans.
125g/4oz canned tomatoes.
1 medium orange and 1 medium apple or pear.

MENU 5
Breakfast or Supper
½ grapefruit.
artificial sweetener (optional).
2 Weetabix.
125ml/4fl oz skimmed milk.

Soup Meal
1 sachet Knorr Golden Vegetable Quick Soup.
1 small packet Chipmunk, Golden Wonder or KP crisps.

Main Meal
Lasagne / Yogurt
250g/9oz pack Birds Eye Lasagne.
25g/4oz cabbage or Brussels sprouts, boiled.
1 small carton Raines or Safeway fruit yogurt.

MENU 6
Breakfast or Supper
½ grapefruit.
artificial sweetener (optional).
50g/2oz muesli.
150ml/¼ pint skimmed milk.

Soup Meal
295g/10.4oz Heinz Low Calorie Chicken or Vegetable & Beef Soup.
1 small slice wholemeal bread (25g/1oz).
1 two-finger Kit Kat.

Main Meal
Ham Omelet
2 eggs, size 3.
30ml/2 tablespoons water.
salt and pepper.
7g/¼oz low-fat spread.
25g/1oz lean, boiled ham.
50g/2oz mushrooms.
125g/4oz broccoli, boiled.
2 small tomatoes.
Beat the eggs with water and season. Grease a frying pan with the low-fat spread and cook the omelet. Fill with chopped ham discarding any fat. Serve with mushrooms poached in stock, broccoli and either raw or grilled tomatoes without fat.

MENU 7
Breakfast or Supper
1 small carton British Home Stores Breakfast Honey & Grapefruit Yogurt or St Ivel Country Prize Muesli, Grapefruit or Walnut Yogurt.
1 medium eating apple.

Soup Meal

295g/10.4oz Boots Low Calorie Vegetable or Tomato Soup.
1 small slice wholemeal bread (25g/1oz) spread with 5ml/1 level teaspoon low-fat spread.
125g/4oz carrots, cut into sticks.

Main Meal
Ham and Mushroom Stuffed Jacket Potato with Salad / Creamed Rice and Fruit

175g/6oz potato.
25g/1oz lean boiled ham.
25g/1oz mushrooms.
pinch chopped fresh chives.
1.25ml/¼ teaspoon mustard.
lettuce.
watercress.
cucumber.
½ small green pepper.
few spring onions or onion rings.
15ml/1 tablespoon oil-free French dressing.
170g/6oz can Ambrosia Creamed Rice.
30ml/1 rounded tablespoon raisins or sultanas or 220g/7.8oz can Boots Fruit Cocktail, Pears or Pineapple in Low Calorie Syrup.
Bake the potato at 200°C/400°F, gas mark 6, until soft when pinched (about 45 minutes). Cut in half and scoop out centre. Add chopped ham (discarding all fat), sliced poached mushrooms, chives and mustard and mix together. Pile filling into potato case and return to oven for 5-10 minutes. Serve with the salad vegetables topped with oil-free French dressing. Follow with creamed rice with raisins or sultanas or canned fruit.

MENU 8
Breakfast or Supper

2 rashers streaky bacon, well grilled.
2 slices Nimble Family bread.
15ml/1 tablespoon tomato ketchup.

Soup Meal

1 can Boots, Waistline or Heinz Low Calorie Oxtail Soup.
2 Ryvita crispbreads.
1 medium apple.

Main Meal
Lamb Chop with Vegetables

150g/5oz lamb chump chop, grilled.
½ medium packet Cadbury's Smash, made up without butter.
125g/4oz cabbage or Brussels sprouts, boiled.
75g/3oz carrots, boiled.

MENU 9
Breakfast or Supper

2 small thin slices wholemeal bread (25g/1oz) each.
7g/¼oz low-fat spread.
10ml/2 level teaspoons jam, honey or marmalade.

Soup Meal
Home-made Vegetable Soup

1 beef or chicken stock cube.
275ml/½ pint boiling water.
1 stick celery.
25g/1oz onion.
50g/2oz carrot.
5ml/1 level teaspoon fresh parsley or pinch dried parsley.
2 Energen crispbreads.
25g/1oz Edam cheese.
Dissolve stock cube in boiling water and add chopped celery and onion, grated carrot and parsley. Cover and simmer for 20 minutes. Season and serve with crispbreads and cheese.

Main Meal
Fish and Vegetables / Berries and Ice Cream

Individual pack Young's Salmon & Mushroom Supreme or Sole & Asparagus Royale or Cod Mornay with Prawns.
125g/4oz green beans, boiled.
50g/2oz frozen sweetcorn, boiled.
50g/2oz vanilla ice cream.
125g/4oz raspberries or strawberries.

MENU 10
Breakfast or Supper
2 Shredded Wheat.
125ml/4fl oz skimmed milk.

Soup Meal
425g/15fl oz can Frank Cooper's French Onion Soup.
50g/2oz slice French bread.
15ml/1 level tablespoon grated Parmesan cheese.
Heat soup. Put into a bowl and top with French bread. Sprinkle on cheese and grill until it bubbles.

Main Meal
Cod in Sauce with Vegetables / Yogurt
1 packet Birds Eye Cod in Mushroom Sauce.
50g/2oz sliced green beans, boiled.
1 tomato, halved and grilled without fat.
50g/2oz peas, boiled.
1 medium orange.
½ small carton natural yogurt.

MENU 11
Breakfast or Supper
125ml/4fl oz unsweetened orange juice.
2 Weetabix.
125ml/4fl oz skimmed milk.
15ml/1 level tablespoon raisins.

Soup Meal
1 sachet Batchelors Slim-a-Soup, Beef & Tomato.
2 slices Sunblest HiBran bread.
1 sliced tomato.
25g/1oz corned beef.

Main Meal
Mushroom and Prawn Omelet / Ice Cream
50g/2oz button mushrooms.
2 eggs, size 3.
salt and pepper.
30ml/2 tablespoons water.
50g/2oz prawns.
175g/6oz courgettes.
1 Lyons Maid Vanilla Bar.

Poach mushrooms in water or stock, drain and halve if necessary. Beat the eggs with water and seasoning. Cook the omelet in a non-stick pan, then add mushrooms and prawns. Fold over. Slice courgettes and boil. Serve with the omelet. Follow with ice cream.

MENU 12
Breakfast or Supper
125ml/4fl oz unsweetened grapefruit juice.
1 Shredded Wheat.
75ml/3fl oz skimmed milk.
15ml/1 level tablespoon raisins.

Soup Meal
Home-made Tomato and Orange Soup / Apple
1 tiny carrot.
½ small onion.
225g/8oz canned tomatoes.
pinch mixed herbs.
salt and pepper.
275ml/½ pint chicken stock.
7g/¼ oz low-fat spread.
7g/¼ oz flour.
30ml/2 tablespoons orange juice.
1 slice Sunblest HiBran bread.
1 medium apple.
Slice the carrot and onion and put in a saucepan with tomatoes, herbs, seasoning and stock. Bring to the boil and simmer for 30 minutes. Push through a sieve. Melt the low-fat spread in a saucepan, stir in flour and soup and bring to boil. Just before serving, add the orange juice. Serve with bread. Follow with an apple.

Main Meal
Beef and Onion Casserole / Mousse
125g/4oz very lean stewing beef.
1 small onion.
1 medium carrot.
5ml/1 level teaspoon flour.
125ml/¼ pint beef stock.
salt and pepper.

10ml/2 level teaspoons tomato purée.
75g/3oz cabbage.
125g/4oz potato, boiled or baked.
1 individual tub Birds Eye or Ross mousse.
Dice the beef, onion and carrot. Put them in a small saucepan. Mix the flour with a little cold water, boil the stock and pour onto the flour, stirring. Add to the pan and bring to the boil. Season. Add tomato purée and simmer for about 1 hour until meat is tender. Serve with potato and cabbage. Follow with mousse.

MENU 13
Breakfast or Supper
25g/1oz Quaker Harvest Crunch.
75ml/3fl oz skimmed milk.
1 small apple.

Soup Meal
283g/10oz can Crosse & Blackwell Country Vegetable and Beef Soup.
1 medium apple.
1 peach or pear.

Main Meal
Juice / Beefburger and Beans
125ml/4fl oz unsweetened orange juice.
2 frozen beefburgers (50g/2oz each) well grilled.
150g/5.3oz can baked beans.
1 tomato, halved and grilled without fat.

MENU 14
Breakfast or Supper
1 Shredded Wheat.
1 small banana (150g/5oz) sliced.
1 small carton natural yogurt.

Soup Meal
1 sachet Batchelors Asparagus Cup-a-Soup.
2 Rich Osborne biscuits.

Main Meal
Braised Kidneys and Sausage / Apple
2 lamb's kidneys.
1 pork chipolata sausage.
5ml/1 teaspoon oil.
1 small onion.
125ml/¼ pint stock (made with stock cube).
5ml/1 level teaspoon tomato purée.
salt and pepper.
pinch mixed herbs.
25g/1oz rice, raw.
75g/3oz broccoli, boiled.
1 large apple (175g/6oz).
Halve kidneys. Grill sausage and cut into four. Heat oil in a small saucepan, add kidneys and onion and fry for a few minutes. Add stock, tomato purée, herbs and seasoning. Simmer for 20 minutes. Add sausage. Serve with boiled rice and boiled broccoli. Follow with the apple.

MENU 15
Breakfast or Supper
125ml/4fl oz unsweetened orange juice.
25g/1oz Quaker Harvest Crunch.
90ml/3fl oz skimmed milk.

Soup Meal
283g/10oz can Waistline Low Calorie Oxtail Soup.
2 cream crackers.
7g/¼oz low-fat spread.

Main Meal
Dressed Egg and Prawns / Biscuit and Cheese
1 egg, size 3.
50g/2oz prawns.
30ml/2 tablespoons Heinz or Waistline low-calorie salad dressing.
lettuce.
cucumber.
1 tomato.
25g/1oz Stilton cheese.
1 digestive biscuit.

Hard boil the egg. Halve and place cut side down on a bed of crisp lettuce. Sprinkle with prawns and top with salad dressing. Decorate with cucumber and tomato slices. Follow with the cheese and biscuit.

gravy.
75g/3oz roast potato.
220g/7.8oz can Boots Pineapple in Low Calorie Syrup.

MENU 16

Breakfast or Supper

1 egg, size 3.
15ml/1 tablespoon skimmed milk.
salt and pepper.
7g/¼ oz low-fat spread.
1 slice wholemeal bread
(40g/1½ oz).

Soup Meal

425g/15oz can Frank Cooper's Consommé.
113g/4oz carton cottage cheese.
2 Nabisco Tea Break Rusks.

Main Meal

Smoked Trout and Coleslaw / Mousse

175g/6oz cold smoked trout.
Half 227g/8oz Eden Vale Coleslaw in Vinaigrette.
lettuce.
cucumber slices.
1 individual tub frozen ripple mousse.

MENU 17

Breakfast or Supper

2 rashers streaky bacon, well grilled.
2 tomatoes, halved and grilled without fat.
1 egg, size 3, poached.

Soup Meal

1 sachet Knorr Chicken Quick Soup.
2 Tuc biscuits.
25g/1oz Edam cheese.

Main Meal

75g/3oz lean roast lamb.
50g/2oz peas, boiled.
50g/2oz Brussels sprouts, boiled.
30ml/2 tablespoons thin fat-free

THE-NO-NEED-TO-COOK DIET

900 calories

If you are the sort of slimmer for whom the kitchen is a disaster area, then this diet is perfect for you. The fact that you don't have to cook a thing means that it fits perfectly into virtually any kind of lifestyle, whether you work full time, do shift work, or are at home all day. Some preparation is involved, but we've kept it to a minimum. All you need to do is wash and chop a few vegetables, spread a crispbread, toss together some fruity mixtures and boil the occasional kettle.

Standing in the kitchen while you wait for a meal to cook can be very dangerous for a dieter. Within arm's reach there are likely to be some nibble-able goodies, and while you are feeling hungry you are at your most vulnerable to temptation. This is just the time when many a slimmer has succumbed to a handful of raisins or a lump of cheese from the fridge.

The No-Need-To-Cook-Diet cuts down on temptation time and offers you a whole variety of delicious and nutritious snacks and meals which add up to two weeks' worth of speedy weight loss. All you need to do is select four meals each day (you can prepare them all in one go if you wish) and eat them whenever you feel hungry. Almost all the meals are suitable for taking to work.

Because this is such a simple, no-trouble diet, you may be tempted to get a bit slap-happy with weighing and measuring quantities. Don't. Errors in calculation by eye instead of scales are always on the generous side – and little errors can add up to a big amount of extra calories that could slow down or even stop your weight loss. We have made it as easy as we can by including a number of convenience foods which come in individual portions so that all the weighing and measuring has been done for you. But count any other items (except salad greens) very carefully.

Don't be worried that you are not going to get a hot meal while on this diet. We have included some quick noodle and rice snack meals which just need boiling water to turn them into a tasty hot dish and some mix-in-the-cup soups.

All you have to do to start your diet tomorrow is to read the rules that follow and then choose your first four meals. Buy all the ingredients you need today. Then take a holiday from the kitchen and in two weeks' time you'll be very glad you did.

DIET RULES

1 You may have four meals a day (each adds up to 200 calories). Eat these whenever you wish, but be sure to leave at least two hours between one meal and the next.

2 To eat as wide a variety of foods as possible – this ensures you get all the nutrients you need – choose one meal from each of the four categories each day. That is one Cereal, Fruit and Sweet Meal; one Bread and Crispbread Meal; one Savoury Meal and one Salad Meal. If you decide to skip one section try to double up on either the savoury meals or salad section.

3 In addition to your four meals, you may have 100 calories' worth of drinks. Black coffee or tea (sweetened with artificial sweetener); any low-calorie label soft drinks; water; Marmite or Oxo made with boiling water can be drunk freely. If you wish to add milk to your tea or coffee, count 100 calories for 150ml/¼ pint Silver Top or 190ml/⅓ pint semi-skimmed milk or 275ml/½ pint skimmed milk. If you don't want to spend your 100 calories' worth on milk, you may choose 100 calories' worth of drinks from the list on pages 154 and 155.

4 Make sure you keep to the stated portions for each meal. The only foods you need not weigh are very low-calorie vegetables, such as lettuce, cucumber and celery.

5 Take very great care when measuring fats. If your scale doesn't weigh accurately under 25g/1oz, then weigh out 25g/1oz and divide this equally into four to give you 7g/¼oz portions. When we use a very small amount of fat, we have given a 5ml/1 teaspoon measure. Use a measuring spoon carefully levelled off at the top. A rounded teaspoon would give you double the amount of fat and calories.

CEREAL, FRUIT AND SWEET MEALS

Milk given in these meals is in addition to your drinks' allowance.

Fruit Juice /Muesli and Yogurt *(pages 80-81)*
150ml/¼ pint Just Juice Grapefruit.
25g/1oz muesli.
1 small carton Chambourcy or Sainsbury's natural yogurt.
Drink juice and serve muesli mixed with yogurt.

Cereal / Bread with Savoury Spread
1 Variety pack Kellogg's Cornflakes or Special K (17g/0.63oz).
5ml/1 level teaspoon sugar.
70ml/2½ fl oz skimmed milk.
2 slices Slimcea bread.
Bovril, Marmite or yeast extract.
Serve cereal with sugar and milk. Follow with bread thinly covered with savoury spread.

Breakfast Bran / Fruit
25g/1oz Kellogg's All-Bran or Sainsbury's Breakfast Bran.
30ml/1 rounded tablespoon raisins or sultanas.
75ml/3fl oz skimmed milk.
1 medium orange or apple.
Serve cereal with dried fruit and milk. Follow with orange or apple.

Yogurt with Fruit and Nuts
1 small banana (150g/5oz).
1 small carton British Home Stores or St Ivel or St Michael natural yogurt.
15ml/1 level tablespoon raisins.
15ml/1 level tablespoon roughly chopped nuts.
Peel and slice banana and mix with other ingredients.

Mandarins and Yogurt
298g/10½ oz can John West Mandarins in natural juice.

1 small carton St Ivel Prize Fruit yogurt.
Mix fruit with yogurt and serve.

Orange Juice / Weetabix
150ml/¼ pint Just Juice Orange.
2 Weetabix.
125ml/4fl oz skimmed milk.
Drink juice and follow with Weetabix and milk.

Egg, Orange and Honey Flip
1 egg, size 3.
150ml/¼ pint Just Juice Orange.
15ml/1 level tablespoon clear honey.
Whisk egg with juice and honey. Serve in a glass.

Fruit with Lemon Curd Yogurt
220g/7.8oz can Boots Fruit Cocktail or Pears in Low Calorie Syrup.
1 small carton Chambourcy Lemon Curd Yogurt.
Mix fruit with yogurt and serve.

Fruit Salad and Ice Cream
1 medium apple.
1 medium orange.
1 small banana (150g/5oz).
15ml/1 level tablespoon lemon juice.
125ml/4fl oz low-calorie bitter lemon drink.
25g/1oz vanilla ice cream.
Peel and slice fruit. Mix with lemon juice and bitter lemon. Serve with the ice cream.

Creamed Rice with Orange Segments
1 medium orange.
170g/6oz can Ambrosia Creamed Rice.
Peel and segment orange. Mix with creamed rice.

Crunchy Bar / Apple
1 Jordan's Original Crunchy Bar.
1 medium apple.

Grapefruit and Celery Munch
2 medium grapefruit.
25g/1oz seedless raisins.

2 sticks celery.
30ml/2 level tablespoons flaked almonds.
Peel and segment grapefruit. Mix with raisins, chopped celery and almonds.

Drinking Chocolate and Biscuit
10ml/1 rounded teaspoon drinking chocolate.
225ml/8fl oz skimmed milk.
1 Huntley & Palmer Milk Chocolate Elevenses or 1 McVitie Bandit or 1 Rowntree Mackintosh Blue Riband or Breakaway.

Flavoured Milk and Biscuit
284ml/½ pint Unigate Low Fat Crazy Drink, Banana or Strawberry Flavour.
1 Marie or Gingerella biscuit.

BREAD AND CRISPBREAD MEALS

Fruit Juice / Bread and Marmalade
125ml/4fl oz Just Juice Orange.
2 slices Nimble Family bread.
7g/¼ oz low-fat spread.
10ml/2 level teaspoons marmalade or jam.

Cheese Spread and Tomato Sandwich / Apple
2 slices Nimble Family bread.
1 triangle cheese spread.
1 tomato, sliced.
1 medium eating apple.

Open Cheese Sandwich
1 small slice wholemeal bread (25g/1oz).
5ml/1 level teaspoon low-fat spread.
1 Kraft Processed Cheese Slice.
30ml/1 rounded tablespoon sweet pickle.
1 tomato.
few sprigs watercress.

Bread with Fish Spread / Soup
2 slices Slimcea bread.
53g/1⅞ oz Princes Lobster or

Salmon Spread.
sliced cucumber.
mustard and cress.
1 sachet Knorr Golden Vegetable Quick Soup.

Chicken Sandwich / Soup
2 small slices wholemeal bread (25g/1oz each).
35g/1¼ oz Sainsbury's Minced Chicken in Jelly.
1 tomato, sliced.
1 sachet Borden's Soup Break, any flavour.

Prawn Sandwich *(pages 80-81)*
50g/2oz peeled prawns.
15ml/1 level tablespoon Waistline Seafood Sauce.
2 small slices wholemeal bread (25g/1oz each).
little shredded lettuce.
Mix prawns with Seafood Sauce. Make into a sandwich with bread and lettuce.

Banana and Cottage Cheese Open Sandwich
50g/2oz cottage cheese.
1 small slice wholemeal bread (25g/1oz).
1 small banana (150g/5oz) sliced.
mustard and cress.
1 medium carrot.
1 stick celery.
Spread cottage cheese on bread and top with sliced banana and mustard and cress. Serve with carrots and celery cut into sticks.

Apple and Cottage Cheese Double Decker
1 dessert apple.
lemon juice.
50g/2oz cottage cheese.
2 lettuce leaves.
3 slices Slimcea bread.
Coarsley grate apple; sprinkle with lemon juice and mix with cottage cheese. Season to taste. Arrange lettuce on two slices of bread and divide apple and cheese mixture between them. Stack one on top of the other and

cover with third slice.

Potted Shrimps and Crispbreads
50g/1.75oz Young's Potted Shrimps.
2 Ryvita crispbreads.
little lettuce or watercress.

Crispbreads, Cottage Cheese / Soup
2 Ryvita crispbreads.
113g/4oz carton Eden Vale cottage cheese, any flavour.
1 sachet Batchelors Slim-a-Soup, any flavour.

Cracottes, Liver Paté / Apple
2 McDougall's Cracottes.
25g/1oz Mattesson's Liver Paté.
2 sticks celery.
1 apple.

Crispbreads, Salmon Paté / Banana
2 Energen crispbreads.
42g/1½oz John West Salmon Paté.
mustard and cress.
1 small banana (150g/5oz).

Tasty Cheese Crispbreads
113g/4oz carton St Ivel cottage cheese with Onion and Chives.
30ml/1 rounded tablespoon Bicks Corn Relish or Cubits Cucumber Relish or Mild Chili Relish.
3 Energen crispbreads.
Mix cheese with relish and spread on crispbreads.

SAVOURY MEALS

Knoodles
1 tub Knorr Knoodles Kashmir Beef Curry or Bombay Chicken Currey or Prawn Curry.

Quick Lunch / Apple
1 tub KP Quick Lunch Curry or Risotto.
1 medium apple.

Prawn Curry
1 tub Knorr Knoodles Prawn Curry.

Savoury Egg / Soup
1 British Home Stores Savoury Egg or St Michael Picnic Egg.
1 sachet Knorr Golden Vegetable Quick Soup.

Baked Beans with Cheese
225g/7.9oz can baked beans.
15g/½oz Edam cheese.
Serve beans topped with grated cheese.

Salmon with Celery Sticks / Apple
99g/3½oz can John West Pink Salmon.
4 sticks celery.
1 medium apple.

Cottage Cheese, Ringos and Tomatoes
113g/4oz carton cottage cheese, any flavour except Onion and Cheddar.
1 small packet Golden Wonder Ringos.
2 tomatoes.

Rollmop, Apple and Cucumber Cocktail
70g/2½oz rollmop herring.
1 red-skinned eating apple.
50g/2oz cucumber.
15ml/1 level tablespoon Waistline Seafood Sauce.
1 Lyons Krispen.
Cut rollmop into slices and mix with cored and chopped apple, diced cucumber and Seafood Sauce. Serve with crispbread.

Snack Noodles / Apple
1 tub KP Quick Lunch, Bolognese.
1 medium apple.

Soup / Cheese Crispbread
(pages 80-81)
1 sachet Batchelors Slim-a-Soup, any flavour.
40g/1½oz Edam cheese.
2 Lyons Krispen.

Crab and Celery Boats with Crispy Snack
2 large sticks celery.

53g/1⅞ oz pot Prince's Crab Spread.
1 small packet Allinson's Wheateats or Golden Wonder Cheesy Wotsits.
Cut celery into 5cm/2in lengths and fill with crab spread. Serve with Wheateats or Wotsits.

Ham and Cheese Rolls with Celery
113g/4oz carton cottage cheese with chives or with onions and peppers.
2 slices (25g/1oz each) Scot's Honey Roast Ham or Virginia Ham.
2 sticks celery.
Divide cottage cheese between slices of ham and roll up. Serve with celery.

Bisks Biscuits / Bovril Drink
1 meal Bisks Cheese Crackers or Cheese 'n' Celery.
1 tomato.
1 stick celery.
1 cup of Bovril.

Shapers Meal Replacement Drink / Apple
1 serving Boots Meal Replacement Drink.
1 medium eating apple.

SALAD MEALS

Coleslaw with Cottage Cheese and Prawns
125g/4oz white cabbage.
1 medium carrot.
1 stick celery.
50g/2oz St Ivel Cottage Cheese with Onion and Chives.
60ml/4 tablespoons natural yogurt.
50g/2oz peeled prawns or shrimps.
salt and pepper.
Shred cabbage and chop celery finely; grate the carrot. Mix cottage cheese with yogurt. Add the prepared vegetables and prawns or shrimps and toss

together gently. Season to taste with salt and pepper.

Chicken, Celery and Apple Salad
50g/2oz cooked chicken, skin removed.
2 sticks celery.
1 medium red-skinned eating apple.
15ml/1 tablespoon lemon juice.
15ml/1 tablespoon Heinz or Waistline low calorie salad dressing.
30ml/2 tablespoons natural yogurt.
salt and pepper.
1 Energen crispbread.
Cut chicken into bite-sized pieces; slice celery. Core and dice apple and toss in lemon juice. Mix together salad dressing and yogurt and season to taste with salt and pepper. Add chicken, celery and apple and mix well. Serve with crispbreaed.

Salmon with Chicory and Orange Salad
99g/3½ oz can John West Pink Salmon.
1 head chicory.
1 medium orange.
30ml/2 tablespoons oil-free French dressing.
Divide chicory into individual leaves and place in a bowl with orange segments. Add the dressing and toss well together. Serve the salmon with the salad.

Tuna, Sweetcorn and Celery Salad
99g/3½ oz can John West Tuna in Brine.
50g/2oz canned sweetcorn with peppers.
2 sticks celery.
15ml/1 level tablespoon oil-free French dressing.
salt and pepper.
lettuce.
2 tomatoes.
cucumber.

Drain and flake tuna. Mix tuna with sweetcorn, chopped celery, dressing and seasoning to taste. Arrange on a bed of lettuce with sliced tomato and cucumber.

Coleslaw in Vinaigrette with Ham Sausage

198g/7oz carton St Ivel Vegetable Salad in Vinaigrette or 225g/8oz carton Sainsbury's Coleslaw in Vinaigrette.
25g/1oz Mattesson's ham sausage.
Mustard and cress.
Mix carton salad with the ham sausage cut into strips. Garnish with mustard and cress and serve.

Garlic Sausage with Carrot and Cauliflower Salad

50g/2oz garlic sausage.
125g/4oz raw carrot.
125g/4oz raw cauliflower sprigs.
45ml/3 tablespoons oil-free French dressing.
½ packet Knorr Salad Days.
Arrange sliced garlic sausage on a serving plate. Cut carrot into small sticks and break cauliflower into small florets. Toss with dressing and Salad Days until well mixed. Serve with the garlic sausage.

Turkey and Ham Loaf with Salad

50g/2oz Mattesson's Turkey and Ham Loaf.
2 tomatoes, sliced.
50g/2oz raw carrot, grated.
few spring onions.
cucumber.
watercress.
lettuce.
15ml/1 tablespoon oil-free French dressing.
1 Energen crispbread.
5ml/1 level teaspoon low-fat spread.
Arrange the slicked turkey and ham loaf with the salad vege-tables on a serving plate. Add the dressing to the salad vegetables and serve with the crispbread and low-fat spread.

Mushroom Salad with Bacon and Liver Sausage *(pages 80-81)*

50g/2oz button mushrooms.
few sprigs watercress.
60ml/4 level tablespoons natural yogurt.
salt and pepper.
lettuce.
50g/2oz Sainsbury's Bacon and Liver Sausage.
2 tomatoes.
2 sticks celery.
Wash, dry and slice mushrooms, chop watercress. Mix mushrooms and watercress with yogurt. Season to taste with salt and pepper. Arrange a few lettuce leaves on a serving plate and pile the mushroom salad on top. Arrange slices of bacon and liver sausage, quartered tomatoes and chopped celery sticks around the mushroom salad.

Silverside of Beef and Salad

125g/4oz Scot's Silverside of Beef.
15ml/1 level tablespoon Bicks Corn Relish or Cucumber Relish.
lettuce.
mustard and cress.
small bunch radishes.
few spring onions.
½ small green pepper, deseeded and sliced.
1 tomato, sliced.
15ml/1 tablespoon oil-free French dressing.
1 Ryvita crispbread.
Arrange the sliced silverside of beef on a serving plate with relish and salad vegetables dressed with oil-free dressing. Serve with crispbread.

Red Cabbage Salad with Cheese

175g/6oz red cabbage.
50g/2oz carrot.

75g/3oz leek.
30ml/2 tablespoons oil-free
French dressing.
15ml/1 tablespoon low-calorie
salad dressing.
25g/1oz Edam cheese.
Mix shredded red cabbage,
grated carrot and thinly sliced
leek together in a bowl. Add the
dressings and toss together until
thoroughly mixed. Serve with
Edam cheese.

Cottage Cheese and Pineapple Salad

113g/4oz carton natural cottage
cheese.
1 ring canned pineapple in
natural juice, drained.
lettuce or chicory.
watercress or mustard and cress.
1 medium carrot.
2 sticks celery.
1 Ryvita crispbread.
5ml/1 level teaspoon low-fat
spread.
Arrange cottage cheese and
pineapple on a bed of lettuce or
chicory leaves. Arrange
watercress or mustard and cress,
grated carrot and chopped celery
around the cottage cheese. Serve
with the crispbread with low-fat
spread.

Blue Cheese and Fruit Salad

15g/½oz Danish Blue or
Roquefort cheese.
45ml/3 tablespoons natural
yogurt.
Few drops lemon juice.
salt and pepper.
1 small grapefruit.
75g/3oz black grapes.
1 medium eating apple.
2 sticks celery.
lettuce.
Crumble blue cheese and mix
with yogurt, lemon juice and
seasoning. Add grapefruit segments, grapes (pips removed),
chopped apple and celery and
toss gently until well mixed.
Serve on a bed of lettuce.

Pear Salad

1 medium dessert pear.
10ml/2 teaspoons lemon juice.
50g/2oz curd cheese.
25g/1oz cooked lean ham.
salt and pepper.
2 walnut halves.
lettuce.
Peel the pear; cut in half; remove
and discard the core. Brush the
pear with lemon juice. Mix
together the curd cheese,
chopped ham, salt and pepper
and chopped walnut halves.
Spoon into the pear hollows.
Serve on a bed of lettuce.

THE VEGETARIAN DIET

850 calories

Meat and fish, although valuable sources of protein, minerals and some vitamins, are not essential to good health. Vegetable protein used to be described as 'second-class protein', but nutritionists now consider it every bit as valuable as that provided by expensive steaks. In this speedy diet, meat and fish have been replaced by cheese, eggs, yogurt, beans, cereals and nuts. When eaten in variety these provide all the nutrients you will need. Even if you are not a vegetarian, this diet may suit you. Meat and fish can be very costly and it is possible to eat the vegetarian way far more economically. Shopping is uncomplicated and only very occasionally have we used a special vegetarian product. The best place to find these is in your local health food shop.

Though this is a strict diet in terms of calories, you will not need to feel hungry, since raw vegetables can be eaten any time of the day when you feel the urge. An interesting thing about hunger is that it seems to be a waxing and waning sensation. Eating experiments have shown that if people delay eating approximately 15-20 minutes after experiencing the first twinges of hunger, more often than not the feeling will diminish. Experiment with your own hunger pangs, seeing what happens when you delay eating – you can stop yourself being bullied by twinges which may, in fact, fade away.

As this diet is very low in calories, we recommend that you stay on it for just two weeks. There are 17 menus to choose from, so that if you dislike any of the meals suggested you can skip that whole day and move on to the next menu. First we give the day's menu, then any recipes you need to cook. If after two weeks you still have weight to lose, then increase your daily calories to 1,000. You can do this by choosing 150 calories' worth of foods from the chart on page 207 or by eating an extra three pieces of fresh fruit each day. To start your diet, read the rules below, then get out a pen and paper and make a list of all the foods you need to shop for. The more shopping you do in advance, the better.

DIET RULES

1 Follow the menus day by day. Do not swap a meal in one day's menu for a meal in another day's menu. If you dislike one of the meals suggested on a certain day then skip that whole day's menu and go on to the next one. You can repeat any daily menu if you wish, but to ensure a balanced diet use at least seven different menus in your two weeks' high-speed slimming campaign.

2 You are allowed two light meals and a main meal each day. The meals may be eaten at any time of the day that suits you. You can also change their order, having the main meal at lunch time or in the evening.

3 Accompany your meals with any of the vegetables from the unlimited list on page 63. These can also be nibbled raw between meals whenever you wish.

4 You may have the following milk allowance for use in tea and coffee or as a milky suppertime drink: 275ml/½ pint soya milk, eg, Itona Soya Beanmilk, measured after it has been diluted with an equal quantity of water as directed, or 275ml/½ pint Silver Top, sterilised, Longlife, or untreated farm milk or 575ml/1 pint skimmed milk or reconstituted dried skimmed milk, eg, Marvel. Tea and coffee with milk from your allowance are unlimited; as is water, Marmite or yeast extract drinks, herbal teas and any bottled soft drink labelled 'low calorie'. If you have a sweet tooth, artificial sweeteners can be used.

5 Vegetarian dishes are enormously enhanced by the use of herbs, spices and flavourings and you may use any of the following as freely as you wish: all herbs and spices, lemon juice, Soy sauce, vinegar, Worcestershire sauce, Waistline Oil-Free French Dressing, Dietade Low-Calorie Salad Dressing.

UNLIMITED VEGETABLES

The following vegetables served raw, boiled or cooked and served without added fat, can be eaten in unlimited quantities with the meals in the following menus. They can be nibbled raw between meals whenever you wish:

Asparagus	Courgettes	Radishes
Aubergines	Cucumber	Runner beans
Bean sprouts	Endive	Salsify
Beetroot	French beans	Seakale
Broccoli	Jerusalem artichokes	Spinach
Brussels sprouts	Leeks	Spring greens
Cabbage, all kinds	Lettuce	Spring onions
Carrots	Marrow	Swedes
Cauliflower	Mushrooms	Tomatoes
Celery	Mustard and cress	Turnips
Chicory	Onions	Watercress
Chinese leaves	Peppers, green or red	

MENU 1
Light Meal 1
125ml/4fl oz unsweetened orange juice.
1 egg, size 3, boiled.
1 Ryvita crispbread.

Light Meal 2
Cheese and Tomato on Toast.*
1 medium orange or pear.

Main Meal
½ grapefruit, no sugar.
Spaghetti with Vegetable Bolognese Sauce.*

Cheese and Tomato on Toast*
1 small slice wholemeal bread (25g/1oz).
1 tomato.
15g/½ oz Edam cheese.
Small bunch watercress.
Toast bread; top with sliced tomato and grated cheese and grill until cheese melts. Serve with watercress.

Spaghetti with Vegetable Bolognese Sauce*
25g/1oz textured vegetable protein mince.
225g/8oz canned tomatoes.
1 small onion.
15ml/1 level tablespoon tomato purée.
2.5ml/½ level teaspoon yeast extract.
Pinch dried oregano or thyme.
50g/2oz wholewheat spaghetti.
Reconstitute the textured vegetable protein mince with water as directed to give 75g/3oz reconstituted weight. Roughly chop canned tomatoes and place them in a pan with peeled and chopped onion, reconstituted textured vegetable protein mince, tomato purée, yeast extract and herbs. Bring to the boil, stirring. Reduce heat, cover and simmer for 15 – 20 minutes. Meanwhile cook the spaghetti in boiling salted water for 12 minutes; drain and arrange in the centre of a warm serving dish. Check the sauce for seasoning and add salt and pepper if necessary. Spoon the sauce over the spaghetti.

MENU 2
Light Meal 1
1 small carton Chambourcy or Sainsbury's natural yogurt.

63

100g/3½oz prunes, stewed without sugar.

Light Meal 2
1 slice Nimble Family bread, toasted.
142g/5oz can baked beans in tomato sauce.

Main Meal
Pasta and Nut Salad.*

Pasta and Nut Salad*
25g/1oz wholewheat spaghetti rings or other pasta shapes.
2 tomatoes.
50g/2oz button mushrooms.
½ small green pepper.
25g/1oz stoned olives.
25g/1oz dry roasted peanuts.
25g/1oz natural cottage cheese.
30ml/2 tablespoons oil-free French dressing.
salt and pepper.
lettuce.
few onion rings, optional.
Cook the spaghetti rings or pasta in boiling salted water for 12 minutes. Drain and rinse through with cold water until cool, then drain again. Cut tomatoes into wedges, slice the mushrooms and chop the pepper. Mix pasta, tomatoes, mushrooms, pepper, olives and nuts together in a bowl. Sieve cottage cheese and mix with salad dressing. Add to the salad with seasoning to taste and toss well to mix. Serve on a bed of lettuce leaves. Garnish with onion rings.

MENU 3
Light Meal 1
1 small slice wholemeal bread (25g/1oz) toasted.
1.25ml/¼ teaspoon Marmite.
50g/2oz low-fat curd cheese.

Light Meal 2
Apple and Nut Salad.*

Main Meal
397g/14oz can Granose Cannelloni.

Salad or boiled vegetables from unlimited list.
Rhubarb Fool.*

Apple and Nut Salad*
(pages 80-81)
1 medium eating apple.
10ml/2 teaspoons lemon juice.
2 sticks celery.
25g/1oz hazelnuts.
15ml/1 tablespoon Heinz or Waistline low-calorie salad dressing.
lettuce.
watercress.
1 tomato.
Core and chop eating apple, then toss in the lemon juice until thoroughly coated. Mix apple with chopped celery and hazelnuts. Stir in low-calorie salad dressing. Arrange a bed of lettuce on a plate and pile the apple and nut salad on top. Accompany with sprigs of watercress and the tomato.

Rhubarb Fool*
125g/4oz rhubarb.
15ml/1 tablespoon water.
1 small carton Raines, Safeway or Sainsbury's natural yogurt.
Granulated sugar-free sweetener, eg Hermesetas Sprinkle Sweet, to taste.
Cut rhubarb into short lengths. Place in a small-lidded pan with the water. Cover and cook over a gentle heat until the rhubarb is tender. Put rhubarb and yogurt in a blender and blend until smooth. Sweeten to taste with granulated sweetener, then pour into a serving dish. Chill then serve.

MENU 4
Light Meal 1
2 Weetabix
125ml/4fl oz skimmed milk (extra to allowance).

Light Meal 2
Baked Cheesy Spinach.*

Main Meal
Vegetable Curry.*

Baked Cheesy Spinach*
125g/4oz frozen spinach, thawed
or 125g/4oz lightly boiled
spinach, chopped.
1 egg, size 3.
45ml/3 tablespoons skimmed
milk.
15g/½ oz Edam cheese.
salt and pepper.
Press any excess moisture out of
the spinach. Beat egg and milk
together, then stir in the grated
cheese. Stir egg mixture into the
spinach and season to taste. Pour
into a lightly greased small
ovenproof dish. Bake at
180°C/350°F, gas mark 4, for 30
minutes. Serve hot.

Vegetable Curry*
25g/1oz brown long-grain rice.
5ml/1 teaspoon vegetable oil.
25g/1oz onion.
50g/2oz cooking apple.
5-10ml/1-2 level teaspoons curry
powder.
150ml/¼ pint water or vegetable
stock.
5ml/1 teaspoon tomato purée.
5ml/1 teaspoon lemon juice.
125g/4oz red kidney beans,
canned.
125g/4oz Birds Eye Cauliflower,
Peas and Carrots.
salt and pepper.
Cook rice in boiling salted water
for 30 minutes. Meanwhile, heat
the oil in a pan. Finely chop the
onion and peel, core and chop
the apple; cook gently in the oil
for 5 minutes, without browning.
Stir in the curry powder, and
cook for 2 minutes stirring all the
time. Add the water or stock,
bring to the boil, stirring, then
add the tomato purée and lemon
juice. Cover and simmer for 5
minutes. Add the drained kidney
beans and thawed mixed
vegetables. Bring to the boil,

cover and simmer gently for 15
minutes. Season to taste with salt
and pepper. Arrange the rice on
a warm serving dish and spoon
the vegetable curry into the
centre. Serve hot.

MENU 5
Light Meal 1
125ml/4fl oz unsweetened orange
juice.
1 small slice wholemeal bread
(25g/1oz).
5ml/1 level teaspoon low-fat
spread.
5ml/1 level teaspoon honey or
marmalade.

Light Meal 2
Three Bean Salad.*

Main Meal
Spanish Omelet.*
Green salad vegetables from
unlimited list.
1 small carton British Home
Stores fruit yogurt or St Ivel
Prize Fruit Yogurt.

Three Bean Salad*
(pages 80-81)
50g/2oz red kidney beans, dried
or canned.
50g/2oz broad beans, fresh or
canned.
125g/4oz green beans, fresh or
frozen.
small piece onion.
30ml/2 tablespoons oil-free
French dressing.
15g/½ oz Edam cheese.
Fresh parsley, chopped.
If using dried kidney beans, soak
overnight then boil until tender.
Boil the fresh broad beans and
green beans and drain. Cut
onion into rings and add to
beans. Mix in dressing. Sprinkle
with grated Edam cheese and
fresh parsley and serve.

Spanish Omelet*
2 eggs, size 3.
30ml/2 tablespoons water.

salt and pepper.
7g/¼ oz low-fat spread.
½ small onion.
1 fresh or canned tomato.
25g/1oz mushrooms.
15ml/1 tablespoon cooked peas.
Beat eggs together with the water
and salt and pepper to taste.
Melt the low-fat spread in a non-
stick omelet pan. Add the
chopped onion, tomato,
mushrooms and peas. Cook over
a gentle heat for 5 minutes,
stirring frequently. Pour the
beaten egg into the pan. Cook
over a moderate heat until the
egg mixture is set on the bottom,
then place under a hot grill to set
the top and brown slightly. Turn
omelet out onto a warm plate
and serve immediately with green
salad vegetables.

MENU 6
Light Meal 1
50g/2oz muesli.
75ml/3fl oz skimmed milk
(additional to allowance).

Light Meal 2
1 small slice wholemeal bread
(25g/1oz).
50g/2oz cottage cheese.
1 small sliced banana (150g/5oz).
mustard and cress.

Main Meal
Sweet and Sour Red Cabbage.*
2 Energen crispbreads.
25g/1oz cottage cheese.

Sweet and Sour Red Cabbage*
½ small cooking apple.
1 small onion.
175g/6oz red cabbage.
5ml/1 level teaspoon brown
sugar.
salt and pepper.
45ml/3 tablespoons vinegar.
30ml/2 tablespoons water.
50g/2oz canned pineapple in
natural juice, drained.
30ml/2 tablespoons natural

yogurt.
watercress.
Peel and chop apple and onion,
finely shred the cabbage and put
with sugar, salt and pepper to
taste, vinegar and water in a
pan. Cover and cook over a low
heat for 45 minutes, stirring
occasionally. Stir in the chopped
pineapple and a little more water
if necessary. Cover again and
continue to simmer for 10-15
minutes. Turn out onto a warm
serving dish, top with the natural
yogurt and serve with watercress.

MENU 7
Light Meal 1
1 small slice wholemeal bread
(25g/1oz) toasted.
2.5ml/½ level teaspoon Marmite
or yeast extract.
50g/2oz mushrooms, poached in
stock or water.
1 medium orange.

Light Meal 2
1 egg, size 3, hard boiled.
15ml/1 tablespoon Heinz or
Waistline low-calorie salad
dressing.
salad vegetables from unlimited
list.
175g/6oz slice cantaloupe, ogen
or yellow melon.

Main Meal
Savoury Crumble.*
Boiled green vegetables from
unlimited list.

Savoury Crumble*
213g/7½ oz can Granose
Meatless Savoury Cuts.
15ml/1 tablespoon low-calorie
tomato ketchup.
piece cucumber.
3 small tomatoes.
salt and pepper.
25g/1oz wholemeal breadcrumbs.
15g/½ oz Edam cheese.
pinch dried basil.
7g/¼ oz low-fat spread.
Chop the meatless savoury cuts

and mix with tomato sauce. Turn into a small ovenproof dish. Peel and dice cucumber and arrange on top. Slice the tomatoes and reserve three slices for garnish. Arrange the remaining tomato slices over the cucumber. Season with salt and pepper to taste. Mix breadcrumbs with grated cheese and basil. Sprinkle over the top of the dish. Dot with tiny pieces of low-fat spread. Arrange reserved tomato slices on top. Bake at 180°C/350°F, gas mark 4, for 20 minutes. Serve at once with the boiled green vegetables.

MENU 8
Light Meal 1
2 Weetabix.
125ml/4fl oz skimmed milk (additional to allowance).

Light Meal 2
Stuffed Tomatoes.*
2 Ryvita crispbreads.
2.5ml/½ teaspoon Marmite or yeast extract.

Main Meal
Cheesy Baked Potato.*
Salad vegetables from unlimited list dressed with 15ml/1 tablespoon oil-free French dressing.

Stuffed Tomatoes*
(pages 80-81)

2 tomatoes.
1 egg, size 3, hard boiled.
15ml/1 tablespoon Waistline Tartare Sauce.
salt and pepper.
watercress.
Cut or slice off the top of each tomato; carefully scoop out pulp and discard. Stand 'shell' upside down to drain. Chop egg and mix with tartare sauce and seasoning to taste. Spoon into the tomato shells and place on a plate. Garnish with watercress and serve.

Cheesy Baked Potato*
200g/7oz potato.
salt and pepper.
50g/2oz cottage cheese with chives.
30ml/2 level tablespoons piccalilli.
15g/½oz Edam cheese.
Scrub potato and bake at 200°C/400°F, gas mark 6, until soft when pinched (about 45 minutes). Cut in half lengthways, scoop out the centre and mash with cottage cheese. Season to taste. Pile back into the potato cases. Top each half with a tablespoon of piccalilli, then sprinkle over the grated cheese. Return to the oven or place under a hot grill until the cheese has melted. Serve with salad vegetables.

MENU 9
Light Meal 1
½ grapefruit.
Artificial sweetener, optional.
1 egg, size 3, boiled.
1 slice Nimble Family bread, toasted.

Light Meal 2
Orange and Cottage Cheese Salad.*
1 Ryvita crispbread.

Main Meal
half a 425g/15oz can Granose Lentil and Vegetable Casserole.
Boiled vegetables from unlimited list.

Orange and Cottage Cheese Salad*
1 medium orange.
113g/4oz carton natural cottage cheese.
salt and pepper.
salad vegetables from unlimited list.
Peel the orange and cut into segments. Season the cottage cheese to taste. Arrange on a plate and place the orange

segments on top. Serve with a selection of salad vegetables.

MENU 10
Light Meal 1
½ grapefruit.
1 egg, size 3, boiled.
1 Energen crispbread.
5ml/1 level teaspoon low-fat spread.

Light Meal 2
Crunchy Carrot Salad.*
1 Energen crispbread.

Main Meal
Vegetable and Nut Risotto.*

Crunchy Carrot Salad*
2 medium carrots.
75g/3oz red cabbage.
25g/1oz fennel or 1 stick celery.
2 spring onions or white part of 1 leek.
15ml/1 level tablespoon raisins.
30ml/2 tablespoons oil-free French dressing.
15ml/1 tablespoon lemon juice.
salt and pepper.
Grate carrots, finely shred cabbage, finely chop the fennel or celery, and thinly slice onions or leek. Mix all the prepared vegetables together in a bowl. Stir in the raisins. Add the dressing and lemon juice and toss together until thoroughly mixed. Season to taste with salt and pepper.

Vegetable and Nut Risotto*
½ small onion.
1 small green pepper.
2 tomatoes.
50g/2oz brown long-grain rice.
225ml/8fl oz boiling water.
1.25ml/¼ teaspoon dried thyme or marjoram.
25g/1oz mushrooms.
salt and pepper.
little grated lemon rind.
25g/1oz salted cashew nuts or peanuts.
Chop onion; remove seeds from

pepper and chop flesh; peel and chop tomatoes. Put into a shallow pan with rice. Add the boiling water and herbs, bring to the boil, stir well, then cover and simmer gently for 25 minutes. Add chopped mushrooms and extra water if necessary. Season to taste with salt and pepper and stir in the grated lemon rind. Cover and continue to simmer for 5 minutes or until the rice is tender and the water is absorbed. Just before serving stir in nuts.

MENU 11
Light Meal 1
125ml/4fl oz unsweetened orange juice.
2 Energen crispbreads.
2.5ml/½ teaspoon Marmite or yeast extract.
50g/2oz low-fat curd cheese.

Light Meal 2
295g/10.4oz can Boots Low Calorie Tomato Soup.
Creamy Mushrooms on Toast.*

Main Meal
175g/6oz slice melon.
Lentil Stew.*
Boiled green vegetables from unlimited list.

Creamy Mushrooms on Toast*
125g/4oz button mushrooms.
10ml/2 level teaspoons low-fat skimmed milk powder.
125ml/4fl oz water or vegetable stock.
salt and pepper.
10ml/2 level teaspoons cornflour.
1 small slice wholemeal bread (25g/1oz).
paprika.
Wash mushrooms and place in a small saucepan. Dissolve skimmed milk powder in the water or stock and pour over mushrooms. Bring to the boil and simmer for 5 minutes. Drain the mushrooms and keep warm.

Blend the cooking liquid with the cornflour. Return to the pan and boil for 1 minute or until thickened. Season to taste and stir in the mushrooms. Toast the bread on both sides. Pile the creamy mushrooms on the bread and lightly dust with paprika.

Lentil Stew*
50g/2oz lentils.
275ml/½ pint vegetable stock or water.
1 small onion.
2 sticks celery.
1 medium carrot.
2.5ml/½ level teaspoon yeast extract.
50g/2oz canned butter beans.
salt and pepper.
Wash lentils and put in a pan with the stock or water. Bring to the boil, reduce heat, cover and simmer gently for 30 minutes. Add the sliced onion and carrot, and chopped celery. Stir in yeast extract. Cover and simmer for a further 30 minutes. Stir in butter beans; season to taste with salt and pepper and heat through. Serve with boiled green vegetables.

MENU 12
Light Meal 1
125ml/4fl oz tomato juice.
275g/10oz wedge melon.
20g/¾oz cornflakes.
75ml/3fl oz skimmed milk.

Light Meal 2
295g/10.4oz can Boots Low Calorie Soup.
1 egg, size 3, hard boiled.
Salad of lettuce, 1 tomato, cucumber.
15ml/1 tablespoon oil-free French dressing.
50g/2oz Sainsbury's Coleslaw in Vinaigrette.

Main Meal
Cauliflower and Leek Cheese.*

Cauliflower and Leek Cheese* *(pages 80-81)*
75g/3oz leeks.
150g/5oz cauliflower.
150ml/¼ pint skimmed milk.
7g/¼oz butter.
7g/¼oz flour.
salt and pepper.
30ml/2 level tablespoons Parmesan cheese, grated.
Slice leeks. Boil them with the cauliflower florets for about 15 minutes until tender. Drain. Meanwhile make a white sauce by beating together the milk, butter, flour and seasoning. Bring to the boil, stirring. Add half the cheese. Put the vegetables in an ovenproof dish, pour over the sauce and sprinkle on the remaining cheese. Grill to brown.

MENU 13
Light Meal 1
1 medium orange.
1 small carton natural yogurt.

Light Meal 2
Bean and Celery Bake.*

Main Meal
Egg Topped Mushrooms.*

Bean and Celery Bake*
1 small head celery.
1 tomato.
150g/5.3oz can baked beans.
15ml/1 level tablespoon fresh breadcrumbs.
Remove leaves from the celery and cut the head in two lengthways. Put in an ovenproof dish and add the sliced tomato. Add 30ml/2 tablespoons water, cover with foil and bake at 180°C/350°F, gas mark 4, for 15 minutes. Remove foil. Pour on the baked beans and top with the crumbs. Bake a further 5 minutes until the beans are hot and the breadcrumbs crisp.

Egg Topped Mushrooms*
1 egg, size 3.
15ml/1 tablespoon skimmed milk.
salt and pepper.
7g/¼ oz low-fat spread.
2 large flat mushrooms.
150ml/¼ pint stock.
30ml/2 level tablespoons fresh breadcrumbs.

Mix the egg, milk and seasoning. Melt low-fat spread and scramble the egg. Meanwhile poach the mushrooms in stock for about 3 minutes. Drain and put on a serving plate. Top with the egg and sprinkle with breadcrumbs. Grill to brown.

MENU 14
Light Meal 1
1 medium apple.
2 Ry-King Wheat Crispbreads.
7g/¼ oz low-fat spread.

Light Meal 2
295g/10.4oz can Heinz Slimway Soup.
50g/2oz French bread.

Main Meal
Stuffed Cabbage Leaves.*

Stuffed Cabbage Leaves*
2 large green cabbage leaves.
15ml/1 level tablespoon rice.
1 small onion.
25g/1oz mushrooms.
5ml/1 level teaspoon oil.
salt and pepper.
15ml/1 level tablespoon fresh breadcrumbs.
15g/½ oz peanuts.
half a 198g/7oz can tomatoes.
salt and pepper.
pinch dried basil.
vegetables from unlimited list.
Boil cabbage leaves for 5 minutes, drain and cool. Boil the rice, drain and cool. Fry onion and sliced mushrooms in the oil. Mix together the rice, onion, mushrooms, seasonings, breadcrumbs and nuts. Divide filling between the cabbage leaves

and fold them to make parcels. Bake in a covered dish at 180°C/350°F, gas mark 4, for about 15 minutes. Make a sauce by heating tomatoes with seasonings, then straining. Serve with boiled vegetables.

MENU 15
Light Meal 1
2 tomatoes, halved.
25g/1oz Edam cheese, grated (grill on top of tomatoes).
50g/2oz poached mushrooms.
1 slice HiBran bread.

Light Meal 2
Pasta Salad.*
175g/6oz raspberries, fresh or frozen.

Main Meal
Sweetcorn Boats.*

Pasta Salad*
25g/1oz pasta shells.
1 stick celery.
2 spring onions.
15ml/1 tablespoon oil-free French dressing.
salt and pepper.
25g/1oz drained, canned red kidney beans.
25g/1oz peas, boiled.
Cook pasta shells in boiling water for about 12 minutes until just soft. Drain and cool. Slice celery and chop spring onions. Mix all ingredients together.

Sweetcorn Boats*
2 slices HiBran bread.
7g/¼ oz low-fat spread.
45ml/3 tablespoons canned sweetcorn and peppers.
1 tomato.
watercress.
cucumber.
Remove crusts from the bread. Spread with low-fat spread and use, fat side down, to line two deep patty tins. Bake at 180°C/350°F, gas mark 4, for 25 minutes. Put the corn in the

cases and top with slices of
tomato. Heat through for a
further 10 minutes. Serve with
watercress and cucumber.

MENU 16
Light Meal 1
125ml/4fl oz unsweetened orange
juice.
20g/¾oz Bran Flakes.
75ml/3fl oz skimmed milk.

Light Meal 2
Stilton Spread.*
2 McDougall's Cracotte biscuits.

Main Meal
Tomato Pasta.*
½ can Weight Watchers
Blackberries.
30ml/2 tablespoons natural
yogurt.

Stilton Spread*
15g/½oz Stilton cheese.
25g/1oz low-fat spread.
15ml/1 tablespoon Heinz or
Waistline low-calorie salad
dressing.
ground black pepper.
Crumble cheese, then mix all
ingredients together with a fork.

Tomato Pasta*
25g/1oz pasta shells.
50g/2oz mushrooms.
1 tomato.
1 small onion.
5ml/1 teaspoon oil.
5ml/1 teaspoon tomato purée.
salt and pepper.
pinch dried mixed herbs.
150ml/¼ pint stock (made with
stock cube).
Boil pasta shells for about 12
minutes; drain. Slice mushrooms
and chop tomato and onion. Fry
the onion for about 5 minutes in
oil. Add tomato, tomato purée,
salt, pepper and herbs. Add
enough stock to make a thick
sauce and simmer for 15
minutes. Pour over the hot pasta
shells.

MENU 17
Light Meal 1
½ papaya (paw paw), puréed
with
1 small carton natural yogurt.

Light Meal 2
half a 227g/8oz packet Birds Eye
Rice, Peas and Mushrooms,
boiled.
1 grilled tomato.
50g/2oz sliced courgettes.

Main Meal
Macaroni and Bean Curry.*
1 apple, pear or orange.

Macaroni and Bean Curry*
25g/1oz short-cut macaroni.
1 small carrot.
1 small onion.
5ml/1 teaspoon oil.
10ml/2 level teaspoons tomato
purée.
pinch each cinnamon, ginger,
salt and sugar.
75ml/3fl oz stock.
25g/1oz drained, canned red
kidney beans.
Boil macaroni and chopped
carrot for about 12 minutes until
just cooked. Drain. Chop onion
and fry in oil for 5 minutes. Add
tomato purée, cinnamon, ginger,
salt, sugar and stock and simmer
for 30 minutes. Add the
macaroni, carrot and red kidney
beans and heat through.

THE BUY-IT DIET 850 calories

If you're more slap-happy than accurate with kitchen scales, or if you're easily tempted by leftovers, this diet will probably work fastest for you.

Knowing how easy it is to make mistakes when you're weighing and measuring food, we've organised this diet around convenience foods which come in individual portions where all the weighing and measuring has been done for you. That way you're less likely to make mistakes and allow extra calories to sneak in which will slow down your weight loss.

A few calorie errors during a day can really mount up. Guess that your muesli is 25g/1oz when it's really 40g/1½oz and you've added 50 calories to your breakfast. Guess that portion of roast lamb to be 125g/4oz instead of the 150g/5oz it is and you've added another 50 calories. Hard cheese is very deceiving and you need only double your 25g/1oz portion of Cheddar to eat 120 more calories. Add to that the milk you tip into your tea cup without bothering to count, and your daily total could be over 250 calories more than you realise. That's why many women claim that they can't lose weight on a diet which they insist they are keeping to.

Another big plus of this diet is that you need to spend less time preparing meals. That means you'll spend less time in the kitchen. Your kitchen presents you with many more eating temptations than almost any other place. Literally hours of the day are often spent within hand's reach of food and often amid the appetite-tempting aroma of cooking. Keep away and there's more chance you'll keep to your strict eating plan.

Most of the foods included in this diet can be bought and stored in the larder or freezer so they are handy to make into a meal when you wish to eat. So there is never a diet-breaking excuse that you forgot to buy your low-calorie meal.

You are allowed three meals a day and you can choose from meals that are practically instant, just requiring to be heated up in a saucepan or popped in the oven. We have also included some interesting recipes so that you can turn your bought meals into something special.

Provided you keep to this diet exactly, this is one of the best ways of losing weight at a high-speed rate.

DIET RULES

1 Each day choose a breakfast/supper meal, a light meal and a main meal. The order in which you eat them is unimportant. You might like to skip breakfast, have a light meal at lunch-time, a main meal early in the evening and supper before you retire. Or you may prefer to have breakfast, a main meal mid-day, and a light meal in the evening.

2 In addition to your three meals, you can have up to 100 calories' worth of drinks each day. You might like to use this allowance on milk in tea and coffee – you can have 275ml/½ pint skimmed milk or 150ml/¼ pint Silver Top each day. Milk given in cereal meals is additional to this allowance. Or you may want to save some of your calories for other drinks (see list on page 154). You can drink unlimited water and unsugared tea and coffee without milk (artificial sweeteners may be used). You can also drink any mixers, squashes or soft drinks labelled 'low-calorie'.

3 Vary your choice of meals to ensure you have all the nutrients you require and make sure you choose one meal from each list every day.

4 Weigh and measure all foods other than those which come in individual portions – especially fat for cooking or spreading. If your scales don't measure accurately under 25g/1oz, weigh out 25g/1oz and divide it into four 7g/¼oz portions.

BREAKFAST/ SUPPERTIME MEALS

150 calories each.

All Bran and Raisins
25g/1oz All Bran.
30ml/2 level tablespoons raisins.
3fl oz skimmed milk.

Shredded Wheat / Orange
1 Shredded Wheat.
75ml/3fl oz skimmed milk.
1 medium orange.

Weetabix
2 Weetabix.
125ml/4fl oz skimmed milk.

Poached Egg on Toast
1 egg (size 4), poached.
1 slice wholemeal bread
(25g/1oz), toasted.
5ml/1 level teaspoon low-fat
spread.

Grapefruit / Boiled Egg
½ grapefruit.
Artificial sweetener.
1 egg (size 4), boiled.
1 slice Sunblest HiBran bread.
5ml/1 level teaspoon low-fat
spread.

Chipolata Grill
2 pork chipolatas, well grilled.
2 tomatoes, grilled without fat.

Cottage Cheese and Crispbread
113g/4oz carton cottage cheese
(natural or with chives, with
onions and peppers, with
sweetcorn and peppers, with
pineapple).
2 Lyons Krispen.
1 stick celery or few slices
cucumber or 1 carton mustard
and cress.

Soup / Chicken Sandwich
1 sachet Borden's Chicken, Beef
or Tomato Soup Break.
2 small slices Slimcea.
35g/1¼ oz pot Sainsbury's
Minced Chicken in Jelly.
slices cucumber and sprigs of
watercress.

Tomato and Vegetable Juice / Fish Paste Sandwich
113ml/4fl oz Campbell's Tomato
and Vegetable Juice.
1 slice wholemeal bread
(25g/1oz).
35g/1.23oz pot Shippams Salmon
and Shrimp or Anchovy Paste.

Soup / Cheese Snack
1 sachet Batchelors Onion and
Beef Cup-a-Soup.
1 Lyons Krispen.
1 processed cheese slice.
1 stick celery.

Soup and Griddles
295g/10.4oz can Boots Low
Calorie Tomato Soup.
1 packet KP Griddles.

Cheese Spread on Crispbreads with Tomato
2 triangles cheese spread.
3 Energen crispbreads.
1 tomato.

Crispbreads and Kipper Spread
2 Ryvita crispbreads.
53g/1 ⅞ oz pot Princes Kipper
Spread.
1 tomato.

Crispbreads and Beef Paste / Banana
35g/1.23oz pot Shippams
Country Pot Paste, Beef and
Horseradish or Beef and Pickle.
2 Lyons Krispen.
1 small banana (150g/5oz).

Ham Sausage and Crispbreads
50g/2oz Scot Ham Sausage,
sliced.
2 Energen crispbreads.
Little made mustard.
1 tomato, sliced.

Soup / Apple
295g/10.4oz can Heinz Chicken
and Vegetable Broth.
1 Ryvita crispbread.
1 medium eating apple.

Toasted Cheese
1 slice Nimble Family bread.
1 processed cheese slice.
2 tomatoes.
Toast bread on one side, top with cheese slice and grill until cheese melts. Serve with tomatoes.

Toasty Griller
1 slice wholemeal bread (25g/1oz).
1 slice Birds Eye Cheese and Ham Griller.
Toast bread on one side; top with Griller and grill.

Golden Wonder Ringos / Apple
1 packet Golden Wonder Ringos.
1 medium apple.

Crisps and Celery
1 small packet KP, Smiths or Walker's crisps.
1 or 2 sticks celery.

Baked Beans on Toast
150g/5oz can Heinz Baked Beans.
1 slice Nimble Family bread, toasted.

Baked Beans and Bacon
150g/5oz can Heinz Baked Beans.
1 rasher streaky bacon, well grilled.

Fish Fingers with Tomatoes and Mushrooms
2 frozen fish fingers, grilled without fat.
198g/7oz can tomatoes.
213g/7½oz can Chesswood Button or Small Whole Mushrooms in Brine.

Grilled Fish Cakes and Tomatoes
2 frozen fish cakes, grilled or baked without fat.
2 large tomatoes, halved and grilled without fat.

Pears and Topping
227g/8oz can Koo Pear Halves in

Apple Juice.
45ml/3 tablespoons Nestlé Tip Top.

Yogurt with Apple and Raisins
1 small carton St Ivel or Chambourcy natural yogurt.
15ml/1 level tablespoon raisins.
1 medium eating apple, cored and chopped.

Yogurt / Orange plus Biscuit
1 small carton St Ivel or Chambourcy natural yogurt.
1 orange, segmented.
1 Nice biscuit.

Hazelnut Yogurt
1 small carton Sainsbury's Hazelnut Yogurt.

Fruit and Bran Bar / Orange
1 Prewett's Fruit and Bran Bar.
1 medium orange.

Milk and Biscuits
150ml/¼ pint Silver Top milk, hot or cold.
2 Marie or Morning Coffee biscuits.

LIGHT MEALS
200 calories each

Scotch Broth / Apple
300g/10.6oz can Heinz Scotch Broth.
1 Ryvita crispbread with Marmite.
1 medium apple.

French Onion Soup with Crispbreads and Cheese
425g/15oz can Frank Cooper's French Onion Soup.
2 Ryvita crispbreads.
2 triangles cheese spread.

Chicken Broth
425g/15oz can Baxters Chicken Broth.
1 slice wholemeal bread (25g/1oz).

Country Vegetable Soup / Fruit
283g/10oz can Crosse & Blackwell Country Vegetable

with Beef Soup.
1 slice Nimble Family bread.
1 medium orange or pear.

Oxtail Soup / Sandwich
1 can Boots (295g/10.4oz), Heinz (300g/10.6oz) or Waistline (283g/10oz) Low Calorie Oxtail Soup.
2 small slices Slimcea.
35g/1.23oz pot Shippams Liver and Bacon Paste.

Soup / Salmon Pâté
295g/10.4oz can Heinz Chicken Low Calorie Soup.
42g/1½oz can John West Salmon Paté.
2 Energen crispbreads.
cucumber slices and watercress.

Ravioli / Apple
213g/7½oz can Tesco Ravioli in Tomato and Meat Sauce.
1 tomato.
1 medium apple.

Quick Lunch
1 carton KP Bolognaise, Curry or Stroganoff Quick Lunch.

Baked Beans and Bacon
225g/7.9oz can Heinz Baked Beans.
1 rasher streaky bacon, well grilled.

Potted Shrimps
50g/1.76oz Young's Potted Shrimps.
2 Ryvita crispbreads.
few sprigs watercress.

Prawn Curry
227g/8oz packet Birds Eye China Dragon Prawn Curry.
125g/4oz drained, canned bean sprouts or lightly boiled fresh bean sprouts.

Poached Egg and Cheese on Toast
1 small slice Slimcea.
1 slice Kraft Processed Cheese.
1 egg (size 4).
2 tomatoes, fresh *or*

Half 212g/7½oz can tomatoes.
Poach egg in water or in a non-stick pan, without fat. Toast bread and top with cheese and poached egg. Serve with grilled fresh tomatoes or heated, canned tomatoes.

Cheese Sandwich / Banana
2 slices Slimcea or Nimble bread.
1 Gervais Danone Petit Suisse Cheese.
little mustard and cress.
1 small banana (150g/5oz).

Spaghetti Hoops on Toast
213g/7½oz can Safeway Spaghetti in Tomato Sauce.
1 slice Nimble Family bread, toasted.
1 medium orange or pear.

Spaghetti Rings and Egg
213g/7½oz can Crosse & Blackwell Spaghetti Rings with Tomato Sauce.
1 egg, size 4, poached.

Prawn Salad
113g/4oz can Princes prawns or shrimps.
15ml/1 tablespoon Waistline Seafood Sauce.
mixed salad of lettuce, mustard and cress, green pepper, spring onions, 1 sliced tomato and 1 stick celery.
1 small slice Slimcea.
5ml/l level teaspoon low-fat spread.

Fish Fingers and Peas
3 frozen fish fingers, grilled without added fat.
50g/2oz frozen peas, boiled.

Cod in Parsley Sauce / Fruit
1 packet Birds Eye Cod in Parsley Sauce.
50g/2oz frozen sweetcorn, boiled.
125g/4oz green beans, boiled.
1 orange or pear.

Cod in Butter Sauce
170g/6oz packet Findus Cod in Butter Sauce.

150g/5oz mixed vegetables, frozen.

Cod in Mushroom Sauce
1 packet Ross Cod Steak in Mushroom Sauce.
50g/2oz peas, boiled.
125g/4oz cauliflower, boiled.

Cheese, Tomato and Pickle Toasty / Apple
1 slice wholemeal bread (25g/1oz).
1 tomato.
1 slice Kraft Processed Cheese.
15ml/1 tablespoon sweet mixed pickle.
1 apple.
Toast bread and top with sliced tomato and cheese. Grill until cheese melts and serve with pickle. Follow with apple.

Cottage Cheese Salad
113g/4oz carton cottage cheese (natural or with chives, with onions and peppers, with sweetcorn and peppers, with pineapple).
mixed salad of lettuce, watercress, cucumber, radishes, green pepper, 2 sticks celery, 1 sliced tomato.
15ml/1 tablespoon low-calorie salad dressing.
1 Ryvita crispbread.

Sausage and Bacon Grill
2 pork chipolatas, well grilled.
1 rasher streaky bacon, well grilled.
2 tomatoes, grilled without fat.

Bacon Fingers, Tomato and Mushrooms
2 Danish Prime Bacon Fingers, grilled without fat.
1 tomato, grilled without fat.
213g/7½oz can Chesswood Button or Small Whole Mushrooms in Brine.
1 medium orange.

Minced Beef and Vegetables.
1 packet Ross Minced Beef and Vegetables.
125g/4oz cauliflower, boiled.
75g/3oz carrots, boiled.

Chicken and Mushroom Casserole
170g/6oz packet Birds Eye Chicken and Mushroom Casserole.
125g/4oz Birds Eye Peas and Baby Carrots.

Liver and Onion Casserole
1 packet Birds Eye Liver with Onion and Gravy.
75g/3oz cabbage, boiled.

Roast Beef / Apple
100g/3½oz Findus Gravy and Roast Beef.
227g/8oz Birds Eye Cauliflower, Peas and Carrots.
1 medium apple.

Roast Chicken / Apple
113g/4oz Birds Eye Gravy and Roast Chicken.
125g/4oz Findus Garden Mix Vegetables.
1 medium apple.

Roast Pork / Fruit
113g/4oz Birds Eye Gravy and Roast Leg of Pork.
125g/4oz Birds Eye Peas and Baby Carrots.
125g/4oz cabbage, boiled.
1 medium orange or pear.

LIGHT MEAL RECIPES

200 calories each

<hr>

Pineapple Burger

<hr>

50g/2oz frozen beefburger.
15g/½oz Kraft Philadelphia
Cheese.
1 slice pineapple in natural juice,
drained.
mixed salad of lettuce,

watercress, spring onions,
cucumber, sliced green pepper,
1 sliced tomato.
15ml/1 tablespoon oil-free French
dressing.

Grill beefburger well. Spread one side of burger with cheese and top
with the slice of pineapple. Heat quickly under a hot grill until the
cheese begins to melt. Serve with mixed salad and dressing.

<hr>

Tomato and Egg Scramble

<hr>

2 eggs (size 4).
10ml/2 level teaspoons skimmed
milk powder.
30ml/2 tablespoons water.
salt and pepper.

125g/4oz canned tomatoes.
10ml/2 level teaspoons chopped
fresh parsley, optional.
1 Ryvita crispbread.
few sprigs watercress, optional.

Beat the eggs, milk powder and water together. Season to taste.
Chop canned tomatoes. Cook the egg mixture in a non-stick pan
over gentle heat, stirring continuously, until thick and creamy. Stir
in the chopped tomatoes and parsley. Heat through gently. Spoon
on to the crispbread or serve with crispbread and with a few sprigs of
watercress.

<hr>

Italian Style Fish

<hr>

2 Findus Cod Steaks.
½ clove garlic, crushed.
pinch dried basil or thyme.

283g/10oz can Buitoni Tomato
Sauce.
125g/4oz broccoli.

Place frozen cod steaks in a small ovenproof dish. Stir garlic and
herbs into tomato sauce and spoon over fish steaks. Cover and bake
in a moderate oven, 190°C/375°F, gas mark 5, for 35-40 minutes.
Serve with broccoli.

Fish Rarebit

170g/6oz Findus Cod Steak in Butter Sauce.
1 slice wholemeal bread (25g/1oz).

15ml/1 tablespoon grated Parmesan cheese.
2 tomatoes.

Cook the fish in butter sauce according to directions. Flake fish into sauce. Spoon onto the toasted bread. Top with cheese and heat under a hot grill with the halved tomatoes until cheese begins to brown. Serve rarebit with tomato halves.

Corned Beef Bake

125g/4oz runner beans, fresh or frozen.
50g/2oz corned beef.

1 sachet Batchelors Cup-a-Soup, Golden Vegetable.

Cook frozen runner beans as directed or trim, slice and boil fresh runner beans until tender, then drain. Slice or dice corned beef and place in the bottom of a small ovenproof dish. Top with runner beans. Make up the soup and pour over beans. Cover and bake at 190°C/375°F, gas mark 5, for 20 minutes.

Mixed Vegetable Soup

125g/4oz mixed vegetables, frozen.
15ml/1 level tablespoon tomato purée.
275ml/½ pint stock prepared from ½ stock cube.
salt and pepper.

pinch ground mace.
dash of Worcestershire sauce.
15ml/1 level tablespoon grated Parmesan cheese.
2 Ryvita crispbreads.
7g/¼oz low-fat spread.
Marmite or yeast extract.

Cook mixed vegetables, tomato purée, stock and seasoning in a covered pan for 15 minutes or until the vegetables are tender. Add the ground mace, Worcestershire sauce and additional seasoning if required. Pour into a serving dish and sprinkle over the Parmesan cheese. Serve with the crispbreads spread with low-fat spread and Marmite or yeast extract.

ONE-MAJOR-MEAL-A-DAY DIET. Curried Chicken and Banana Salad; followed by Strawberry Mousse with Raspberries.

NO-NEED-TO-COOK DIET. Fruit Juice
with Muesli and Yogurt; Soup with Cheese
Crispbread; Mushroom Salad with Bacon and
Liver Sausage; Prawn Sandwich.

VEGETARIAN DIET. Three Bean Salad;
Cauliflower and Leek Cheese, Stuffed
Tomatoes and Apple and Nut Salad.

BIG BOWLFUL DIET. Potato and Bacon
Salad; Stewed Fruit and Nuts; Prawn and
Pasta Hot Pot.

Vegetable and Tomato au Gratin

125g/4oz Birds Eye Cauliflower, Peas and Carrots.
½ packet Chef, Sainsbury's or Knorr Cheese Sauce Mix.

150ml/¼ pint skimmed milk.
2 tomatoes.
15ml/1 level tablespoon grated Parmesan cheese.

Cook vegetables according to pack instructions. Make up cheese sauce mix with skimmed milk. Skin and roughly chop tomatoes. Stir all the vegetables into the cheese sauce, check the seasoning and turn into an ovenproof dish. Sprinkle the top with Parmesan cheese and brown under the grill.

Salmon Coleslaw

99g/3½oz can John West Pink Salmon.
125g/4oz white cabbage, shredded.
1 carrot, grated.

2 sticks celery, finely chopped.
30ml/2 tablespoons oil-free French dressing.
15ml/1 tablespoon chopped fresh parsley.

Drain and flake salmon. Mix shredded cabbage, grated carrot and finely chopped celery together with salmon. Add the dressing and chopped fresh parsley. and toss gently. Turn onto a serving dish.

Cauliflower Soup with Frankfurter

15ml/1 tablespoon dried onion flakes.
150g/5oz frozen cauliflower florets.
150ml/¼ pint chicken stock prepared from ½ stock cube.

salt and pepper.
5ml/1 level teaspoon cornflour.
120ml/8 tablespoons skimmed milk.
25g/1oz frankfurter, sliced.

Cook onion and cauliflower florets with stock in a covered pan until tender, about 10 minutes. Sieve or liquidise in a blender. Return to pan and season with salt and pepper. Blend the cornflour with a little milk, then add to soup with remaining milk. Cook, stirring, until the soup boils: add the sliced frankfurter and heat through gently. Serve hot.

MAIN MEALS

400 calories each

Chicken Soup / Banana
425g/15oz can Campbell's Main
Course Chicken and Vegetable
Soup.
1 slice wholemeal bread
(25g/1oz).
1 large banana (200g/7oz).

Grapefruit / Ham, Turkey and Vegetable Soup
½ grapefruit.
artificial sweetener, optional.
425g/15oz can Campbell's Main
Course Ham, Turkey and
Vegetable Soup.
2 slices wholemeal bread (25g/1oz
each).
7g/¼oz low-fat spread.

Ravioli / Apple
397g/14oz can Buitoni Ravioli.
1 medium apple.

Macaroni Cheese and Egg
210g/7.4oz can Heinz Macaroni
Cheese.
1 egg, size 4, poached.
1 tomato, sliced.
2 Lyons Krispen.
1 orange.

Spaghetti Bolognese / Apple
283g/10oz can Buitoni Bolognese
Sauce.
50g/2oz spaghetti.
1 medium apple.
Heat sauce and serve with boiled
spaghetti. Follow with apple.

Lasagne / Fruit Sundae
250g/9oz Birds Eye Lasagne.
1 Eden Vale Fruit Sundae.

Silverside and Coleslaw
125g/4oz Scot's Silverside of
Beef.
227g/8oz carton Mattesson's
Coleslaw in Vinaigrette.
1 tomato, sliced.
lettuce.
watercress.

Fish Steaks with Vegetables / Yogurt
2 Birds Eye Haddock or Cod
Steaks.
5ml/1 teaspoon oil.
15ml/1 tablespoon Waistline
Tartare Sauce.
125g/4oz Birds Eye Peas and
Baby Carrots.
213g/7½oz can Chesswood
Button or Small Whole
Mushrooms in Brine.
small carton St Ivel Prize Fruit
Yogurt, any flavour.
Brush fish with oil and grill.
Serve with tartare sauce and
vegetables. Follow with yogurt.

Smoked Haddock with Tomatoes
198g/7oz Ross Smoked Haddock
with Butter.
227g/8oz can tomatoes.
125g/4oz canned or new
potatoes, boiled.

Cod in Cheese Sauce / Doughnut
170g/6oz pack Findus Cod in
Cheese Sauce.
175g/6oz cauliflower, boiled.
50g/2oz peas, boiled.
1 Birds Eye Dairy Cream
Doughnut.

Cod Steaks and Chips
2 Findus Cod Steaks.
5ml/1 teaspoon oil.
1 tomato.
75g/3oz McCain Oven Chips.
50g/2oz sweetcorn, frozen.
Brush fish with oil and grill with
tomatoes. Cook oven chips as
instructed and serve with fish
and boiled sweetcorn.

Salmon Fish Cakes / Chocolate Mousse
2 Birds Eye or Ross Salmon Fish
Cakes, grilled or baked without
fat.
15ml/1 tablespoon Waistline
Tartare Sauce.
125g/4oz frozen mixed

vegetables, boiled.
125g/4oz canned or new
potatoes, boiled.
1 Ross Chocolate Mousse Cup.

Shepherd's Pie / Cheese Crispbread
227g/8oz Birds Eye Shepherd's
Pie.
125g/4oz green beans, boiled.
1 Ryvita crispbread, spread with
2 triangles cheese spread.

Steakburger / Fruit Salad
100g/3½ oz Tiffany's Angus
Steakburger, grilled.
125g/4oz frozen mixed
vegetables, boiled.
125g/4oz broccoli, boiled.
198g/7oz can Weight Watchers
Fruit Salad in Low Calorie
Syrup.
30ml/2 tablespoons Nestlé Tip
Top.

Steak and Kidney Pie / Orange
128g/4½ oz Sainsbury's Steak
and Kidney Pie.
125g/4oz cabbage, boiled.
125g/4oz carrots, boiled.
1 orange.

Minced Beef / Peaches and Topping
170g/6oz pack Birds Eye Minced
Beef with Vegetables in Gravy.
175g/6oz canned or new
potatoes, boiled.
220g/7.8oz can Boots Peaches in
Low Calorie Syrup.
15ml/1 tablespoon Nestlé Tip
Top.

Melon / Beef Curry
175g/6oz slice of Canteloupe,
Ogen, Honeydew or Yellow
melon.
283g/10oz can Crosse &
Blackwell Beef Curry and Rice.
side salad of sliced cucumber and
1 sliced tomato.

Shepherd's Pie / Trifle
227g/8oz Findus Shepherd's Pie.
125g/4oz cabbage, boiled.

1 Sainsbury's Fruit Dessert or
Ross Devonshire Trifle.

Grapefruit / Chicken in Barbecue Sauce
½ grapefruit.
artificial sweetener, optional.
205g/7¼ oz can Shippams
Chunky Chicken in Barbecue
Sauce.
25g/1oz rice.
75g/3oz bean sprouts, fresh or
drained canned.
Serve grapefruit with artificial
sweetener. Serve chicken in
barbecue sauce with boiled rice
mixed with bean sprouts.

Roast Chicken Dinner / Fruit Sundae
1 Birds Eye Roast Chicken
Dinner.
1 Eden Vale Fruit Sundae.

Chicken Curry / Orange
Individual pack Findus Chicken
Curry with Rice.
side salad of watercress,
cucumber and 1 sliced tomato.
1 orange.

Pizza / Choc Ice and Pear
Individual (2cm/5 inch) Ross
Cheese and Tomato Pizza.
green salad of lettuce, spring
onions, cucumber and green
pepper, dressed with 15ml/1
tablespoon oil-free French
dressing.
1 Wall's Dark and Golden or
Golden Vanilla Choc Ice.
1 medium pear.

Melon / French Bread Pizza
175g/6oz slice of Cantaloupe,
Ogen or Honeydew melon.
Findus French Bread Pizza with
bacon, tomatoes, cheese, peppers
and mushrooms.
mixed salad of lettuce,
watercress, cucumber, 1 sliced
tomato, 2 sticks celery and sliced
green pepper, dressed with
15ml/1 tablespoon oil-free French
dressing.

MAIN MEAL RECIPES
400 calories each

Eggs and Mushrooms in Creamed Sauce

2 eggs, size 4.
213g/7½oz can Chesswood
Sliced Mushrooms in Creamed
Sauce.

125g/4oz mixed vegetables,
frozen.
5ml/1 level teaspoon chopped
parsley.

Boil the eggs for 7 minutes; rinse under cold water to cool, then shell. Heat the mushrooms in creamed sauce and cook the mixed vegetables as instructed. Arrange a border of mixed vegetables on a warm serving plate. Halve eggs lengthwise and place, cut sides down, in the middle of the vegetables. Spoon over the hot mushrooms in creamed sauce and sprinkle with chopped parsley.

Mackerel and Tomato Bake

125g/4.4oz canned mackerel in
tomato sauce.
2 tomatoes.
213g/7½oz can button or small
whole mushrooms in brine,

drained.
salt and pepper.
1 Birds Eye Mushroom and
Bacon Griller.
125g/4oz broccoli or cauliflower.

Flake the canned mackerel. Cover the base of a small ovenproof dish with 1 sliced tomato and half the mushrooms. Season, then cover with the flaked mackerel. Arrange the remaining mushrooms and sliced tomato on top and season again. Cover and bake at 180°C/350°F, gas mark 4, for 20 minutes. Remove from the oven, uncover and arrange the Griller on top. Place under a hot grill until the Griller is cooked. Serve with boiled broccoli or cauliflower.

Cod with Mushrooms and Prawn Sauce and Rice

175g/6oz cod fillets, frozen.
water.
5ml/1 teaspoon lemon juice.
salt and pepper.
140g/4.9oz can Campbell's
Condensed Cream of Mushroom
Soup.

30ml/2 tablespoons skimmed
milk.
25g/1oz prawns, fresh, defrosted
or drained canned.
25g/1oz long grain rice.
25g/1oz green or red pepper.
parsley.

Place the frozen fish fillets in a pan with sufficient water to cover and add the lemon juice and seasoning. Simmer the fish for 15 minutes, then drain. Meanwhile heat mushroom soup with skimmed milk and prawns until hot. Boil the rice in lightly salted water for 10 minutes, add the chopped pepper and continue to boil for a further 5 minutes or until the rice is tender. Drain, if necessary and arrange on a serving dish with the fish on top. Pour over the hot mushroom and prawn sauce and garnish with sprigs of parsely.

Baked Fish and Tomato Custard

175g/6oz cod or coley fillets,
frozen.
2 tomatoes.
2 eggs, size 3.
175ml/6fl oz skimmed milk.

15ml/1 tablespoon grated
Parmesan cheese.
5ml/1 teaspoon chopped fresh
parsley.
salt and pepper.

Thaw fish for 1 hour at room temperature. Place in a small lightly-greased ovenproof dish. Cover with skinned and sliced tomatoes. Beat the eggs and skimmed milk together. Stir in cheese and parsley. Season to taste. Pour egg mixture over the tomatoes and fish. Bake at 180°C/350°F, gas mark 4, for 40 to 45 minutes or until set. Serve hot.

Prawn Risotto

227g/8oz pack Birds Eye Rice with Sweetcorn and Peppers.
50g/2oz prawns, fresh or defrosted.
5ml/1 teaspoon chopped fresh parsley.

Cook the vegetable rice as instructed on the packet but omitting any butter. Stir in the prawns and heat through gently. Turn onto a serving dish and sprinkle with chopped parsley.

Cheesy Bacon and Onions

142g/5oz Birds Eye Small Onions and White Sauce.
1 rasher streaky bacon.
1 slice Nimble Family bread.
1 processed cheese slice.
1 tomato.

Cook onions and white sauce according to the instructions on the pack. Remove rind from bacon and grill rasher until crisp then crumble. Toast bread and top with onions and sauce. Sprinkle over the bacon and chopped cheese. Place under a hot grill with halved tomatoes and grill until the cheese begins to melt.

Chilli Beef and Beans

170g/6oz packet Birds Eye Minced Beef with Vegetables in Gravy.
5ml/1 level teaspoon chilli powder.
283g/10oz can Smedley Red Kidney Beans.
227g/8oz cauliflower florets.

Heat the minced beef in gravy according to packet instructions. Pour into a saucepan and add the chilli powder and drained red kidney beans. Heat through stirring well. Serve in a border of boiled cauliflower florets.

Beefburger and Orange

1 Birds Eye Quarterpounder (beefburger).
½ medium orange.
75g/3oz sweetcorn, frozen or canned.
175g/6oz broccoli.
50g/2oz button mushrooms.

Cut a slice from the orange and squeeze the juice from the remainder. Grill the beefburger as packet instructions, spooning over the orange juice during the cooking. Just before cooking is complete, place the slice of orange on top of the beefburger and allow to warm through. Serve with boiled broccoli and mushrooms poached in stock or salted water.

Curried Chicken with Coleslaw Salad

225g/8oz chicken portion.
½ small carton natural yogurt.
lemon rind, grated.
2.5ml/½ level teaspoon curry powder.
salt and pepper.
15ml/1 tablespoon raisins or sultanas.
227g/8oz carton Mattesson's Coleslaw in Vinaigrette.

Skin the chicken portion and place in a dish. Place the yogurt in a basin and stir in a little lemon rind, curry powder and seasoning. Pour the yogurt over the chicken portion and marinade for at least 2 hours. Bake chicken with marinade at 200°C/400°F, gas mark 6, for 30 minutes or until cooked. Stir the raisins or sultanas into the coleslaw and serve with the chicken.

THE METABOLIC DIET

900 calories

S limming's scientists say eating little and often can speed up metabolic rate to a modest but helpful degree. In the hour and a half immediately after you've eaten a meal your metabolism works faster. So if you eat five small meals a day instead of three larger ones, your body is in a state of high burn-up more often.

What exactly is your metabolic rate? The body needs calories for two reasons; firstly to keep functioning and secondly to provide energy for activity. Even if you are just lying in bed all day your body still needs calories – and the number you burn up is called your basal metabolic rate. Your body uses these calories to keep your heart beating, to keep breathing and control your body temperature. An average woman's resting metabolic rate is 1,400 calories a day; for an average man, the figure is 1,700 calories. It is your basal metabolic rate that this diet is designed to speed up.

In addition to the calories which your body uses automatically, it also burns up extra calories when you start moving around. The more you move, the more calories you burn up. That is why activity is important. The average woman will use around 700 calories during the day walking, doing the housework, driving to work, shopping and so on.

In addition to speeding up your metabolism, this diet is ideal if you are a compulsive nibbler and find it difficult to go for long stretches without food. The little-and-often dieting method caters to appetite. Appetite is what makes you want to eat irrespective of whether you're physically hungry or not, because you see food, smell food, think of food, feel bored or happy or sad or for any of dozens of other reasons.

Many slimmers are more dominated by appetite than hunger. That's why they find it almost impossible to keep to three meals a day, and put it down to lack of willpower. On this metabolic diet, which consists of four easy-to-prepare meals and one snack a day, you can virtually eat when your appetite urges you to. And the comforting thought that there is a little meal never far away cancels out the temptation to eat illicit extras.

DIET RULES

1 Choose four of any of the 180-calorie meals each day and one 80-calorie snack. Leave at least two hours between each meal.

2 In addition to the meals you can have 100 calories' worth of drinks. You could use this drinks allowance either on milk in tea or coffee – 150ml/¼ pint Silver Top or 275ml/½ pint skimmed milk – or keep it for drinks from the list on page 154. If you do not want to use your drinks allowance you could choose an 180-calorie meal instead of an 80-calorie snack (but ensure that one of your meals includes some milk).

3 Vary your meals, choosing at least one meat, fish, cheese or egg meal each day so that you have a good supply of nutrients.

4 Keep to the stated portions of ingredients for each meal. Use your kitchen scales to ensure accuracy.

5 Plan ahead and make sure your next low-calorie meal is readily available.

CEREAL AND BREAD MEALS

Grapefruit Juice / Weetabix
125ml/4fl oz Libby's Grapefruit 'C' Calorie Reduced Juice.
2 Weetabix served with 125ml/4fl oz skimmed milk.

All Bran and Banana
25g/1oz Kellogg's All Bran served with 75ml/3fl oz skimmed milk and 1 medium banana (170g/6oz).

Breakfast Bran / Boiled Egg
25g/1oz Sainsbury's Breakfast Bran served with 75ml/3fl oz skimmed milk and followed by 1 egg, size 4, boiled.

Cornflakes and Dried Fruit
25g/1oz cornflakes served with 75ml/3fl oz skimmed milk and 30ml/2 level tablespoons sultanas or raisins.

Muesli and Yogurt
25g/1oz muesli served with 142g/5oz carton St Ivel natural yogurt.

Bread with Jam, Marmalade or Honey
Spread a 40g/1½oz slice of white or wholemeal bread with 7g/¼oz butter and 7.5ml/1½ level teaspoons jam, marmalade or honey.

Porridge / Fruit Juice
25g/1oz oatmeal made into porridge with 75ml/3fl oz skimmed milk and 75ml/3fl oz water.
Serve with Hermesetas Sprinkle Sweet. Follow with 150ml/¼ pint unsweetened orange juice.

Juice / Ryvita and Marmalade
150ml/¼ pint unsweetened grapefruit juice; 2 Ryvita spread with 10g/⅓oz low-fat spread and 10ml/2 teaspoons marmalade or jam.

EGG MEALS

Orange Juice / Poached Egg on Toast
115ml/4fl oz Kellogg's Rise and Shine Orange made up; 1 egg, size 3, poached and served on 1 slice Nimble Family bread, toasted.

Scrambled Egg and Ham on Toast
Beat together 1 egg, size 3, 15ml/1 tablespoon skimmed milk, salt and pepper. Add 25g/1oz chopped lean boiled ham and scramble in a non-stick pan. Serve on 1 small slice toasted Slimcea.

Cheesy Egg and Tomato
Beat together 1 egg, size 3, 50g/2oz cottage cheese with chives and salt and pepper. Scramble in a non-stick pan and serve on 1 small slice toasted Slimcea with one tomato.

Egg and Bacon
Poach 1 egg, size 3, and serve with 2 rashers streaky bacon, well grilled.

Picnic Egg
1 St Michael Picnic Egg or British Home Stores Savoury Egg served with 1 stick celery. Follow with 1 medium orange.

Baked Egg with Chicken Livers and Mushrooms
Chop 50g/2oz chicken livers and 50g/2oz mushrooms and place in a small saucepan with 60ml/4 tablespoons tomato juice. Cover and cook gently for 10 minutes. Season to taste and pour into a small ovenproof dish. Break an egg, size 3, on top and bake at 350°F/180°C, gas mark 4, for 10 minutes until the egg white is just set. Serve with a few sprigs of watercress.

Egg Florentine
1 poached egg, size 3, served on 175g/6oz cooked spinach and topped with 15g/½ oz grated Edam cheese.

Potato Egg
Make up half a medium packet of Cadbury's Smash. Press into an individual ovenproof dish and hollow out the centre. Break 1 egg, size 3, into the hollow and bake at 350°F/180°C, gas mark 4, for about 10 minutes. Serve with lettuce, cucumber and watercress salad.

CHEESE MEALS

Snack Pizza
Toast a 45g/1½oz crumpet, top with 1 large sliced tomato and 25g/1oz grated Edam cheese. Place under a hot grill until the cheese melts.

Cheese and Pickle on Toast
Mix 25g/1oz grated Edam cheese with 15ml/1 level tablespoon sweet pickle and spread on 1 slice toasted Nimble Family bread. Heat under a hot grill until the cheese is melted and serve with sprigs of watercress or mustard and cress.

Mushrooms and Cheese on Toast
Heat a 213g/7½oz can mushrooms in brine or poach 125g/4oz fresh mushrooms in stock or water. Drain and place on a 25g/1oz slice toasted wholemeal bread spread with 5ml/1 level teaspoon low-fat spread. Cover with 25g/1oz grated Edam cheese. Heat under a grill until cheese is melted.

Banana and Cottage Cheese
Slice a small (150g/5oz) banana and mix with 113g/4oz carton natural cottage cheese.

Cheese, Celery and Apple
25g/1oz Edam cheese served with 1 Ryvita crispbread spread with 5ml/1 level teaspoon low-fat spread and 2 sticks celery. Follow with 1 medium eating apple.

Crisps and Cheese
1 small packet KP Griddles, Rancheros or Skips and 25g/1oz Edam cheese, 1 tomato and 2 sticks celery.

Cheese Open Sandwich
On 2 slices of Sunblest HiBran bread, arrange lettuce leaves, 1 sliced tomato, 50g/2oz cottage cheese and 6 grapes, halved with pips removed.

Grilled Cheese and Tomato
Cut 3 tomatoes in half. Grate 50g/2oz Edam cheese and spread this over the cut surfaces of the tomatoes. Sprinkle with Worcestershire sauce and grill until the cheese bubbles and browns.

Cheese and Cucumber Logs
Cut a quarter of a large cucumber in half lengthways. Scoop out some of the flesh and discard it. Grate 40g/1½oz Edam cheese and mix with 15ml/1 tablespoon finely chopped onion, some chopped parsley and a very little sage or thyme. Pile back into the cucumber shells. Serve with 1 Lyons Krispen.

FISH MEALS

Grilled Fish
Brush 175g/6oz cod, coley or haddock fillets with 7g/¼oz low-fat spread, grill and serve with 50g/2oz boiled peas and ½ tomato grilled without fat.

Fish Steak au Gratin
Bake a Birds Eye Cod or Haddock Steak with 75g/3oz canned tomatoes and seasoning, topped with 15g/½oz grated

Edam cheese at 375°F/190°C, gas mark 5, for 30 minutes. Serve with 75g/3oz frozen mixed vegetables, boiled.

Fish Fingers with Mushrooms and Sweetcorn
Grill 2 fish fingers without fat. Serve with 15ml/1 tablespoon tomato ketchup, 213g/7½oz can mushrooms in brine, heated and drained and 50g/2oz frozen sweetcorn, boiled.

Fish Cakes and Tartare Sauce
Grill or bake 2 frozen fish cakes without fat. Serve with 15ml/1 tablespoon Waistline Tartare Sauce and 75g/3oz runner beans and 2 tomatoes, grilled without fat.

Cod Steak in Mushroom Sauce
Cook an individual packet Ross Cod Steak in Mushroom Sauce as directed. Turn into a small ovenproof dish, sprinkle with 15ml/1 level tablespoon grated Parmesan cheese and brown under a hot grill. Serve with 75g/3oz boiled cauliflower and 50g/2oz French beans.

Plaice and Grapes
Brush 150g/5oz plaice fillets with 7g/¼oz low-fat spread and grill. Serve with 25g/1oz green grapes, 50g/2oz green beans and 50g/2oz broccoli.

Cod Parcel
Put a 100g/3½oz frozen cod steak onto a square of foil. Chop 1 small onion, 1 tomato and 50g/2oz mushrooms. Mix vegetables together and pile them on the fish. Season and fold the foil over. Bake at 375°F/190°C, gas mark 5, for 30 minutes. Serve with 125g/4oz boiled potato and 75g/3oz broccoli.

MEAT MEALS

Sausage, Bacon and Tomato
Grill 2 pork and beef chipolata sausages and 1 rasher streaky bacon until well done. Serve with 1 tomato, halved and heated under the grill.

Bacon Steak, Tomato Sauce and Vegetables
Well grill an average bacon steak (100g/3½oz raw weight) and serve with 15ml/1 tablespoon tomato sauce, 125g/4oz mushrooms poached in stock or water and 125g/4oz boiled cabbage.

Roast Beef and Vegetables
75g/3oz roast topside beef with all fat removed, served with 50ml/2fl oz gravy made from Boots, Birds, Bisto or McCormick Lite Gravy Mix and with 150g/5oz boiled cauliflower and 75g/3oz boiled carrots.

Drumstick Casserole
Skin a chicken drumstick and place in a small ovenproof casserole with 175g/6oz Findus Country or Garden Mix vegetables. Dissolve ½ chicken stock cube in 150ml/¼ pint boiling water and pour over chicken and vegetables. Cover and cook at 350°F/180°C, gas mark 4, for 40 minutes until the chicken is tender.

Braised Kidneys with Cauliflower
Wash, skin, core and quarter 2 lamb's kidneys. Make up 1 sachet Batchelor's Beef and Tomato or Oxtail Cup-a-Soup as directed. Put the kidneys, soup and 1 drained 213g/7½oz can mushrooms in brine in a small saucepan. Cover and simmer gently for 15 minutes or until the kidneys are tender. Serve in a border of 150g/5oz boiled cauliflower florets.

Beefburger and Vegetables

Grill 1 Ross Beefburger well and serve with 15ml/1 tablespoon low-calorie tomato ketchup, 125g/4oz boiled runner beans, 75g/3oz boiled carrots and 1 slice Sunblest HiBran bread.

Roast Pork Dinner

Heat an individual packet Birds Eye Gravy and Lean Roast Pork as instructed. Serve with 125g/4oz boiled Brussels sprouts and 75g/3oz boiled carrots. Follow with 1 medium apple or a 198g/7oz can Weight Watchers Fruit Cocktail or Fruit Salad in Low-calorie Syrup.

Beefburger Sandwich

Well grill a 50g/2oz frozen beefburger. Spread 1 small slice Nimble or Slimcea bread with a little made mustard, top with the grilled beefburger and a second small slice of Nimble or Slimcea. Serve with 1 sliced tomato and a little sliced onion or spring onions.

SALAD MEALS

Potted Shrimps and Salad

Serve 50g/1.76oz Young's Potted Shrimps with lettuce, watercress, 1 stick celery, 1 sliced tomato and 1 Lyons Krispen, unbuttered.

Sardine Salad

Serve 2 sardines in tomato sauce with coleslaw made from 125g/4oz shredded white cabbage, 1 grated carrot, 5ml/ 1 teaspoon chopped onion or 1 chopped spring onion mixed with 15ml/1 level tablespoon low-calorie salad cream. Add 1 sliced tomato and a few lettuce leaves and sprigs of watercress.

Prawn and Egg Salad

Serve 50g/2oz fresh or thawed frozen prawns and 1 egg, size 3, hard boiled, with 15ml/1 tablespoon low-calorie salad cream and a green salad of lettuce, mustard and cress, sliced or chopped green pepper and sliced cucumber.

Ham, Mushroom and Sweetcorn Salad

Slice 50g/2oz raw button mushrooms and mix with 15ml/1 tablespoon natural yogurt seasoned with salt and pepper. Cook 50g/2oz sweetcorn kernels, drain and cool. Mix with 15ml/1 tablespoon seasoned soured cream. Serve the mushroom and sweetcorn salads with 1 rolled slice of ham (25g/1oz) and a few sprigs of watercress.

Strip Chicken

Cut 50g/2oz cooked chicken meat into strips. Arrange a few lettuce leaves on a plate, then the chicken. Sprinkle on 15ml/1 tablespoon oil-free French dressing and 15g/½ oz broken walnuts. Arrange small piles of grated carrot, chopped celery, diced beetroot and cold cut beans around the rim of the plate.

Peach and Cheese Salad

Put 2 drained peach halves (canned in natural juice) on a bed of lettuce, cut side up. Pile 113g/4oz cottage cheese on the halves. Serve with 1 Ryvita.

Corned Beef and Coleslaw

Serve 40g/1½ oz corned beef with 227g/8oz Eden Vale Coleslaw in Vinaigrette.

Ham Sausage and Beetroot

Put 50g/2oz Mattesson's Ham Sausage on ¼ bunch chopped watercress. Arrange segments from ½ fresh grapefruit on top and serve with 30ml/2 tablespoons diced beetroot mixed with 15ml/1 tablespoon natural yogurt. Serve with 1 slice Sunblest HiBran bread.

SOUP MEALS

French Onion Soup

Toast a 25g/1oz slice wholemeal bread, then sprinkle over 15g/½oz grated Edam cheese and grill until the cheese melts. Cut into cubes and place in the bottom of a soup bowl. Heat a 425g/15oz can Crosse & Blackwell or Frank Cooper's French Onion Soup and pour over the cheesy bread in the soup bowl.

Spring Vegetable Soup and French Bread

Serve 283ml/½ pint Knorr Florida Spring Vegetable Soup sprinkled with 5ml/1 level teaspoon grated Parmesan cheese and a 50g/2oz piece French bread.

Beef Soup and Sandwich

Serve a 295g/10.4oz can Heinz Low Calorie Beef and Mushroom or Vegetable and Beef Soup with a sandwich made from 2 small slices Slimcea filled with 35g/1¼oz Sainsbury's Beef Spread or 35g/1.23oz Shippams Beef and Pickle Country Pot Paste and ½ carton mustard and cress.

Chicken Broth

Serve a 425g/15oz can Campbell's Granny's Soup, Chicken and Vegetable Broth with Rice with 1 Ryvita crispbread.

Soup and Open Sandwich

Make up 1 sachet Batchelors Beef and Tomato Cup-a-Soup as directed. Spread a 25g/1oz slice wholemeal bread with 15ml/1 level tablespoon low-calorie salad dressing, cover with 1 lettuce leaf, 1 sliced tomato, 15ml/1 level tablespoon cottage cheese and a few slices cucumber.

Soup and Cheese / Fruit

Serve a 295g/10.4oz can Boots or Heinz Low Calorie Tomato soup with 25g/1oz Riccotta cheese spread on 2 Lyons Krispen. Follow with 1 orange.

Oxtail Soup / Cheese and Crackers

Serve a 295g/10.4oz can Heinz Slimway Oxtail Soup, with 2 Lyons Krispen and 25g/1oz Edam cheese.

Orange Tomato Soup and Toast

Heat a 295g/10.4oz can Heinz Slimway Tomato Soup, then add 30ml/2 tablespoons unsweetened orange juice. Serve with 2 slices of Sunblest HiBran bread, toasted.

Lobster Bisque and Crudités

Heat a 425g/15oz can Crosse & Blackwell Lobster Bisque. Serve with 1 stick celery, 1 carrot and 75g/3oz cucumber, all cut into thin strips.

BAKED BEANS, RICE AND PASTA MEALS

Baked Beans

Heat a 220g/7¾oz can Sainsbury's Baked Beans in Tomato Sauce and serve with 1 Ryvita crispbread.

Spaghetti Bolognese

Heat and serve a 210g/7.4oz can Heinz Spaghetti Bolognese.

Spaghetti Rings with Tomato Sauce

Heat a 213g/7½oz can Crosse & Blackwell Spaghetti Rings in Tomato Sauce, sprinkle over 15ml/1 tablespoon grated Parmesan cheese and serve with 1 Energen crispbread.

Beans, Sausage and Tomato

Heat a 150g/5.3oz can Heinz Baked Beans in Tomato Sauce and serve with 1 beef chipolata sausage, well grilled and 2 tomatoes, grilled without fat.

Beans and Bacon
Heat a 150g/5.3oz can Heinz Baked Beans in Tomato Sauce. Well grill 1 rasher streaky bacon and crumble over the beans. Serve with 1 Ryvita crispbread.

Rice Quick Lunch
Make up 1 pot KP Quick Lunch with Rice, curry or risotto. Serve with 2 Lyons Krispen.

Ravioli
Heat 213g/7½oz can Tesco Ravioli in Tomato and Meat Sauce. Serve with 1 tomato, grilled without fat.

Cheesy Pasta Shells
Boil 25g/1oz pasta shells until tender – about 12 minutes. Drain. Make up ½ packet Sainsbury's Cheese Sauce with 150ml/¼ pint skimmed milk. Toss the hot pasta in the sauce.

Macaroni and Burger
Boil 25g/1oz macaroni for about 12 minutes. Drain. Toss in 15ml/1 tablespoon Waistline Low Calorie Tomato Ketchup. Grill 1 Birds Eye Beefburger well and serve with the macaroni.

Kedgeree
Boil 25g/1oz rice for about 15 minutes until tender. Drain. Grill 50g/2oz smoked haddock fillet with 7g/¼oz low-fat spread. Flake the fish and mix with the hot rice, seasoning well.

FRUIT AND YOGURT MEALS

Banana and Yogurt
Slice a small (150g/5oz) banana and mix with a 142g/5oz carton Dessert Farm Strawberry Yogurt.

Apple and Muesli Yogurt
Chop up 1 medium apple and mix with 1 small carton St Ivel Country Prize Muesli Yogurt.

Orange and Yogurt
Peel and segment a medium orange and serve with 1 small carton Eden Vale Natural Yogurt with Honey.

Prune and Orange Yogurt
Soak and cook 6 prunes. Remove stones and cut each prune in half. Mix with 1 small carton natural yogurt. Peel and segment 1 small orange and add to the yogurt.

Peaches and Cherry Yogurt
Slice 2 fresh peaches or 4 peach halves, canned in natural juice, drained. Spoon over 60ml/4 tablespoons black cherry yogurt.

Winter Fruit Salad and Yogurt
Soak 25g/1oz raisins and 15g/½oz chopped, dried apricots and boil gently in water until tender. Drain and add 1 small chopped apple. Mix with 1 small carton natural yogurt.

Grapefruit, Mint and Ginger Yogurt
Halve a medium grapefruit and scoop out the segments. Discard the membrane. Mix segments with 5ml/1 teaspoon chopped mint, segments from 1 small orange and 1 piece chopped stem ginger. Put the mixture back into the two grapefruit shells and serve with 1 small carton natural yogurt.

Chocolate Banana
Slice 1 medium (175g/6oz) banana. Pour over ½ small carton Eden Vale Chocolate Yogurt. Top with 5ml/1 level teaspoon chopped mixed nuts, toasted.

Chocolate Pear
Put 2 pear halves canned in natural juice, drained in a small dish. Pour over ½ small carton Eden Vale Chocolate Yogurt.

Serve with 1 McDougall's Cracotte crispbread.

Fruit and Natural Yogurt
Mix 1 small carton natural yogurt with 1 medium eating apple and 1 large pear.

DESSERT MEALS

Canned Fruit and Ice Cream
Serve the contents of a 227g/8oz can Koo Pear Halves in Apple Juice with ¼ Lyons Maid Cornish Dairy or Vanilla Handy Pack.

Carton Dessert and Fruit
Serve an individual carton St Ivel Strawberry Sundae Best or St Michael Strawberry Delight or a Findus Strawberry Ripple Mousse or Sainsbury's Mousse (any flavour) with 1 medium orange.

Fruit Juice and Dessert
Serve 150ml/¼ pint of one of the following orange juices: Adams Just Juice, Chambourcy unsweetened Pure Orange, reconstituted Findus Jaffa Orange. Follow with an individual carton Chambourcy Strawberry Dessert a la Creme or Eden Vale Chocolate, Raspberry or Strawberry Fool.

Muesli Bar and Grapes
Serve 1 Prewett's Muesli Bar with 125g/4oz black grapes.

Mousse and Cherries
Turn out 1 individual tub (57g/2oz) frozen strawberry mousse. Allow to thaw for 1 hour. Halve and remove stones from 50g/2oz fresh cherries and arrange halves around the mousse. Pour over 30ml/2 table-spoons Wall's Raspberry Dessert Sauce.

Creme Caramel with Fruit Sauce
Turn out a 142g/5oz St Ivel Creme Caramel. Put 50g/2oz blackberries in a small pan with 15ml/1 tablespoon water. Stew until pulpy and sieve. Cool and sweeten with Hermesetas Sprinkle Sweet. Pour over the creme caramel.

Lime and Grape Jelly
Make up a quarter of a lime jelly. Pour half into an individual serving dish and allow to set. Meanwhile halve and remove pips from 75g/3oz grapes. Arrange these on the set jelly, then pour on the remaining jelly. Allow to set. Serve with 1 small (125g/4oz) eating apple.

Baked Banana and Ice Cream
Peel 1 medium banana (175g/6oz) and wrap in foil. Bake at 350°F/180°C, gas mark 4, for 15 minutes. Open the foil and sprinkle with a pinch of cinnamon and 5ml/1 level teaspoon soft brown sugar. Grill until the sugar melts. Serve with 1 Lyons Maid Vanilla Bar.

Sorbet and Pineapple
Serve 50g/2oz Wall's Lemon Sorbet with 2 rings pineapple, drained and chopped. Top with 15ml/1 tablespoon ginger syrup.

Apple Charlotte
Peel, core and slice 1 medium cooking apple (175g/6oz). Put into an ovenproof dish with 10ml/2 level teaspoons brown sugar and a good pinch cinnamon. Sprinkle over 25g/1oz fresh breadcrumbs and dot with 15g/½ oz low-fat spread. Bake at 375°F/190°C, gas mark 5, for 25 minutes or until the top is golden.

BISCUIT MEALS

Chocolate Biscuit and Apple
Serve 1 Macdonald's Penguin biscuit with 1 medium apple.

Fruit Juice and Chocolate Biscuit or Bar

Serve 125ml/4fl oz Libby's Natural Orange Juice or Orange 'C', Sweetened, with 1 Jacob's Club biscuit (any flavour) or 1 McVitie's Milk Chocolate Sport or 1 Sainsbury's Milk Chocolate Caramel Wafer or 1 bar Cadbury's Super Mousse.

Drinking Chocolate and Biscuits

Make up a cup of drinking chocolate from 20ml/2 rounded teaspoons drinking chocolate and 225ml/8fl oz skimmed milk (extra to daily allowance) and serve with 2 Marie, Thin Arrowroot or Petit Beurre biscuits.

Wholemeal Biscuits and Juice

Serve 2 Fox's Wholemeal and Bran biscuits with 125ml/4fl oz fresh or frozen orange juice.

Kit Kat and Milk

Serve 2 fingers Rowntree Kit Kat with 190ml/⅓ pint skimmed milk.

Digestive Biscuit and Cheese

Serve 1 McVitie's Digestive Wheatmeal biscuit with 25g/1oz Stilton or Cheddar cheese.

Tea Breaks

Serve 2 Nabisco Tea Breaks spread with 15g/½oz low-fat spread and 10ml/2 level teaspoons jam.

Tuc 'n' Egg

Serve 4 Tuc biscuits with 1 hard-boiled egg, size 3.

Ginger Nut and Milk

Serve 1 McVitie's Ginger Nut with 150ml/¼ pint whole milk *or* 275ml/½ pint skimmed milk.

Cornish Wafers

Spread 2 Jacob's Cornish Wafers with 25g/1oz low-fat curd cheese and 10ml/2 level teaspoons jam.

Harvest Crunch Biscuits and Fruit

Serve 2 Quaker Almond and Honey Harvest Crunch Bars with 1 small apple or pear.

80-calorie snacks

Fruit snacks

1 medium banana (175g/6oz).
2 small eating apples (125g/4oz each).
6 fresh apricots and 1 small eating apple (125g/4oz).
25g/1oz raisins or sultanas or dried currants.
5 dates.
25g/1oz stem ginger.
1 medium grapefruit (340g/12oz) and 1 small eating apple (125g/4oz).
150g/5oz grapes.
125g/4oz canned lychees.
275g/10oz wedge any melon (weight includes skin) and 1 small eating apple (125g/4oz).
1 large orange (275g/10oz).
1 small orange (150g/5oz) and 1 small apple (125g/4oz).
2 fresh peaches (125g/4oz each).
2 pears (150g/5oz each).
75g/3oz fresh pineapple and 1 small orange (150g/5oz).
3 fresh plums and 75g/3oz fresh cherries.
8 prunes.
150g/5oz fresh or frozen raspberries and 1 fresh peach (125g/4oz).
175g/6oz fresh strawberries and 1 peach (125g/4oz).
4 tangerines.

Biscuit snacks

1 Cadbury's Chocolate Sandwich.
1 Cadbury's Orange Cream.
2 Cadbury's Shortcake.
3 Chiltonian Gingerellas.
2 Crawford's Ginger Snaps.
1 Crawford's Milk Chocolate Wholemeal.
2 Pennywise Garibaldi.

4 Pennywise Morning Coffee.
2 Cream Crackers.
3 Tuc.
1 Fox's Wholemeal Bran.
1 Digestive Wheatmeal.
1 McVitie's Munchmallow.
1 Bourbon.
1 Jaffa Cake and 1 Marie.
2 Dutch Tea Breaks (no butter).
1 Taxi.
1 Quaker Harvest Crunch Bar, Peanut.
2 Sainsbury's Caramel Wafers.
1 Sainsbury's Chocolate Malted Milk and 1 Fruit Shortcake.

Soup snacks
275ml/½ pint or ½ packet Batchelors Oxtail or Savoury Beef or Vegetable and Beef Soup.
1 sachet Batchelors Cup-a-Soup in Golden Vegetable or Oxtail or Tomato.
1 Batchelors Slim-a-Soup and 1 Cream Cracker.
295g/10.4oz can Boots Low Calorie Soup, Chicken or Chicken and Vegetable.
284ml/½ pint Chef Boxes – Chicken and Leek or Golden Vegetable or Minestrone or Mushroom or Oxtail.
425g/15oz can Frank Cooper's French Onion Soup.
1 pot Crosse & Blackwell Pot Soup, Rich Tomato.
295g/10.4oz can Heinz Slimway Soup, any flavour,
1 sachet Knorr Quick Soup, Tomato or Onion.
2 sachets Knorr Quick Soup, Beef and Onion.
1 pint Maggi Chicken Noodle Soup.
2 pints Maggi Spring Vegetable Soup.

Savoury snacks
1 hard-boiled egg, size 3.
1 cream cracker with 10g/⅓oz low-fat spread.

1 Ryvita with 15g/½oz Edam cheese, 1 tomato and cucumber slices.
1 Energen Brancrisp with 25g/1oz Mattesson's Ham Sausage and 10ml/2 level teaspoons Branston Pickle.
2 Lyons Krispen with half a 53g/1⅞oz pot of Princes Lobster or Salmon and Shrimp Spread and cucumber slices.
1 Ryvita and 50g/2oz cottage cheese.
2 triangles cheese spread with celery sticks.
1 frozen fish cake, grilled without fat, 1 tomato and watercress.
1 Lyons Krispen with 25g/1oz cooked chicken meat and 10ml/2 level teaspoons mango chutney.
1 rasher streaky bacon, well grilled, with 2 tomatoes, grilled without fat.
1 chipolata sausage, well grilled.
70g/2½oz cooked, shelled prawns.

Sweet snacks
40g/1½oz ice cream.
15g/½oz chocolate.
2 toffees.
8 Maltesers.
1 Fun Size Milky Way.
5 Spangles.
15g/½oz Milky Bar.
25g/1oz ice cream with 15ml/1 tablespoon Wall's Dessert Sauce.
1 Sainsbury's Junior Jam Roll.
1 Sainsbury's Mini Madeira Cake.
1 individual meringue nest filled with fresh fruit.
⅛ frozen Dairy Cream Sponge.
1 Mr Kipling Viennese Split or Sponge Drop.
2 slices Buitoni Melba Toast with 7g/¼oz low-fat spread and 7ml/1 rounded teaspoon jam or honey.
150ml/¼ pint jelly made with water.
150ml/5fl oz fresh or frozen unsweetened orange juice.

THE MUNCHING DIET

about 900 calories

This diet allows you to munch all day long if you wish while still speeding off those surplus pounds. It allows you a limited amount of high-protein foods but gives you a whole range of unlimited fruits and vegetables from which you can choose as much as you wish.

In order to achieve the maximum speedy weight loss from this diet, it is worth considering your normal eating behaviour. In one experiment carried out in America a few years ago, two groups of people were invited to help themselves to a plate piled high with sandwiches. The subjects did not realise that this was an experiment nor that they were being observed through a two-way mirror. Faced with the enormous pile of sandwiches the overweight group ate their way through a very large quantity of food. The slim people stopped eating when they had had a moderate amount. It would seem that overweight people do not have the same 'stop' mechanism that their skinnier sisters and brothers have. So don't pile up your plate with unlimited foods. Start with a reasonable portion and if you are not completely satisfied you can always have another helping.

What effortlessly-slim people can do by 'automatic pilot', over-weight people have to do by very determined effort. They don't have less willpower than slim people; it is simply that the slim people don't need the willpower. One way to change this situation is to practise being hungry. Deliberately delay one daily meal for at least an hour and repeat this for several weeks. If you learn to recognise when you are hungry, you will have a chance of learning to know when you are full. What you are aiming for is the situation where your body will eventually take control and you will find, as many slim people do, that you simply can't face eating any more food than your body needs.

The Munching Diet provides one of the fastest ways of losing weight without weighing everything you eat. There is one important point, though. This diet does not allow alcohol so it is not suitable for those who find it difficult to make this sacrifice.

DIET RULES

1 You can eat anything on the list of unlimited fruit and vegetables freely. In addition each day you can eat three portions of any fruit and one portion of any vegetable on the list of limited fruit and vegetables.

2 Choose two items from the list of high-protein foods each day.

3 Include all the foods listed under daily essentials each day.

4 Drink as much tea and coffee as you wish – without sugar (use artificial low-calorie sweeteners and milk from your allowance). Bovril, Marmite and other beef drinks, drinks labelled 'low calorie' and water are unlimited.

5 Vary your meals each day to ensure that you have a good supply of all nutrients.

6 Follow all the preparation and cooking tips when preparing meals.

7 Always have a plentiful supply of unlimited foods available so that you can nibble whenever you feel the need.

UNLIMITED FRUIT AND VEGETABLES

Fruit
Raw or stewed without sugar or sweetened with artificial sweetener

Apricots, fresh
Bilberries
Blackberries
Blackcurrants
Cherries, fresh
Cooking apples
Damsons

Gooseberries
Grapefruit
Kiwi fruit
Lemons
Loganberries
Melon, all types
Plums

Raspberries
Redcurrants
Satsumas
Strawberries
Tangerines

Vegetables
Raw or boiled or cooked and served without added fat.

Asparagus
Aubergine
Bean sprouts
Beetroot
Broccoli
Brussels sprouts
Cabbage, all kinds
Carrots
Cauliflower
Celery
Chicory
Chinese leaves
Courgettes

Cucumber
Endive
French beans
Gherkins
Globe artichokes
Jerusalem artichokes
Leeks
Lettuce
Marrow
Mushrooms
Mustard and cress
Onions
Peppers, green or red

Radishes
Runner beans
Salsify
Seakale
Spinach
Spring greens
Spring onions
Swede
Tomatoes
Turnips
Watercress

LIMITED FRUIT AND VEGETABLES

Allow up to three portions each day, if you wish, of the fruits listed below:

125g/4oz fresh pineapple.
125g/4oz black grapes.
1 average pomegranate.
1 small banana (150g/5oz).
125g/4oz white grapes.

1 medium orange (150g/5oz).
1 medium peach (125g/4oz).
1 medium pear (125g/4oz).
1 medium eating apple (125g/4oz).

Allow one portion each day, if you wish, of one of the vegetables listed below:

125g/4oz broad beans.
125g/4oz parsnips.
125g/4oz peas.
125g/4oz baked beans.
175g/6oz new potatoes.

175g/6oz old potatoes.
50g/2oz sweetcorn kernels.
125g/4oz red kidney beans.
125g/4oz butter beans.

HIGH PROTEIN FOODS

Choose two items each day from the list below:

225g/8oz white fish.
150g/5oz kipper, on the bone.
125g/4oz canned pilchards in tomato sauce.
50g/2oz prawns and 113g/4oz carton cottage cheese.
50g/2oz Edam, Brie or Camembert cheese.
40g/1½ oz Caerphilly, Cheddar Cheviot, Lancashire, Cheshire or Derby cheese.
175g/6oz cottage cheese.
125g/4oz raw weight minced beef, pre-fried in a non-stick pan and drained of fat.
100g/3½oz lean stewing steak.
125g/4oz roast topside beef, lean only.
50g/2oz liver sausage.
75g/3oz boiled lean ham.
3 pork and beef chipolatas, well grilled.
75g/3oz lamb's liver.
150g/5oz chicken liver.
125g/4oz roast chicken, without skin.
250g/9oz raw weight chicken joint, skin removed.
50g/2oz luncheon meat.
75g/3oz roast leg of lamb, lean only.
125g/4oz pork fillet, lean only.
75g/3oz roast leg of pork, lean only.
3 lamb's kidneys.
150g/5oz roast turkey, without skin.
2 eggs, size 3.

DAILY ESSENTIALS

275ml/½ pint Silver Top milk or 575ml/1 pint skimmed milk.
15g/½ oz butter or margarine or 25g/1oz any low-fat spread for cooking and spreading.
25g/1oz breakfast cereal.
2 small slices slimmer's bread or 25g/1oz slice white or wholemeal bread or 3 Energen or Ryvita crispbreads.

UNLIMITED EXTRAS

Herbs and spices; Worcestershire sauce; lemon juice; vinegar; Waistline Oil-free French dressing or Dietade Low-Calorie Salad Dressing.

Drinks: sugarless tea and coffee (using artificial low-calorie sweeteners only and milk from allowance); Marmite and Bovril; drinks labelled 'low-calorie'; water.

PREPARATION AND COOKING TIPS

1 Boil or stew fruit in a little water then add artificial sweetener to taste.
2 Prepare fruit salads from raw fruits and use low-calorie ginger ale or lemonade as juice.
3 Sweeten grapefruit with artificial sweetener in powder or liquid form.
4 Boil vegetables, if necessary, in a minimum quantity of lightly salted water until just tender. Do not add butter.
5 Add vegetables to casseroles without pre-frying – they taste just as good.
6 Toss raw salad vegetables in oil-free French dressing.
7 Poach or bake white fish in a little water with lemon juice and seasoning or grill using fat from allowance.
8 Cover fish or meat with sliced vegetables and a little water if necessary, and bake in the oven.
9 Grill chicken joints with the skin on but without added fat, then remove skin and serve.
10 Remove all skin from roast chicken and turkey before serving.

11 Remove all visible fat from roast beef, lamb or pork before serving.

12 Brush liver or kidneys with a little fat from allowance and grill or cover with vegetables and a little water and bake in the oven.

13 Eggs can be boiled, poached in water or scrambled in a non-stick pan using a little milk from allowance.

14 To prepare an omelet, beat the eggs with a little water, seasoning and herbs, if liked, and cook in a non-stick pan lightly greased with a little fat from allowance. Boiled vegetables or mushrooms poached in water can be used to fill the omelet.

THE BIG BOWLFUL DIET

900 calories

For years and years, every dieter has been urged to introduce plenty of variety into slimming menus – partly because ringing the changes means there is less risk of becoming bored. We have always gone along with this theory. Certainly if you are on a long-term slimming campaign, a diet that allows you many different foods will help you keep your resolution and, even more vital, ensure good nutrition. But stand by for a surprise. Much evidence is now emerging to indicate that, in the short term, eating 'the same old thing' can have some positive advantages.

One of the main reasons for overeating is that sitting down to a delicious variety actually entices our 'apppetites' to demand more – and more – long after we have eaten enough to satisfy any real hunger. Let us explain in grisly dinner-table detail exactly what we mean. You finish the tasty large savoury course and feel absolutely full without a scrap of room left for one more bite of tender steak or one more morsel of potato. Then along comes the pudding with its quite different texture and taste – and, suddenly, there is room! In fact, it's no trouble at all to polish off quite a lot of it.

Limiting food choice can be a most effective way for dieters to reduce their calorie consumption. But for most people, it's impossible to go on and on eating the same old thing without coming slap up against a willpower problem. You get so sick at the prospect of eggs or bananas or whatever that you won't be able to face the idea of carrying on. But done the right way, eating the same thing all day has real advantages for short-term dieting. With the Big Bowlful Diet we have devised some good-looking, good-tasting dishes. All you have to do is make up one bowl of food for your whole day's diet. This means you weigh, measure and cook or prepare just once in 24 hours, thus cutting down on calorie errors. It also means that there is far less time spent in that dieter's danger zone, the kitchen. Vary your bowlfuls from day to day to ensure that you get a good mixture of all the nutrients you require for good health.

If you are one of those people who are tempted to nibble a little of this and a little of that, this diet is ideal for you. Go ahead and nibble. If you've eaten the lot by the middle of the afternoon – well you'll have to spend the rest of the day drinking black tea or coffee or no-calorie water. But it's unlikely that you will have finished all your dish by then. For one thing, there's a generous amount – quite enough for three meals if that's how you prefer to eat it. And because you aren't changing flavours, you should find yourself far less tempted to exceed your calorie allowance anyway. Another advantage is that once you've made up your bowlful you can literally forget about calories and calorie counting for the rest of the day.

So there you are. Eating one big bowlful a day can be very good for your figure. We highly recommend it for a super-fast short-term diet. But please don't be tempted to carry on for longer than two weeks. Switch after that to one of the other diets in this book.

DIET RULES

1 There are 22 different Bowlful recipes to choose from for your fortnight's diet. You may omit those recipes you do not care for, but try to introduce as much variety in your different Bowlfuls as you can. If you try to stick to one or two favourites only, you will end up hating the sight of them and that could be the end of your diet! Also, variety on a weekly basis is the key to ensuring a nutritionally balanced diet.

2 You will find each Bowlful sufficiently generous to last you all day and you may dip into it whenever you wish. If you like to eat in nibbles, go ahead and nibble! If you prefer a three-meals-a-day pattern, divide your bowl accordingly.

3 As you are not changing flavours, you may find you haven't even finished your bowlful at the end of the day. Don't worry. Just throw it away. It means you didn't really need those extra calories anyway.

4 You are not allowed milk on this diet, except when it is part of a recipe.

5 Water, soft drinks labelled 'low-calorie', and black coffee and tea or lemon tea are unlimited. No sugar, please! Use artificial sweetener if you must.

6 If you are the sort of person who is always tempted to add a little bit more of this and that when you are preparing food, it's a good idea to make up your Bowlful just after your last nibble the evening beforehand and store it in the fridge overnight. It is always easier to obey slimming rules when you do food preparation on a satisfied stomach!

COLD SAVOURY BOWLFULS

Potato and Bacon Salad *(pages 80-81)*

350g/12oz new potatoes.
3 bacon steaks (100g/3½oz each).
175g/6oz broad beans, frozen.
175g/6oz white cabbage.
6 radishes.
25g/1oz gherkins.

75ml/5 tablespoons low-calorie salad dressing.
30ml/2 tablespoons oil-free French dressing.
5ml/1 level teaspoon mustard.
salt and pepper.

Scrub potatoes and boil them in their skins until just tender. Drain, cool and cube. Grill bacon steaks, then cube. Boil broad beans as instructed, drain, rinse under cold water and drain again. Shred cabbage, slice radishes and chop gherkins. Mix all ingredients together and season with salt and pepper. Keep in the refrigerator and help yourself to a bowlful whenever you want one.

Frankfurter and Wholewheat Macaroni

75g/3oz wholewheat macaroni.
1 egg, size 3.
150g/5oz frankfurters.
6 radishes.
1 red or green pepper.
150g/5oz red cabbage.

30ml/2 tablespoons low-calorie salad dressing.
30ml/2 tablespoons oil-free French dressing.
25g/1oz cucumber relish.
salt and pepper.

Cook the macaroni as instructed on the packet. Drain, rinse under cold running water and drain again. Hard boil the egg. Cool, shell and chop. Slice frankfurters. Top and tail radishes and slice thinly. Discard white pith and seeds from pepper and dice flesh. Shred red cabbage. Mix all the ingredients together and season with salt and pepper. Keep in the refrigerator and serve yourself a bowful whenever you want one.

Rice and Ham Salad

125g/4oz long-grain rice.
125g/4oz lean cooked ham.
125g/4oz sweetcorn, frozen or canned, drained.
150g/5oz peas, frozen.
1 red pepper.

175g/6oz cucumber.
4 rings pineapple, canned in natural juice, drained.
90ml/6 tablespoons oil-free French dressing.
salt and pepper.

Boil rice as instructed. Drain, rinse under cold water and drain again. Discard all visible fat from ham and dice the lean meat. Boil sweetcorn (if frozen) and peas. Drain, rinse under cold water and drain again. Discard white pith and seeds from pepper and dice flesh. Dice cucumber. Cut pineapple into small pieces. Mix all ingredients together and season. Keep in the refrigerator and serve yourself a bowlful whenever you want one.

Mixed Bean and Tuna Salad

225g/8oz French beans or haricots verts, frozen.
1 medium onion.
4 sticks celery.
4 tomatoes.
223g/7.9oz can Batchelors Canellini Beans.
223g/7.9oz can Batchelors Red

Kidney Beans.
99g/3½oz can tuna in brine.
198g/7oz can tuna in brine.
225g/7.9oz can baked beans in tomato sauce.
60ml/4 tablespoons oil-free French dressing.
salt and pepper.

Cook French beans or haricots verts as instructed on the packet. Drain, rinse under cold water and drain again. Finely chop onion. Slice celery. Cut each tomato into eight wedges. Drain canellini beans and red kidney beans. Drain and flake both cans of tuna. Mix all ingredients together and season with salt and pepper. Keep in the refrigerator and serve yourself a bowlful whenever you want one.

Salmon and Pasta Salad

75g/3oz pasta shells or shapes.
198g/7oz can salmon.
99g/3½oz can salmon.
1 green pepper.
3 tomatoes.
6 stuffed olives.

25g/1oz tomato and chilli
chutney or relish.
45ml/3 tablespoons oil-free
French dressing.
15ml/1 tablespoon vinegar.
salt and pepper.

Cook pasta in boiling, salted water until just tender. Drain, rinse under cold water and drain again. Empty cans of salmon into a basin and flake roughly. Discard pith and seeds from pepper and dice flesh. Cut each tomato into eight wedges. Slice olives. Mix together tomato and chilli chutney, oil-free French dressing and vinegar. Season, then mix with all other ingredients. Keep in the refrigerator and help yourself to a bowlful whenever you want one.

Waldorf Salad

10 sticks celery.
675g/1½lb eating apples.
juice ½ lemon.
40g/1½oz toasted hazelnuts.
75g/3oz Edam cheese.

2 cartons St Ivel natural yogurt
(142g/5oz each).
5ml/1 level teaspoon caster sugar.
salt and pepper.

Slice celery. Core and dice apples, but leave the skin on. Toss in the lemon juice. Roughly chop hazelnuts. Cube Edam. Mix all ingredients together and season with salt and pepper. Keep in the refrigerator and help yourself to a bowlful whenever you want one.

Chicken, Nut and Raisin Salad

225g/8oz cooked chicken.
450g/1lb celery.
50g/2oz dry roasted peanuts.
75g/3oz raisins.

50ml/4 tablespoons oil-free
French dressing.
salt and pepper.

Discard any skin from chicken and cut flesh into bite-size pieces. Cut celery into 6mm/¼-inch slices and mix with the chicken, peanuts, raisins and oil-free French dressing. Season. Keep in the refrigerator and serve yourself a bowlful whenever you want one.

Chicken and Rice Salad

75g/3oz long-grain rice.
225g/8oz cooked chicken.
175g/6oz mushrooms.
1 green pepper
175g/6oz cucumber.
3 spring onions.
50g/2oz raisins.

30ml/2 tablespoons oil-free French dressing.
15ml/1 tablespoon low-calorie salad dressing.
15ml/1 tablespoon Soy sauce.
salt and pepper.

Cook rice as instructed. Drain, rinse under cold water and drain again. Discard any skin from chicken and cut flesh into bite-size pieces. Slice mushrooms. Discard roots and tough green leaves from spring onions and thinly slice white bulbs. Mix together oil-free French dressing, low-calorie salad dressing and Soy sauce; stir in rice, chicken, vegetables and raisins. Season with salt and pepper. Keep in refrigerator and serve yourself a bowlful whenever you want one.

HOT SAVOURY BOWLFULS

Saucy Tuna and Rice

75g/3oz long-grain rice.
175g/6oz runner beans, frozen.
150g/5oz button mushrooms.
275ml/½ pint skimmed milk.
198g/7oz can sweetcorn kernels.

1 packet Knorr White Sauce
Mix.
198g/7oz can tuna in brine.
salt and pepper.

Boil rice and runner beans as instructed on the packets. Drain and set aside. Slice button mushrooms and simmer in 250ml/9fl oz skimmed milk for 5 minutes. Drain milk into a measuring jug and make up to 250ml/9fl oz with liquid from sweetcorn if necessary. Empty the sauce mix into a milk pan and blend with remaining 25ml/1fl oz skimmed milk until smooth. Add milk in which the mushrooms were cooked and bring to the boil, stirring continuously. Simmer for 1 minute. Drain and flake tuna. Drain any remaining liquid from the sweetcorn. Mix all ingredients together and season with salt and pepper. Whenever you want a bowl of Saucy Tuna and Rice place your portion in a small pan and warm through, stirring to prevent sticking.

Pea and Ham Soup

75g/3oz onion.
1 stick celery.
75g/3oz carrot.
175g/6oz potato, weighed, peeled.
675g/1½ lb peas, frozen.
2 chicken stock cubes.

5ml/1 level teaspoon dried mixed herbs.
1.4 litres/2½ pints water.
25g/1oz skimmed milk powder e.g. Marvel.
125g/4oz lean cooked ham.
salt and pepper.

Chop onion. Thinly slice celery, carrot and potato and place in a saucepan with the onion, peas, stock cubes, herbs and water. Bring to the boil, cover the pan and simmer for 20 minutes, or until all the vegetables are tender. Purée in a blender with the powdered skimmed milk or rub through a sieve, then whisk in the powdered skimmed milk. Discard all visible fat from ham and chop the lean. Stir into soup and season with salt and pepper. Help yourself to a bowlful whenever you want one – just place your portion in a small pan and heat.

Chinese Crab and Sweetcorn Soup

75g/3oz onion.
15ml/1 tablespoon Soy sauce.
2 chicken stock cubes.
1.1 litres/2 pints water.
½ red or green pepper.
2 cans cream-style sweetcorn
(283g/10oz each) or 2 cans

sweetcorn kernels (312g/11oz
each).
30ml/2 level tablespoons
cornflour.
175g/6oz crab meat.
salt and pepper.

Chop onion and place in a saucepan with the Soy sauce, stock cubes
and water. Bring to the boil, cover and simmer for 10 minutes.
Discard pith and seeds from pepper and dice flesh. Add to pan and
simmer for 5 minutes longer. If sweetcorn kernels are used, purée
them in a blender with their liquid until almost smooth – a few
whole kernels should remain. Add sweetcorn purée or cream-style
corn to pan. Blend cornflour with a little cold water until smooth
then add to pan. Bring back to the boil, stirring continuously and
simmer for 2 minutes. Flake crab meat, add to pan and season with
salt and pepper. Whenever you want a bowl of soup, pour portion
into a small pan and heat through thoroughly.

Smoked Haddock Chowder

175g/6oz potato, weighed peeled.
125g/4oz carrots, weighed peeled.
75g/3oz onion, weighed peeled.
1.1 litres/2 pints water.
450g/1lb smoked haddock fillet.
125g/4oz sweetcorn, frozen or

drained canned.
25g/1oz powdered skimmed milk.
30ml/2 level tablespoons
cornflour.
salt and pepper.

Cut potatoes and carrots into small dice. Chop onion and place in a
saucepan with the potatoes, carrots and water. Bring to the boil,
cover pan and simmer for 10 minutes. Add the smoked haddock and
cook for another 10-15 minutes or until fish flakes easily. Lift out fish
and remove any skin and bones. Flake and return to the pan with
the sweetcorn. Bring back to the boil and cook for another 5
minutes. Blend the powdered skimmed milk and the cornflour with
a little cold water until smooth. Add to the pan, stirring
continuously and simmer for 1-2 minutes. Taste and season with
pepper and a little salt if necessary. The haddock may be salty
enough. Help yourself to a bowlful of chowder whenever you want
one. Just place your portion in a small pan and heat through.

Prawn and Pasta Hot Pot *(pages 176-7)*

125g/4oz pasta shells.
125g/4oz onion.
225g/8oz courgettes.
2 cans chopped tomatoes
(400g/14oz each).

225g/8oz button mushrooms.
5ml/1 level teaspoon dried basil.
350g/12oz prawns, fresh peeled
or frozen.
salt and pepper.

Cook pasta shells in boiling, salted water for 10-12 minutes or until just tender. Drain and set aside. Chop onion. Cut courgettes into ¼-inch slices. Thinly slice mushrooms and place in a saucepan with the tomatoes and their juice, onion, courgettes and basil. Cover the pan and simmer gently for 15 minutes. Stir in the pasta and prawns and season with salt and pepper. Help yourself to a bowlful whenever you want one – just transfer your portion to a small pan and warm through.

Kidney and Chilli Beans

275g/10oz lamb's or pig's
kidneys.
175g/6oz onions.
1 red or green pepper.
2 cans tomatoes (567g/1lb 4oz
each).
5ml/1 level teaspoon chilli
powder.
1.25ml/¼ level teaspoon ground

cumin, optional.
2 red Oxo cubes.
275ml/½ pint water.
salt and pepper.
223g/7.9oz can Batchelors Red
Kidney Beans.
45ml/3 level tablespoons
cornflour.

Halve and core kidneys and cut into small pieces. Chop onions. Discard pith and seeds from pepper and chop flesh. Place kidneys, onion, pepper, tomatoes and their juice, chilli powder, cumin, Oxo cubes and water in a saucepan and season with salt and pepper. Cover the pan and simmer for 15 minutes. Drain beans and add to pan. Blend cornflour with a little cold water until smooth then add to the pan, stirring all the time. Bring back to the boil and simmer for 2 minutes, stirring continuously. Whenever you want a bowl of chilli just place your portion in a small pan and heat.

Mushroom and Chicken Supreme

225g/8oz skinless chicken breast
fillet.
675g/1½lb button mushrooms.
1 green pepper.
900ml/1½ pints water.
2 Chicken Oxo cubes.

1 bouquet garni.
125g/4oz peas, frozen.
50g/2oz cornflour.
50g/2oz powdered skimmed milk.
salt and pepper.

Cut chicken into bite-size pieces and place in a large saucepan. Quarter the mushrooms if large, leave whole if small. Discard pith and seeds from pepper and dice flesh. Add mushrooms, pepper, water, Oxo cubes and bouquet garni to pan. Bring to the boil, cover and simmer gently for 15 minutes. Add peas and simmer for 5 minutes longer. Blend cornflour and powdered skimmed milk with a little water until smooth. Add to the pan, stirring all the time and bring back to the boil. Simmer for 2 minutes, stirring all the time and then remove bouquet garni. Season with salt and pepper. Heat yourself a bowlful of Mushroom and Chicken Supreme whenever you want one – stirring to prevent sticking.

Cheese and Vegetables

225g/8oz cauliflower.
225g/8oz carrots.
125g/4oz onion.
225g/8oz courgettes.

275g/10oz broad beans, frozen.
3 packets Knorr Cheese Sauce
Mix.
900ml/1½ pints skimmed milk.

Break cauliflower into florets and slice carrots. Chop onion and cook with cauliflower and carrots in boiling salted water for 10 minutes. Slice the courgettes and add to pan with the broad beans. Bring back to the boil and simmer for another 5-10 minutes or until all vegetables are tender. Stir the sauce mix into a little of the skimmed milk in another saucepan until smooth. Add remaining milk and bring to the boil, stirring all the time. Simmer for 1-2 minutes then stir in all the vegetables. Help yourself to a bowlful whenever you fancy one – just transfer your portion to a small pan and warm through.

SWEET BOWLFULS

Cottage Cheese and Fruit

2 cartons Eden Vale Cottage
Cheese with Pineapple (227g/8oz
each).
60ml/4 tablespoons low-calorie
salad dressing.

2 medium apples.
2 medium bananas.
juice of 1 lemon.
225g/8oz black grapes.
275g/10oz melon.

Mix together the cottage cheese and low-calorie salad dressing. Core apples and cut into ¼-inch cubes. Slice bananas; toss in the lemon juice with the apple so that all cut sides come into contact with the juice. Drain off excess lemon juice then add fruit to the cottage cheese. Halve and pip grapes. Skin melon and cube. Stir into the cheese mixture. Keep in the refrigerator and help yourself whenever you feel peckish.

Apricot and Honey Rice Pudding

75g/3oz dried apricots.
70g/2¾oz round grain or
pudding rice.
pinch salt.
15ml/1 tablespoon liquid honey.

1.1 litres/2 pints skimmed milk.
15ml/1 level tablespoon
Hermesetas Sprinkle Sweet,
optional.

Cut each dried apricot into four pieces and place in a large ovenproof dish with the rice, salt, honey and skimmed milk. Stir and then bake at 150°C/300°F, gas mark 2, for 3 hours. Stir after 1 hour then after 2 hours. Taste and if necessary sweeten with Sprinkle Sweet. Serve yourself a bowlful whenever you want one; serve pudding cold or place your portion in a small ovenproof dish and heat through in the oven.

Stewed Fruit and Nuts *(pages 176-7)*

1.4kg/3lb cooking apples, preferably Bramleys.
225g/8oz blackberries, fresh or frozen.
60ml/4 tablespoons water.
60g/2¼oz roasted hazelnuts.
225g/8oz raspberries, fresh or frozen.
15ml/1 level tablespoon honey.

Peel, core and slice apples. Place in a saucepan with blackberries and water. Cover the pan and cook over a low heat until the fruits are soft. Roughly chop hazelnuts and stir into the cooked fruit with the raspberries and honey. Serve yourself a bowlful that has been chilled or place your portion in a saucepan and heat it through on a cold day.

Winter Fruit Salad and Yogurt

4 mandarins or tangerines.
175g/6oz grapes.
2 medium bananas.
2 medium apples.
2 medium pears.
lemon juice.
2 cartons Eden Vale Natural Yogurt with Honey (150g/5.3oz each).
150g/5.3oz carton Eden Vale natural yogurt.

Peel and segment mandarins or tangerines. Halve and pip grapes. Peel and slice bananas. Core apples and pears and cut into ¼-inch pieces. Toss the bananas, apples and pears in lemon juice until thoroughly coated. Drain and mix with the other fruits and yogurts. Keep in the refrigerator and serve chilled.

Yogurt and Summer Fruit Salad

225g/8oz strawberries.
2 large peaches.
3 kiwi fruit.
450g/1lb melon.
225g/8oz cherries.
225g/8oz raspberries.
1 large carton St Ivel Prize Fruit Yogurt, any flavour (454g/16oz).

Hull strawberries and halve or quarter if large. Halve and stone peaches, then cube. Peel and slice kiwi fruit; cut each slice in half. Skin melon and cube flesh. Mix all the fruit with the yogurt. Keep in the refrigerator and serve yourself a bowlful whenever you like.

Melon and Muesli Yogurt

75g/3oz rolled oats.
25g/1oz roasted hazelnuts.
25g/1oz dried apricots.
500g/1lb 2oz melon.

25g/1oz raisins.
3 cartons Chambourcy natural
yogurt (142g/5oz each).
15ml/1 tablespoon honey.

Spread the rolled oats on a baking dish and bake at 190°C/375°F, gas mark 5, for 5-10 minutes or until just starting to brown. Place in a bowl and leave to cool. Roughly chop hazelnuts and dried apricots. Remove skin from melon and cube flesh. Mix all the ingredients together and chill. Keep in the refrigerator and help yourself to a bowlful whenever you want one.

FAST FOLLOWERS

These 1,000-calorie diets can be continued until you have lost all your surplus flab. Although they are slightly higher in calories than the Superfaster Starters they are still high-speed diets which are guaranteed to lose those excess pounds in the quickest possible time, safely and nutritiously. These seven diets again cater for different tastes and eating habits.

The **High Fibre Diet** follows the latest research in slimming. Foods high in dietary fibre not only fill you up but also pass through the body without it extracting every single calorie.

If you respond well to a bit of bullying, the **Maxi-Discipline Diet** guarantees success because it tells you precisely what to eat.

The **Slim and Sin Diet** keeps you in tow for five days a week and lets you sin for two. This is an ideal diet for anyone who finds it easy to be saintly during weekdays but whose good intentions tend to go out of the window at weekends.

Everyone has sunny days and blue days, but if you suffer from mood changes rather frequently we have just the diet for you. The **Marvellous Moody Diet** gives you a selection of low-calorie menus for good days and allows you to comfort-eat on days when you feel blue.

The **Easy Freezer Diet** is just right for people who are willing to spend one weekend shopping and preparing for their diet, so they can forget about planning, cooking and counting for two weeks. Take your prepared meals from the freezer each day and you will lose weight without even having to think about slimming.

Bad eating habits are often the biggest stumbling block when you are trying to lose weight and in the **Big Brother Diet** we teach you a few new habits on a daily basis. Every day we look over your shoulder, anticipating those mistakes and making sure that this time you really do follow our diet exactly as we intended.

If you have more than two stone to lose, then turn to the section on **Extras for Big Losers**, before you start your chosen diet.

None of these high-speed diets promises you a specific weight loss of so many pounds each week for the simple reason that no diet can make this promise. Rate of weight loss varies a great deal among individuals and depends on many personal factors. What these diets do promise is that they will help you to achieve your personal best in speed of weight loss if you follow the diet of your choice carefully. Good luck.

THE HIGH FIBRE DIET

1,000 calories

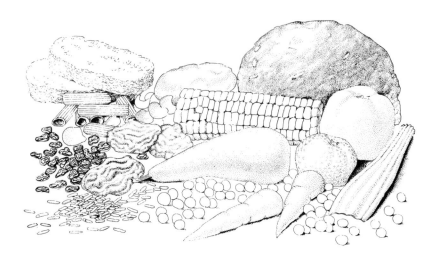

This diet follows all the current nutritional recommendations for healthy eating. Ten years ago nutritionists were urging us to eat plenty of protein food and go easy on the carbohydrates. Steaks with salad were in; potatoes, rice and bread were out. Now, aware that many protein foods are high in fat content, and increasingly alarmed by indications that excess fat intake is causing health problems, nutritionists are advising us to moderate our intake of most proteins. At the same time, they realise that we tend to need more fibre in our diets; and fibre is found in some of those once-despised carbohydrate foods. No, not in sugar but in such wholegrain cereal foods as wholemeal bread, bran products, brown rice and pasta, vegetables and fruit. So today's dietary advice packed in a nutshell is this. Eat a lot less fat and sugar, a little less protein and more fibrous carbohydrate foods. Happily for dieters, those 'good' carbohydrate foods like bread and baked beans are particularly comforting. An added bonus is that research has shown that, although fibre foods make you feel full, their calories aren't fully digested and quite a few pass straight through the body.

This diet contains plenty of fresh fruit and vegetables which are an excellent source of fibre, vitamins and minerals. It is also high in wholegrain cereals which are good sources of fibre and other nutrients. You'll find beans, bread, pasta and potatoes included. If you bake a potato, eat the skin for that is where the fibre lies. Likewise, boil and eat new potatoes in their skins.

There is very little fat in this diet, but you'll probably not miss it. Indeed, meals and menus are so attractive that perhaps it will encourage you to permanently forego the high amounts of butter and vegetable fats that you have been used to in the past – with consequent benefit to your health and your figure.

So here is a very modern diet that old-time slimmers never thought would happen: The High Fibre Diet – ideal for your health and comfortingly easy on your slimming willpower.

DIET RULES

1 Choose any breakfast from the list given. If you don't wish to eat this meal at breakfast-time you may save it for later in the day.

2 Choose one of the lunch and dinner menus each day. You may eat the meals in any order you wish and at any time of day. However, do not mix daily menus and choose a lunch from one day and a dinner from another. Each day's food selection is carefully balanced in terms of both calories and nutrients. If you dislike a particular meal, skip a menu altogether – there are 20 to choose from.

3 In addition to your three meals a day you may have 100 calories' worth of drinks. This means you may have 275ml/½ pint skimmed milk or 190ml/⅓ pint semi-skimmed milk. Water, tea and coffee (taken either black or with milk from your allowance), are unlimited. Other drinks can be selected from the list on page 154. Please do not use sugar to sweeten, use artificial sweetener if you must.

4 This diet has been very precisely worked out, so you too must weigh and measure all foods equally carefully. The only exceptions to this important rule are very low-calorie vegetables, such as lettuce, cress and cucumber, which couldn't possibly sabotage your diet.

BREAKFASTS

Cereal
2 Weetabix or 40g/1½oz
All-Bran.
15ml/1 level tablespoon raisins.
125ml/4fl oz skimmed milk.

Cheese on Toast / Fruit
1 slice wholemeal bread,
40g/1½oz, toasted.
50g/2oz cottage cheese, plain or
flavoured.
1 medium apple or pear.

Juice / Toast and Marmalade
125ml/4fl oz unsweetened orange
juice.
1 slice wholemeal bread, 40g/
1½oz, toasted.
7g/¼oz low-fat spread.
10ml/2 level teaspoons
marmalade.

Fruit and Yogurt
1 medium peach or apple.
1 small banana (150g/5oz).
1 small carton St Ivel or St
Michael natural yogurt.

Muesli
25g/1oz muesli.
10ml/2 level teaspoons raisins.
1 small banana (150g/5oz).
70ml/2½fl oz skimmed milk.

Cereal and Dried Fruit
25g/1oz Kellogg's 30% Bran
Flakes.
25g/1oz raisins.
125ml/4fl oz skimmed milk.

Prunes and Yogurt *(page 128)*
6 prunes, rehydrated if
necessary.
1 small carton orange yogurt.

Fruit and Nuts
1 medium apple, diced.
1 small banana (150g/5oz) sliced.
10ml/2 level teaspoons flaked
almonds.
½ small carton natural yogurt.

Bacon and Bread
2 rashers streaky bacon, well
grilled.
2 tomatoes, grilled without fat.
1 slice wholemeal bread (40g/
1½oz).

Biscuit and Cheese
1 Fox's Wholemeal Bran Biscuit.
25g/1oz Edam cheese.
1 medium apple or pear.

Bran Toast and Egg
2 slices Sunblest HiBran bread,
toasted.
7g/¼oz low-fat spread.
1 egg, size 3, boiled or poached.

Fruit Porridge
25g/1oz porridge oats.
75ml/3fl oz skimmed milk.
75ml/3fl oz water.
5ml/1 level teaspoon sugar.
15g/½oz raisins.

Bacon and Tomatoes on Toast
2 slices Sunblest HiBran bread,
toasted.
1 rasher streaky bacon, well
grilled.
227g/8oz can tomatoes.

Juice / Jam Crispbreads
125ml/4fl oz unsweetened orange
juice.
3 Energen Brancrisp.
15g/½oz low-fat spread.
15ml/1 level tablespoon
marmalade or jam.

DAY 1

Lunch
Nutty Cheese Sandwich / Orange

2 slices wholemeal bread (40g/1½oz each).
50g/2oz cottage cheese with pineapple.
2 walnut halves.
1 medium orange.

Mix cottage cheese with chopped walnuts and use to fill two slices of bread. Serve with a few sprigs of watercress. Follow with orange.

Dinner
Baked Chicken and Vegetables

225g/8oz chicken joint.
salt and pepper.
175g/6oz potato.
30ml/2 level tablespoons natural yogurt.
125g/4oz broccoli or Brussels sprouts, boiled.
125g/4oz carrots, boiled.

Season chicken joint and wrap in foil (do not add fat). Wash potato and bake with chicken at 190°C/375°F, gas mark 5, for 45 minutes or until the chicken and potato are tender. Halve the baked potato and top each half with a tablespoon of natural yogurt and seasoning to taste. Serve with chicken, carrots and broccoli or Brussels sprouts.

DAY 2

Lunch
Baked Beans on Toast / Apple

225g/7.9oz can baked beans.
1 slice wholemeal bread (40g/1½oz).
1 large apple.

Heat the beans. Toast the slice of bread on both sides and add beans. Follow with apple.

Dinner
Wholewheat Pasta and Tuna Salad / Orange

40g/1½oz wholewheat pasta rings or macaroni.
99g/3½oz can tuna in brine.
50g/2oz peas, frozen.
1 pickled baby beetroot.
2 or 3 spring onions.
30ml/2 tablespoons of Waistline or Heinz low-calorie salad dressing.
salt and pepper.
lettuce.
1 orange.

Cook pasta in boiling salted water until just tender, then drain. Rinse in cold water and drain again. Drain and roughly flake tuna. Cook peas and drain. Chop beetroot and spring onions. Mix together pasta, tuna, beetroot, spring onions and low-calorie salad dressing. Season to taste and serve on a bed of lettuce. Follow with orange.

DAY 3

Lunch
Salmon Salad

100g/3½oz John West or Princes canned salmon.
1 tomato.
few lettuce leaves.
piece cucumber.
2 sticks celery.
½ carton mustard and cress.
15ml/1 tablespoon Waistline or Heinz low-calorie salad dressing.
2 Energen Brancrisp.
7g/¼oz low-fat spread.

Serve the salmon with the prepared salad vegetables, salad dressing and crispbreads spread with low-fat spread.

DINNER
Cheesy Spinach Omelet / Fruit and Yogurt

2 eggs, size 3.
125g/4oz cooked spinach, fresh or frozen.
salt and pepper.

pinch of grated nutmeg.
7g/¼ oz low-fat spread.
25g/1oz Edam cheese, grated.
75g/3oz button mushrooms.
125g/4oz raspberries or
strawberries.
½ small carton natural yogurt.
Separate the eggs and mix yolks
with chopped spinach. Season
well with salt and pepper and
nutmeg. Whisk the egg whites
until stiff. Fold whites into the
egg yolk and spinach mixture.
Melt low-fat spread in an omelet
pan, pour in the mixture and
cook for 3 minutes. Place the
omelet under a hot grill and cook
until firm. Sprinkle with cheese
and fold in half. Serve with the
mushrooms, poached in stock or
salted water. Follow with
raspberries or strawberries
topped with natural yogurt.

DAY 4
Lunch
Sardine Sandwich
2 sardines canned in tomato
sauce.
15ml/1 level tablespoon cottage
cheese.
salt and pepper.
2 slices wholemeal bread
(40g/1½ oz each).
lettuce leaves.
few slices cucumber.
Mash sardines with cottage
cheese and season to taste. Fill
the two slices of bread with the
sardine mixture, lettuce leaves
and sliced cucumber. Cut into
four and serve.

Dinner
Kidney and Mushroom
Jacket Potato with Salad /
Grapes *(pages 176-7)*
200g/7oz potato for baking.
2 lamb's kidneys.
5ml/1 teaspoon chopped onion.
50g/2oz button mushrooms.
50ml/2fl oz beef stock or water.
salt and pepper.

5ml/1 level teaspoon cornflour.
lettuce leaves.
small bunch watercress.
few slices cucumber.
1 sliced tomato.
½ small green pepper, sliced.
15ml/1 tablespoon oil-free French
dressing.
125g/4oz grapes.
Bake potato at 200°C/400°F, gas
mark 6, for 45 minutes or until
soft when pinched (or boil in its
skin until tender then place in
hot oven for 5-10 minutes to
crisp the skin). Skin, core and
slice kidneys. Place in a small
pan with the onion, sliced
mushrooms, stock or water and
seasoning to taste. Bring to the
boil, reduce heat, cover and
simmer gently for 20 minutes,
adding more stock if necessary.
Blend the cornflour to a smooth
paste with a little cold water then
stir into the pan. Continue to
heat and stir until the sauce
thickens. Halve potato and scoop
out inside. Stir into the kidney
mixture. Pile back into the potato
shells and serve at once with
mixed salad. Follow with grapes.

DAY 5
Lunch
Egg and Tomato Open
Sandwich / Yogurt
1 slice wholemeal bread
(40g/1½ oz).
15ml/1 level tablespoon Waistline
or Heinz low-calorie salad
dressing.
lettuce.
1 egg, size 3, hard boiled.
1 tomato.
salt and pepper.
mustard and cress.
1 small carrot.
1 small carton Dessert Farm Pear
and Banana Yogurt or 1 small
carton Raines, Safeway or
Sainsbury's natural yogurt.
5ml/1 level teaspoon honey.

Spread bread with low-calorie salad dressing, then cover with lettuce leaves. Slice egg and tomato and arrange in alternate slices over the lettuce. Season with salt and pepper. Garnish with grated carrot and mustard and cress. Follow with a small carton Pear and Banana Yogurt or natural yogurt mixed with honey.

Dinner
Stuffed Green Pepper with Mixed Vegetables / Apple

1 medium green pepper (about 150g/5oz).
125g/4oz minced beef, raw.
1 fresh tomato or 50g/2oz canned tomatoes.
25g/1oz onion.
25g/1oz mushrooms.
15g/½oz brown rice.
60ml/4 tablespoons beef stock or water.
salt and pepper.
1.25ml/¼ level teaspoon dried mixed herbs.
175g/6oz mixed vegetables, frozen.
1 medium apple.
Cut top off the green pepper and remove seeds. Put pepper into a pan of boiling water and boil for 3 minutes. Drain well then stand it upright in a small ovenproof dish. Fry minced beef, without added fat, until well browned. Drain off and discard any fat which has cooked out of the meat. Chop the fresh or canned tomatoes and add, with the chopped onion and mushrooms, rice and stock or water to the meat in the pan. Season to taste with salt and pepper and add herbs. Stir well and heat to simmering point. Cover and simmer gently for 30 minutes. Spoon mixture into the pepper. Cover with a lid or foil and bake at 190°C/375°F, gas mark 5, for 20 minutes. Boil mixed

vegetables as directed and serve with the stuffed pepper. Follow with apple.

DAY 6
Lunch
White Onion Soup with Frankfurter / Apple

50g/2oz onion.
½ beef stock cube.
200ml/7fl oz boiling water.
15ml/1 level tablespoon skimmed milk powder.
salt and pepper.
pinch dried or chopped fresh sage.
25g/1oz frankfurter, thinly sliced.
1 wholemeal roll.
1 large apple.
Put sliced onion in a pan. Dissolve stock cube in the boiling water and add to the pan. Cover and simmer for 20 minutes. Sieve or liquidise onions and stock together. Whisk a little of the onion purée with the milk powder, then return to the pan with the remainder of the purée. Season to taste and add the sage. Reheat, then serve topped with slices of frankfurter and accompanied by the bread roll. Follow with apple.

Dinner
Roast Lamb with Vegetables
75g/3oz roast lean leg of lamb.
15ml/1 tablespoon mint sauce.
30ml/2 tablespoons fat-free gravy.
125g/4oz cauliflower.
75g/3oz carrots.
125g/4oz broad beans.
Trim any fat from the lamb and serve with the mint sauce, gravy and boiled vegetables.

Fresh Fruit Salad
1 small orange, peeled and segmented.
1 small apple, cored and chopped.

50g/2oz raspberries or strawberries, fresh or frozen.
50g/2oz green or black grapes.
125ml/4fl oz low-calorie lemonade.
30ml/2 level tablespoons natural yogurt.
Mix fruit together and stir in the lemonade. Leave to stand in a cool place for 30 minutes then serve topped with the yogurt.

DAY 7
Lunch
Lamb Coleslaw Salad / Grapes
75g/3oz raw white cabbage.
1 medium carrot.
1 stick celery.
5ml/1 teaspoon finely chopped or grated onion.
50g/2oz cold lean roast leg of lamb.
15ml/1 tablespoon Waistline or Heinz low-calorie salad dressing.
15ml/1 tablespoon natural yogurt.
salt and pepper.
lettuce.
2 Ryvita crispbreads.
125g/4oz grapes.
Mix shredded cabbage, grated carrot, finely chopped onion and celery together. Trim off any visible fat from the lamb and cut meat into strips or cubes. Add to the vegetables, then add the salad dressing and yogurt and mix well until all the ingredients are thoroughly blended. Season to taste with salt and pepper.
Arrange on a bed of lettuce leaves and serve with the crispbreads. Follow with the grapes.

Dinner
Bacon Steaks and Pineapple
2 bacon steaks (100g/3½oz each).
2 pineapple rings, fresh or canned in natural juice.
75g/3oz sweetcorn.

125g/4oz runner beans.
Grill bacon steaks on both sides without added fat until cooked, then grill pineapple rings until hot. Serve with boiled sweetcorn and runner beans.

DAY 8
Lunch
Grapefruit and Prawn Salad / Biscuit and Apple
½ medium grapefruit.
50g/2oz shelled prawns.
1 stick celery.
15ml/1 tablespoon Waistline Seafood Sauce or Waistline or Heinz low-calorie salad dressing.
lettuce.
2 Energen Brancrisp.
7g/¼oz low-fat spread.
1 Fox's Wholemeal Bran Biscuit.
1 large apple.
Cut segments from the grapefruit. Remove and discard any pith from the grapefruit shell and reserve the shell. Mix the prawns, grapefruit segments, chopped celery and seafood sauce or salad dressing in a bowl. Line the grapefruit shell with the shredded lettuce, then spoon in the grapefruit and prawn mixture. Serve with the crispbreads and low-fat spread. Follow with wholemeal bran biscuit and apple.

Dinner
Spaghetti Bolognese
125g/4oz raw minced beef.
25g/1oz onion.
1 stick celery.
125g/4oz canned tomatoes.
15ml/1 tablespoon Worcestershire sauce.
75ml/3fl oz water or beef stock.
salt and pepper.
pinch dried mixed herbs or oregano.
50g/2oz wholewheat spaghetti.
chopped fresh parsley, optional.
Fry minced beef without added fat until browned, then drain off

and discard the fat which has cooked out. Add the finely chopped onion and celery, roughly chopped tomatoes, Worcestershire sauce and water or stock to the browned meat. Stir well, then season with salt and pepper and add the mixed herbs or oregano. Bring to simmering point, then cover and simmer for 25 minutes. Meanwhile cook the spaghetti in boiling salted water for about 12 minutes or until tender. Drain the spaghetti and arrange on a warm serving dish. Pour the minced beef sauce over the spaghetti and serve sprinkled with parsley.

DAY 9

Lunch
Cheese and Crispbreads / Fruit

50g/2oz Edam cheese.
3 Energen Brancrisp or Ryvita crispbreads.
15ml/1 tablespoon pickle.
2 sticks celery.
1 medium orange or pear.
Serve the cheese with the crispbreads, pickle and celery. Follow with orange or pear.

Dinner
Crispy Topped Fish with Pasta and Greens / Banana
(pages 176-7)

175g/6oz cod, coley or haddock fillets.
125g/4oz canned drained tomatoes.
25g/1oz mushrooms.
pinch dried mixed herbs.
salt and pepper.
25g/1oz wholemeal breadcrumbs.
25g/1oz wholewheat short-cut macaroni or spaghetti rings.
125g/4oz spring greens or broccoli.
1 small banana (150g/5oz).
Place fish fillets in an ovenproof dish. Roughly chop the tomatoes

and mix with the chopped mushrooms. Stir in the mixed herbs and season to taste with salt and pepper. Spread the tomato mixture over the fish. Cover the dish with foil and bake at 180°C/350°F, gas mark 4, for 15 minutes. Uncover the fish and sprinkle the breadcrumbs over the top. Return to the oven for about 10 minutes until the breadcrumbs are crisp. Meanwhile cook the macaroni or spaghetti rings in boiling salted water for 12 minutes and boil the spring greens or broccoli until just tender. Drain the pasta and spring greens or broccoli and serve with the fish. Follow with banana.

DAY 10

Lunch
Fruity Chicken Salad with Crispbreads / Fruit

1 medium eating apple.
10ml/2 teaspoons lemon juice.
50g/2oz black grapes.
2 large sticks celery.
50g/2oz cooked chicken.
30ml/2 tablespoons natural yogurt.
pinch curry powder.
salt and pepper.
few lettuce leaves.
1 tomato.
2 Energen Brancrisp.
7g/¼ oz low-fat spread.
1 medium orange, pear or peach.
Toss the cored and chopped apple in the lemon juice, then add the halved and pipped grapes and chopped celery. Remove any skin from the chicken, cut into bite-size pieces and add to the fruit and celery. Mix the yogurt with the curry powder then stir into the salad ingredients until well mixed. Season to taste with salt and pepper. Arrange the salad on a bed of lettuce and garnish with the tomato cut in

wedges. Serve with the crispbreads spread with the low-fat spread. Follow with orange, pear or peach.

Dinner
Tangy Pork with Pasta

125g/4oz pork fillet.
8 squirts Limmits Spray & Fry.
1 small onion.
50g/2oz button mushrooms.
1.25ml/¼ level teaspoon dried thyme.
salt and freshly ground pepper.
5ml/1 level teaspoon flour.
30ml/2 tablespoons chicken stock.
10ml/2 teaspoons lemon juice.
30ml/2 level tablespoons natural yogurt.
40g/1½oz wholewheat short-cut macaroni.
75g/3oz carrots.
parsley and lemon to garnish, optional.

Trim all fat from the pork fillets and cut the meat into bite-size pieces. Spray a frying pan with the Spray & Fry and add the chopped onion. Cook over a low heat stirring frequently until transparent. Add the pork, sliced mushrooms, thyme and salt and pepper to taste. Cover and cook for 5-10 minutes until tender, stirring occasionally. Sprinkle in the flour, stir well and cook for 1 minute. Add the chicken stock and lemon juice and bring to the boil. Turn heat down very low and stir in the yogurt carefully. Do not allow to boil. Cook the wholewheat macaroni as directed and cook the carrots in salted water, then drain and serve with the Tangy Pork. Garnish with a slice of lemon and sprig of parsley.

DAY 11
Lunch
Cheese, Apple and Ham Toasty

1 slice wholemeal bread (40g/1½oz).
little made mustard.
25g/1oz cooked lean ham.
1 medium eating apple.
25g/1oz Edam cheese, grated.
1 medium carrot.
1 stick celery.

Toast the slice of bread on both sides, then spread one side very lightly with the mustard. Remove and discard all visible fat from the ham. Lay the ham on the toast. Core and slice the apple and arrange the slices on the ham. Place under a hot grill for about 2 minutes until the apple starts to soften. Cover the apple with the grated cheese and then return to the grill until the cheese melts. Cut the carrot and celery into small sticks and serve with the cheese, apple and ham toasty.

Dinner
Beef Casserole with Cauliflower / Melon

125g/4oz lean stewing beef.
25g/1oz onion.
50g/2oz carrot.
25g/1oz turnip or swede.
125g/4oz canned tomatoes.
½ beef stock cube.
275ml/½ pint boiling water.
salt and pepper.
pinch of chilli powder.
1 bouquet garni.
50g/2oz drained canned red kidney beans.
15g/½oz wholewheat pasta shapes.
150g/5oz cauliflower.
175g/6oz slice Canteloupe, Honeydew or Yellow melon.

Trim off and discard all fat from the stewing beef then cut the meat into cubes. Put the meat, sliced onion and carrot, diced turnip or swede and canned

131

tomatoes into a pan. Dissolve the stock cube in the boiling water and add to the meat and vegetables. Bring to the boil, then season to taste with salt and pepper. Add the chilli powder and bouquet garni. Cover and simmer gently for 1½ hours. Remove bouquet garni. Add the red kidney beans and pasta, stir well, return to simmering point, cover and continue to cook for a further 20 minutes. Boil the cauliflower in salted water until just tender then drain. Arrange the cauliflower in a ring on a warm serving dish and serve the beef casserole in the centre.

Serve a slice of melon before or after the casserole.

DAY 12
Lunch
Sweetcorn and Pineapple Open Sandwich / Apple

50g/2oz sweetcorn, canned or frozen.
1 ring pineapple, canned in natural juice.
1 stick celery.
15ml/1 tablespoon oil-free French dressing.
1 slice wholemeal bread (40g/1½oz).
1 medium apple.
Cook sweetcorn if frozen, drain and cool. Cut the pineapple into small pieces and slice the celery. Mix sweetcorn, pineapple and celery with the dressing and spread over the bread. Follow with the apple.

Dinner
Stuffed Aubergine / Biscuit and Orange

1 small aubergine, 175g/6oz.
1 small onion.
50g/2oz button mushrooms.
25g/1oz butter beans, canned.
salt and pepper.
7g/¼oz low-fat spread.

10ml/2 level teaspoons wholemeal flour.
125ml/¼ pint skimmed milk.
salt and pepper.
25g/1oz Edam cheese.
1 Fox's Wholemeal Bran biscuit.
1 medium orange.
Halve the aubergine. Scoop out some of the flesh and chop. Peel and chop the onion and simmer in stock or water for about 5 minutes; drain. Slice the mushrooms. Mix together the aubergine flesh, onion, butter beans, mushrooms and seasoning. Pile back into the aubergine shells. Make cheese sauce by mixing the low-fat spread, flour, milk and seasoning in a saucepan and, stirring, bring to the boil. Grate the cheese and stir in. Pour the sauce over the aubergine halves and bake at 180°C/350°F, gas mark 4, for about 35-40 minutes until the aubergine is cooked. Follow with the biscuit and orange.

DAY 13
Lunch
Baked Beans and Bacon

2 rashers streaky bacon.
150g/5.3oz can Heinz baked beans.
1 slice wholemeal bread (40g/1½oz).
Grill the bacon until very crisp. Drain. Either crumble it into the cold baked beans or heat the beans and toast the bread.

Dinner
Pork Fillet with Apricots / Stewed Apple

125g/4oz pork fillet.
5ml/1 teaspoon vegetable oil.
1 small onion.
5ml/1 level teaspoon cornflour.
150ml/¼ pint stock (made with stock cube).
salt and pepper.
5ml/1 teaspoon vinegar.
5 dried apricot halves.

75g/3oz peas.
75g/3oz green beans.
175g/6oz cooking apple.
15ml/1 tablespoon water.
pinch cinnamon.
Hermesetas Sprinkle Sweet.
Cut pork into cubes. Heat the oil in a saucepan and fry the pork. Chop the onion and add to the pan. Cook for 5 minutes. Stir in the cornflour, then the stock, seasoning, vinegar and apricots. Simmer for about 35 minutes until the pork is tender. Add a little water if necessary during cooking. Serve with boiled peas and green beans. Peel, core and slice the apple. Put in a saucepan with the water and cinnamon and cook until tender. Cool slightly and sweeten to taste with Sprinkle Sweet.

DAY 14
Lunch
Beetroot and Sardine Salad
2 baby beetroot.
2 sticks celery.
1 small apple.
120g/4½oz can John West Sardines in Tomato Sauce.
5ml/1 teaspoon lemon juice.
black pepper.
cucumber.
Slice the beetroot and celery. Dice the apple. Flake the sardines and mix with lemon juice. Season with black pepper. Top with cucumber slices.

Dinner
Swiss Steak / Ice Cream
175g/6oz stewing steak.
½ small onion.
227g/8oz can tomatoes.
125ml/¼ pint boiling water.
half a beef stock cube.
5ml/1 level teaspoon cornflour.
salt and pepper.
half a 217g/7½oz can butter beans.
125g/4oz green beans.
50g/2oz ice cream.

1 piece stem ginger.
Cut steak in two and remove all visible fat. Slice onion and drain the tomatoes but keep the juice. Put the meat, onion and 30ml/2 tablespoons tomato juice in a saucepan. Bring to the boil. Dissolve stock cube in boiling water and add to meat. Mix cornflour with a little water and add to steak mixture. Season and simmer gently for 1-1½ hours until the meat is tender. Add more tomato juice during cooking if necessary. Just before serving add the tomatoes. Serve with boiled butter and green beans. Follow with ice cream mixed with chopped ginger.

DAY 15
Lunch
Cucumber Boats
½ small cucumber
25g/1oz prawns.
113g/4oz carton cottage cheese with chives.
25g/1oz sweetcorn, canned or frozen.
salt and pepper.
2 slices Sunblest HiBran bread.
15g/½oz low-fat spread.
Cut cucumber in half lengthways. Scoop out some of the flesh and dice it. Chop prawns and mix with the cucumber flesh, cottage cheese, sweetcorn and seasoning. Pile back into cucumber shells. Serve with bread and low-fat spread.

Dinner
Pizza and Salad / Grapes
170g/6oz Findus French Bread Pizza.
green salad including lettuce, cucumber and watercress.
15ml/1 tablespoon oil-free French dressing.
125g/4oz grapes.
Prepare salad by tearing lettuce, slicing cucumber and tossing ingredients with dressing. Cook

the pizza according to pack instructions. Serve with salad. Follow with grapes.

DAY 16
Lunch
Fish Cakes and Baked Beans/ Fruit
2 Birds Eye or Findus Fish Cakes.
150g/5.3oz can baked beans.
1 peach or medium apple.
Grill fish cakes without added fat. Heat beans and serve with fish cakes. Follow with fruit.

Dinner
Stuffed Chicken Breast and Vegetables
150g/5oz chicken breast.
50g/2oz onion.
25g/1oz wholemeal breadcrumbs.
15g/½oz broken walnuts.
pinch dried herbs.
1 stick celery.
10ml/2 teaspoons skimmed milk.
salt and pepper.
75g/3oz peas.
75g/3oz carrots.
Remove skin from chicken and beat the flesh between two pieces of non-stick paper, using a meat hammer or heavy frying pan. Chop onion and boil for 5 minutes, drain. Mix bread-crumbs, walnuts, onion, herbs, celery, milk and seasoning together and use to stuff the chicken. Secure with wooden cocktail sticks. Wrap in foil and bake at 180°C/350°F, gas mark 4, for 1¼-1½ hours. Serve with boiled peas and carrots.

DAY 17
Lunch
Pear, Cheese and Walnut Open Sandwich
50g/2oz cottage cheese.
1 slice wholemeal bread (40g/1½oz).
1 small fresh pear.
1 tomato.
15g/½oz walnut halves.

cucumber.
Spread cottage cheese on the bread. Peel, core and slice pear and arrange on the cheese. Top with sliced tomato and walnuts. Serve with cucumber slices.

Dinner
Pork Chop with Apple / Melon
200g/7oz loin pork chop.
1 thick slice cooking apple.
1 slice onion.
salt and pepper.
75ml/3fl oz cider.
50ml/2fl oz stock (made with stock cube).
75g/3oz cabbage.
125g/4oz potato, boiled.
225g/8oz melon.
Remove and discard all fat from the chop. Remove core from apple. Put the chop in an oven-proof dish, add apple, onion and seasoning. Pour on the cider and stock, cover and bake at 180°C/350°F, gas mark 4, for 1¼-1½ hours. Serve with boiled cabbage and potato. Follow with melon.

DAY 18
Lunch
Cod in Sauce / Biscuit
1 packet frozen cod in parsley sauce.
125g/4oz peas and sweetcorn, frozen.
1 Fox's Wholemeal Bran Biscuit.
Cook the fish according to pack instructions. Serve with the boiled vegetables and follow with the biscuit.

Dinner
Lemony Liver
125g/4oz calves' liver.
7g/¼oz flour.
salt and pepper.
5ml/1 teaspoon oil.
½ small onion.
125ml/¼ pint stock (made with stock cube).
10ml/2 teaspoons lemon juice.

25g/1oz wholewheat pasta, raw.
lettuce, cucumber, carrot.
½ apple.
Cut liver into thin strips. Toss in
seasoned flour. Heat oil in a
small pan and drop in the liver.
Cook gently for 5 minutes and
remove. Add the onion then stir
in the stock and lemon juice.
Simmer for 5 minutes. Replace
the liver and simmer for a
further 10 minutes. Serve with
boiled pasta and a salad of
lettuce, cucumber, apple, carrot.

DAY 19
Lunch
Mushroom Omelet / Prunes and Yogurt

2 eggs, size 3.
15ml/1 tablespoon skimmed milk.
salt and pepper.
50g/2oz button mushrooms.
125ml/¼ pint stock (made with
stock cube).
50g/2oz peas.
1 tomato.
8 prunes.
30ml/2 tablespoons natural
yogurt.
Beat together the eggs, milk and
seasoning. Pour into a non-stick
omelet pan and cook gently until
set. Meanwhile, slice and poach
mushrooms in the stock, drain
and use to fill omelet. Serve with
boiled peas and sliced tomato.
Follow with prunes and yogurt.

Dinner
Minestrone Soup *(pages 176-7)* / Cake

25g/1oz haricot beans, dried.
1 rasher streaky bacon.
1 small onion.
1 small carrot.
50g/2oz cabbage.
250ml/½ pint stock (made with
stock cube).
10ml/2 teaspoons tomato purée.
1 tomato.
15g/½ oz wholewheat macaroni,
raw.

1 slice Sunblest HiBran bread.
1 Sainsbury's Mini-Madeira
Cake.
Soak the beans overnight, drain
and boil in fresh water for 1-2
hours until tender. Drain. Chop
the bacon and heat in a
saucepan, pressing with a spoon
to extract the fat. Chop onion
and carrot and shred cabbage
finely. Add to the pan. Add the
remaining ingredients and cook
until the pasta is tender. Serve
with the bread. Follow with a
mini-Madeira cake.

DAY 20
Lunch
Baked Beans on Toast / Apple

225g/7.9oz can baked beans.
1 slice wholemeal bread
(40g/1½ oz).
1 large apple.
Heat the beans. Toast the slice of
bread on both sides and add
beans. Follow with apple.

Dinner
Wholewheat Pasta and Tuna Salad / Orange

40g/1½ oz wholewheat pasta
rings or macaroni.
99g/3½ oz can tuna in brine.
50g/2oz peas, frozen.
1 pickled baby beetroot.
2 or 3 spring onions.
30ml/2 tablespoons low-calorie
salad dressing.
salt and pepper.
lettuce.
1 orange.
Cook pasta in boiling salted
water until just tender, then
drain. Rinse in cold water and
drain again. Drain and roughly
flake tuna. Cook peas and drain.
Chop beetroot and spring onions.
Mix pasta, tuna, beetroot, spring
onions and low-calorie dressing.
Season and serve on a bed of
lettuce. Follow with orange.

THE MAXI-DISCIPLINE DIET

1,000 calories

Look, we're sick and tired of listening to you moan about wanting to lose weight. The plain truth is you're not even trying. You're just a greedy, self-indulgent lazybones who's going to spend the rest of your days looking frumpy. Yes, we know you say you hate being fat, that it's awful to feel like a slob, to watch yet more buttons pop and zips come unstuck. And you'd love not to feel so miserable. But it's all talk, isn't it? Plain old fashioned poppycock. You can't mean what you say and eat the way you do. Yes, we know about that last glorious binge of yours, the one that went on for five days and nights . . . remember?

Blushing, eh? Well, so you should. When was the last time you weighed yourself? Stop hedging . . . go and get your scales and bring them back here. Look at that horror story . . . no, we don't want to hear about your fluid retention. That's not fluid retention, it's just plain old-fashioned piggery. To be blunt the rot has got to stop . . . listen to us and do exactly what we say. You're going on a diet and you're going to stick to it once and for all. You've got one last chance to lose weight – and this time you'd better take it.

We're going to allow you just 1,000 calories every day, spread around a breakfast, light meal, main meal and snack – and, by golly, you're going to follow it to the last half a calorie. You will not be allowed to change a thing: just follow the diet exactly as it is. And you are not going to cheat. Got that? Right, then get on this diet this instant and don't come back until you've reached your target.

DIET RULES

This diet requires your full cooperation. It does not allow you to substitute one food for another or cheat, however innocently, by having a little more of this or that. It is one of the surest ways to lose weight because it guarantees that you will not exceed the correct number of calories.

1 Follow the menus precisely. Don't change anything or substitute one food for another.

2 You may choose the times you eat your meals. The breakfast meal may be eaten later in the day if you wish; and the main and lighter meals may be taken in any order.

3 As well as the three meals and a snack each day, you are allowed 100 calories' worth of drinks. You may use all your allowance on milk for your tea and coffee if you like; or you can choose 100 calories' worth of drinks from the list on page 154. Measure milk carefully. You can have 275ml/½ pint skimmed milk for your 100 calories or 150ml/¼ pint Silver Top.

4 You may drink unlimited quantities of sugarless black coffee or tea, water and any soft drinks labelled 'low calorie'.

5 Because this diet is so precise, it means you must have every single food you need ready to hand. Plan and shop before you even start on day one. To make this easier for you we have given shopping lists for each week. It is best to get in a whole week's supply of food in one go if you can: but if, for any reason, you need to shop more frequently, take the greatest care to shop accurately. Don't be tempted to buy more than you are allowed. As we said, this diet is very precise; and it is bossy for your own good!

SHOPPING LIST

In addition to the foods listed, small quantities of marmalade or jam, raisins, low-calorie tomato ketchup, low-calorie salad dressing, oil-free French dressing, Waistline Tartare Sauce, mint sauce, mild mustard pickle or piccalilli are required. If these are not already in your store cupboard, add them to the shopping list.

Some of the foods listed require chilled or frozen storage. If you do not have a refrigerator and/or freezer these items will have to be bought as and when needed. We have marked them with a * and put the day on which they are required in brackets.

Shopping List: Week 1
Groceries, Meat and Fish

1 Slimcea loaf.

1 packet Ryvita crispbreads (for 2 weeks).

1 packet Weetabix (for 2 weeks).

250g/9oz carton low-fat spread (for 2 weeks).

125g/4oz Edam cheese.

1 can or packet instant low-fat skimmed milk powder.

6 eggs, size 3 (for 2 weeks).

2 x 283g/10oz cans Heinz Low Calorie Scotch Broth or Tomato or Vegetable Soup.

1 sachet Batchelors Cup-a-Soup, Chicken and Leek or Vegetable and Beef.

1 sachet Knorr Oxtail Quick Soup.

227g/8oz can tomatoes.

225g/7.9oz can Heinz Baked Beans in Tomato Sauce.

35g/1.23oz Shippams Country Pot Paste, Beef and Horseradish or Beef and Pickle.

* 1 small chicken for roasting or 175g/6oz roast chicken meat (Sunday and Monday).

* 1 small carton Chambourcy Black Cherry, Raspberry or Strawberry Yogurt (Monday).

* 125g/4oz lamb's liver (Tuesday).

* 2 rashers back bacon (Tuesday).

* 175g/6oz cod, coley or haddock fillets (Wednesday).

* 2 small cartons Chambourcy, Sainsbury's or Safeway natural yogurt (Wednesday, 1; Thursday and Saturday, ½ each).

* 2 Matthews Turkey & Beef-burgers (Wednesday and Saturday).

* 200g/7oz pork chop (Thursday).

* 113g/4oz carton Eden Vale or St Ivel cottage cheese, any flavour except 'with Onion and Cheddar' (Friday).

* 200g/7oz packet Findus Cod Steaks in Batter (for 2 weeks), two on Friday, week 1; two on Tuesday, week 2.

* Small sliceable block vanilla ice cream (for 2 weeks).

Fresh Fruit and Vegetables

3 grapefruit (approx. 250g/9oz each).

4 medium eating apples (approx. 150g/5oz each).

125g/4oz grapes.

3 medium oranges (approx. 225g/8oz each).

2 medium pears (approx. 125g/4oz each).

2 small bananas (approx. 150g/5oz each).

1 lettuce.

6 medium tomatoes.

1-2 bunches watercress.

1 cucumber.

1 small green or red pepper.

1 bunch spring onions.

125g/4oz button mushrooms.

350g/12oz new potatoes, fresh or canned.

175g/6oz potato for baking.

350g/12oz carrots.
1 small cabbage.
1 head celery.
* 125g/4oz raspberries, fresh or
frozen (Sunday).
* 250g/8oz broccoli, fresh or
frozen (Sunday and Friday).
* 175g/6oz peas, frozen (Tuesday
and Friday).
* 125g/4oz runner beans, fresh
or frozen (Wednesday).

Week 1 Sunday
Breakfast
Grapefruit / Egg and bread
½ grapefruit.
artificial sweetener, optional.
1 egg, size 3, boiled or poached.
1 slice Slimcea bread.
5ml/1 level teaspoon low-fat
spread.

Light Meal
Cheese and Tomato Sandwich
2 slices Slimcea bread.
7g/¼ oz low-fat spread.
25g/1oz Edam cheese, grated.
15ml/1 level tablespoon mild
mustard pickle or piccalilli.
1 tomato, sliced.
1 medium pear.

Main Meal
**Roast Chicken and Vegetables /
Fruit and Ice Cream**
75g/3oz roast chicken, all skin
removed.
45ml/3 tablespoons thin fat-free
gravy.
175g/6oz new potatoes, boiled or
canned.
125g/4oz broccoli, boiled.
75g/3oz carrots, boiled.
125g/4oz strawberries or
raspberries, fresh or frozen.
25g/1oz slice vanilla ice cream.

Snack
1 Weetabix.
150ml/¼ pint skimmed milk.

Week 1 Monday
Breakfast
**Grapefruit / Toast and
Marmalade**
½ grapefruit
artificial sweetener, optional.
2 slices Slimcea bread, toasted.
7g/¼ oz low-fat spread.
10ml/2 level teaspoons jam or
marmalade.

Light Meal
**Soup, Crispbreads / Cheese and
Apple**
295g/10.4oz can Heinz Low
Calorie Scotch Broth, Tomato or
Vegetable Soup.
2 Ryvita crispbreads.
7g/¼ oz low-fat spread.
25g/1oz Edam cheese.
1 medium apple.

Main Meal
Chicken Salad
75g/3oz roast chicken, all skin
removed.
mixed salad: lettuce, 1 tomato,
watercress, cucumber, half small
green pepper, few spring onions.
15ml/1 tablespoon low-calorie
salad dressing.
125g/4oz grapes.
1 small carton Chambourcy
Black Cherry or Raspberry or
Strawberry yogurt.

Snack
2 Ryvita crispbreads.
35g/1.23oz pot Shippams
Country Pot Paste, Beef and
Horseradish or Beef and Pickle.

Week 1 Tuesday
Breakfast
Cereal
2 Weetabix.
150ml/¼ pint skimmed milk.

Light Meal
Soup / Bacon Sandwich
1 sachet Knorr Oxtail Quick
Soup.
2 rashers back bacon, well
grilled.

2 slices Slimcea bread.
15ml/1 tablespoon low-calorie
tomato ketchup.

Main Meal
Grilled Liver and Vegetables / Orange
125g/4oz lamb's liver, grilled with
15g/½oz low-fat spread.
half a 227g/8oz can tomatoes.
50g/2oz button mushrooms,
poached in stock or salted water.
75g/3oz peas, boiled.
1 medium orange.

Snack
25g/1oz raisins.
1 small apple.

Week 1 Wednesday
Breakfast
Yogurt and Banana
1 small carton Chambourcy,
Sainsbury's or Safeway natural
yogurt.
1 small banana.

Light Meal
Turkey / Beefburger and Salad
1 Matthews Turkey &
Beefburger, grilled.
mixed salad: lettuce, watercress,
cucumber, spring onions, 1
tomato and ½ small red or green
pepper.
15ml/1 tablespoon low-calorie
salad dressing.
1 slice Slimcea bread.
5ml/1 level teaspoon low-fat
spread.

Main Meal
Grilled Fish and Vegetables / Apple
175g/6oz cod, coley or haddock
fillets, grilled or baked with
15g/½oz low-fat spread.
125g/4oz runner beans, boiled.
half a 227g/8oz can tomatoes.
175g/6oz new potatoes, canned
or boiled.
1 medium apple.

Snack
2 slices Slimcea bread.

10ml/2 level teaspoons low-fat
spread.
1 tomato, sliced.

Week 1 Thursday
Breakfast
Grapefruit / Egg and Crispbreads
½ grapefruit.
artificial sweetener, optional.
1 egg, size 3, boiled or poached.
2 Ryvita crispbreads.
7g/¼oz low-fat spread.

Light Meal
Beans on Toast / Apple
2 slices Slimcea bread, toasted.
225g/7.9oz can Heinz Baked
Beans in Tomato Sauce.
1 medium apple.

Main Meal
Pork Chop and Vegetables
200g/7oz pork chop (weighed
raw), well grilled and all visible
fat removed.
50g/2oz button mushrooms,
poached in stock or salted water.
125g/4oz cabbage, boiled.

Snack
1 small banana.
½ small carton natural yogurt.

Week 1 Friday
Breakfast
Cereal
2 Weetabix.
150ml/¼ pint skimmed milk.

Light Meal
Cottage Cheese Salad / Pear
113g/4oz carton Eden Vale or St
Ivel Cottage Cheese, any flavour.
2 medium carrots, grated or cut
into sticks.
2 sticks celery.
lettuce, watercress and 1 tomato.
15ml/1 tablespoon low-calorie
salad dressing.
2 Ryvita crispbreads.
7g/¼oz low-fat spread.
1 medium pear.

Main Meal
Cod Steaks in Batter with Vegetables / Orange

2 Findus Cod Steaks in Batter,
45g/1¾oz each, grilled or baked
without added fat.
15ml/1 tablespoon Waistline
Tartare Sauce.
75g/3oz peas, boiled.
75g/3oz carrots, boiled.
125g/4oz broccoli, boiled.
1 medium orange.

Snack
1 sachet Batchelors Cup-a-Soup,
Chicken and Leek or Vegetable
and Beef.

Week 1 Saturday
Breakfast
Grapefruit / Toast and Marmalade
½ grapefruit.
artificial sweetener, optional.
2 slices Slimcea bread, toasted
and spread with
7g/¼oz low-fat spread.
10ml/2 level teaspoons
marmalade or jam.

Light Meal
Soup / Crispbreads and Cheese
295g/10.4oz can Heinz Low
Calorie Scotch Broth, Tomato or
Vegetable Soup.
1 Ryvita crispbread.
50g/2oz Edam cheese.
2 sticks celery.

Main Meal
Turkey & Beefburger, Jacket Potato and Salad
1 Matthews Turkey & Beef-
burger, grilled.
170g/6oz baked jacket potato,
topped with
7g/¼oz low-fat spread.
mixed salad: lettuce, cucumber,
watercress, spring onions, 1
tomato and
15ml/1 tablespoon oil-free French
dressing.

Snack
1 small grapefruit.
1 medium orange.
½ small carton natural yogurt.

Shopping List: Week 2
Groceries, Meat and Fish
1 small loaf wholemeal bread.
125g/4oz Edam cheese.
128g/4½oz can Heinz Pizza
Toast Topper.
1 sachet Batchelors Beef &
Tomato Cup-a-Soup.
295g/10.4oz can Boots Low
Calorie Soup.
227g/8oz can pineapple rings in
natural juice.
575ml/1 pint unsweetened orange
juice.
2 x 227g/8oz can tomatoes.
150g/5.3oz can baked beans in
tomato sauce.
* 150g/5oz lamb chump chop
(Sunday).
* 50g/2oz cooked lean ham
(Monday).
* 2 lamb's kidneys (Monday).
* 4 pork chipolata sausages (two
on Monday, two on Tuesday).
* 227g/8oz packet Birds Eye
Cauliflower, Peas & Carrots
(Monday and Thursday).
* 225g/8oz chicken joint
(Wednesday).
* 1 small carton Eden Vale
Creme Caramel or Ross Devonshire Trifle (Wednesday).
* 113g/4oz carton Eden Vale or
St Ivel Cottage Cheese, any
flavour except 'with Onion and
Cheddar' (Thursday).
* 1 small carton natural yogurt
(Saturday).
* 50g/2oz corned beef
(Thursday).
* 175g/6oz cod, coley or haddock
fillets (Friday).
* 125g/4oz sweetcorn, canned or
frozen (Friday).
*125g/4oz peas, frozen
(Wednesday and Friday).

* 2 bacon or ham steaks (100g/
3½ oz each) (Saturday).

Fresh Fruit and Vegetables
2 medium pears (approx.
125g/4oz each).
5 medium oranges (approx.
225g/8oz each).
4 medium eating apples (approx.
150g/5oz each).
1 small banana (approx.
150g/5oz).
1 medium banana (approx.
175g/6oz).
1 bunch watercress.
1 lettuce.
½ cucumber.
1 bunch spring onions.
6 medium tomatoes.
1 bunch radishes.
1 carton mustard and cress.
250g/8oz cabbage suitable for
coleslaw and boiling.
1 head celery.
125g/4oz button mushrooms.
250g/8oz carrots.
450g/1lb potatoes for boiling.
* 250g/8oz broccoli, fresh or
frozen (Sunday and Wednesday).
* 125g/4oz raspberries or strawberries, fresh or frozen
(Saturday).

Week 2 Sunday
Breakfast
Tomatoes on Toast
2 small slices wholemeal bread
(25g/1oz each) toasted.
227g/8oz can tomatoes.

Light Meal
Egg Salad
1 egg, size 3, hard boiled.
mixed salad: lettuce, cucumber,
spring onion, 1 carrot, grated, 1
tomato, few radishes and
mustard and cress.
15ml/1 tablespoon low-calorie
salad dressing.
1 Ryvita crispbread.

Main Meal
**Lamb Chop with Vegetables /
Orange**
150g/5oz lamb chump chop
(weighed raw), grilled and all
visible fat removed.
10ml/2 teaspoons mint sauce.
175g/6oz potatoes, boiled.
125g/4oz broccoli, boiled.
75g/3oz carrots, boiled.
1 medium orange.

Snack
2 tomatoes.
25g/1oz Edam cheese.

Week 2 Monday
Breakfast
Cereal
2 Weetabix.
150ml/¼ pint skimmed milk.

Light Meal
Ham and Salad Sandwich / Apple
2 small slices wholemeal bread
(25g/1oz each).
7g/¼ oz low-fat spread.
50g/2oz lean ham, all visible fat
removed.
1 tomato, sliced.
little lettuce and cucumber.
1 medium apple.

Main Meal
**Grilled Kidneys and Sausages
with Vegetables / Orange**
2 lamb's kidneys, grilled.
2 pork chipolata sausages, well
grilled.
15ml/1 tablespoon low-calorie
tomato ketchup.
125g/4oz Birds Eye Cauliflower,
Peas & Carrots.
125g/4oz cabbage, boiled.
1 medium orange.

Snack
2 Ryvita crispbreads.
7g/¼ oz low-fat spread.
10ml/2 level teaspoons marmalade or jam.

Week 2 Tuesday

Breakfast
Orange Juice / Scrambled Egg on Toast
150ml/¼ pint unsweetened orange juice.
1 small slice wholemeal bread (25g/1oz) toasted.
1 egg, size 3, scrambled with 45ml/3 tablespoons skimmed milk and
7g/¼oz low-fat spread.

Light Meal
Sausages and Coleslaw
2 pork chipolata sausages, well grilled and cooled.
125g/4oz white cabbage, shredded.
1 medium carrot, grated.
1 stick celery, finely chopped.
15ml/1 tablespoon low-calorie salad dressing.

Main Meal
Cod Steaks in Batter with Vegetables / Banana
2 Findus Cod Steaks in Batter, 50g/1¾oz each, grilled or baked without added fat.
150g/5.3oz can baked beans in tomato sauce.
1 tomato, grilled without fat.
1 small banana.

Snack
1 medium apple.
1 medium pear.

Week 2 Wednesday

Breakfast
Cereal
2 Weetabix.
150ml/¼ pint skimmed milk.

Light Meal
Pizza Toast Toppers / Carton Dessert
2 small slices wholemeal bread (25g/1oz each) toasted.
128g/4½oz can Heinz Pizza Toast Topper.
1 small carton Eden Vale Creme Caramel or Ross Devonshire

Trifle.

Main Meal
Grilled Chicken and Vegetables / Orange
225g/8oz chicken joint, grilled and skin removed.
50g/2oz sweetcorn, frozen or canned.
50g/2oz button mushrooms, poached.
125g/4oz broccoli, boiled.
1 medium orange.

Snack
295g/10.4oz can Boots Low Calorie Soup, any flavour.
1 Ryvita crispbread.

Week 2 Thursday

Breakfast
Orange Juice / Egg and Crispbreads
150ml/¼ pint unsweetened orange juice.
1 egg, size 3, boiled or poached.
2 Ryvita crispbreads.
7g/¼oz low-fat spread.

Light Meal
Soup / Cottage Cheese and Bread
1 sachet Batchelors Beef & Tomato Cup-a-Soup.
113g/4oz carton Eden Vale or St Ivel Cottage Cheese, any flavour except 'with Onion and Cheddar'.
1 small slice wholemeal bread (25g/1oz).
3 sticks celery.

Main Meal
Corned Beef and Vegetables / Banana
50g/2oz corned beef.
½ 227g/8oz can tomatoes.
125g/4oz Birds Eye Cauliflower, Peas and Carrots.
125g/4oz potato, boiled.
1 medium banana.

Snack
1 medium orange.
1 medium apple.

Week 2 Friday

Breakfast
Cereal
2 Weetabix.
150ml/¼ pint skimmed milk.

Light Meal
Orange Juice / Cheese Salad
150ml/¼ pint unsweetened orange juice.
50g/2oz Edam cheese.
mixed salad: lettuce, cucumber, watercress, few radishes and few spring onions.
15ml/1 tablespoon oil-free French dressing.

Main Meal
Grilled Fish with Vegetables / Pineapple
175g/6oz cod, coley or haddock fillets, grilled or baked, brushed with
15g/½ oz low-fat spread.
50g/2oz peas, boiled.
50g/2oz sweetcorn, canned or frozen.
½ 227g/8oz can tomatoes.
227g/8oz can pineapple rings in natural juice (save 2 rings for Saturday).

Snack
1 slice Slimcea bread.
7g/¼ oz low-fat spread.
1 medium apple.

Week 2 Saturday

Breakfast
Orange Juice / Egg and Bread
150ml/¼ pint unsweetened orange juice.
1 egg, size 3, boiled or poached.
1 small slice wholemeal bread (25g/1oz).
7g/¼ oz low-fat spread.

Light Meal
Cheese & Tomato Toast / Pear
1 small slice wholemeal bread (25g/1oz) toasted.
1 sliced tomato.
25g/1oz Edam cheese, grilled.
1 medium pear.

Main Meal
Bacon Steaks with Pineapple and Vegetables / Fruit and Ice Cream
2 bacon or ham steaks, 100g/3½ oz each raw weight, well grilled.
2 pineapple rings in natural juice (reserved from Friday), heated under grill.
small bunch watercress.
50g/2oz button mushrooms, poached in stock or water.
50g/2oz peas, boiled.
125g/4oz raspberries or strawberries, fresh or frozen.
25g/1oz portion vanilla ice cream.

Snack
1 small carton natural yogurt.
1 small orange, sliced.

THE SLIM AND SIN DIET

about 1,000 calories

A full social life and a lovely slim figure aren't incompatible. The Slim and Sin Diet is the sociable way to slim. Provided that you keep to SlimDay meals from Monday to Friday you can "sin" all weekend and yet still lose weight. Our researches have shown that many diets work well enough on weekdays but then along comes the weekend with extra leisure (to think about food!) and extra time (in which to eat it!) – or along comes the unexpected party or dinner out and bang go the good resolutions. This diet has been specially planned for just such emergencies.

On the diet you will be able to eat biscuits, cakes and crisps; and if you have the family around you at weekends the likelihood of someone commenting: 'I thought you were supposed to be dieting!' is quite high. Remarks like these are likely to infuriate you into eating extra rather than restrain you from eating more. There is a fairly common tendency in overweight people to eat certain foods only in private; they may feel self-conscious about eating sugary or starchy foods when others are watching and may even go to the lengths of sneaking down to the kitchen in the middle of the night to lessen the risk of being found out. In modern dieting, the emphasis has moved away from banning certain foods towards stricter fat control and more freedom with carbohydrate foods. To protect yourself from being infuriated out of eating-control by other people's old-hat ideas of what you should eat, you need to come out into the open. Explain to the family beforehand that your calorie allowance does permit foods which they might consider to be 'indulgent' and that they will be seeing you eating these foods as part of your weight loss plan.

The Slim and Sin Diet gives you five strict days and two treat days in every seven. On strict days you will eat a maximum of 800 calories; and you are allowed 1,500 calories on the other two days of the week. If you do your sums, you will see that this allowance balances you to an overall fast-slimming 1,000 calories a day; so even though you can quite indulge yourself twice a week, your weight will still come down (as long as you observe your strict diet on the other five days). The Slim and Sin Diet is ideal for people who follow a busy Monday to Friday routine, but for whom the weekend signals a break in strict eating patterns; or for anybody for whom a weekend represents weakened willpower. But it is just as good and effective for those who find it easy to follow a diet except for the days when business or social commitments demand a less strict eating pattern.

DIET RULES

1 Each SlimDay diet meal has been carefully worked out at 200 calories. You may therefore choose any four meals to have on each strict diet day. Vary your choice to ensure a good supply of nutrients. Have five SlimDays every week.

2 You may eat your four SlimDay meals at any time of the day that suits you. If you are one of those people who can go happily without breakfast but feels starving in the evenings, for example, then by all means do without food until you feel hungry: and eat two or three of your 200-calorie meals at short intervals, or even together later in the day.
It really doesn't matter *when* you eat, or how much of your food allowance you eat at any one time. The important thing is not to exceed the daily 800 calories your four-meals choice allows you.

3 On each SinDay you can have 700 calories' worth of treats *as well as* your choice of four meals from the SlimDay section. To make it easy for you to know precisely how many extra calories your treats are costing you, they are divided into 50-calorie, 100-calorie and 200-calorie lists. You may choose your extras from any of these, but be sure your treats do not total more than 700 calories each SinDay. You may have two SinDays every week.

4 This diet does not include milk for use in drinks unless you take it as one of your treats on SinDays. You are allowed as much black coffee, lemon or black tea, soft drinks labelled 'low-calorie' and water as you wish which will make no difference to your total calorie intake.

SLIMDAY CEREAL MEALS

Grapefruit / Weetabix
½ medium grapefruit.
5ml/1 level teaspoon sugar.
2 Weetabix.
125ml/4fl oz skimmed milk.
5ml/1 level teaspoon sugar.

Bran Flakes and Banana
25g/1oz Kellogg's 30% Bran
Flakes.
1 small banana.
125ml/4fl oz skimmed milk.

Muesli and Yogurt
25g/1oz muesli.
1 individual carton natural
yogurt, any brand.

Orange Juice / Cornflakes
125ml/4fl oz unsweetened orange
juice.
25g/1oz cornflakes.
5ml/1 level teaspoon sugar.
125ml/4fl oz skimmed milk.

All Bran and Raisins
50g/2oz All Bran.
15ml/1 level tablespoon raisins.
125ml/4fl oz skimmed milk.

Apple Juice / Sugar Puffs
150ml/¼ pint apple juice.
25g/1oz Sugar Puffs.
125ml/4fl oz skimmed milk.

Porridge
25g/1oz Ready Brek or Warm
Start.
150ml/¼ pint skimmed milk,
hot.
5ml/1 level teaspoon honey or
sugar.

Shredded Wheat / Boiled Egg
1 Shredded Wheat.
125ml/4fl oz skimmed milk.
5ml/1 level teaspoon Hermesetas
Sprinkle Sweet.
1 egg, size 3, boiled.

Muesli
40g/1½oz muesli.
125ml/4fl oz skimmed milk.

Bran Flakes with Dried
Apricots *(pages 176-7)*
25g/1oz 30% Bran Flakes.
25g/1oz dried apricots, chopped.
125ml/4fl oz skimmed milk.

SLIMDAY BREAD AND TOAST MEALS

Cheese and Marmite on Toast
2 small slices Slimcea, toasted.
a little Marmite.
40g/1½oz Edam cheese.

Orange Juice / Toast and Marmalade
150ml/¼ pint unsweetened
orange juice.
1 medium slice bread
(40g/1½oz).
7g/¼oz low-fat spread.
10ml/2 level teaspoons
marmalade or jam.

Crumpets
2 crumpets.
15g/½oz low-fat spread.

Ham and Vegetable Sandwich
2 small slices brown or
wholemeal bread (25g/1oz each).
30ml/2 level tablespoons
Waistline Country Vegetable
Spread.
25g/1oz lean cooked ham.

Banana Sandwich
1 small banana.
2 small slices bread (25g/1oz
each).

Pizza Toast / Banana
1 small slice bread (25g/1oz),
toasted.
1 Birds Eye Pizza Griller.
1 small banana.

Cheese Spread and Salad Roll
1 crusty roll.
1 triangle cheese spread.
1 tomato, sliced.
few slices cucumber.

Toasted Sandwich / Apple
1 Findus Toasted Sandwich, Beef
or Ham & Cheese flavour.
1 apple.

Buttered Currant Bun
1 currant bun, 45g/1¾oz.
7g/¼oz butter.

Herring Roes on Toast / Pear
125g/4oz herring roes, poached
in water with a dash of lemon
juice or vinegar.
1 small slice bread (25g/1oz)
toasted.
1 medium pear.

Toast and Honey
2 small slices wholemeal bread
(25g/1oz each) toasted.
15g/½oz low-fat spread.
10ml/2 level teaspoons honey.

Fish Spread and Cucumber Roll
1 crusty roll.
half a 53g/1⅞oz pot Princes
Kipper or Smoked Mackerel
Spread.
Few slices cucumber.

French Bread and Salad Sandwich
1 piece French bread (50g/2oz).
15g/½oz low-fat spread.
1 tomato, sliced.
unlimited lettuce, cucumber,
spring onions and watercress or
mustard and cress.

SLIMDAY EGG MEALS

Open Egg and Tomato Sandwich
1 egg, size 3, hard boiled.
15ml/1 tablespoon low-calorie
salad dressing.
1 large slice bread (40g/1½oz).
1 tomato, sliced.

Apple Juice / Poached Egg on Toast
150ml/5fl oz apple juice.
1 egg, size 3, poached.
1 small slice bread (25g/1oz)
toasted.

Boiled Egg and Crispbreads
2 eggs, size 3, boiled.
2 Energen or Krispen
crispbreads.

Egg and Bacon
1 egg, size 3, poached.
2 streaky bacon rashers, crisply
grilled.
1 Energen or Krispen crispbread.

Tomato and Onion Omelet with Broccoli
125g/4oz broccoli.
2 eggs, size 3.
10ml/2 teaspoons water.
Limmits Spray & Fry.
salt and pepper.
1 tomato.
1 spring onion.
Boil broccoli, drain and keep
warm. Lightly beat together eggs
with water and season. Spray a
small non-stick omelet pan with
Limmits Spray & Fry and heat.
Pour in egg mixture and cook;
lifting omelet edges and tilting
pan until all mixture is set. Slice
tomato and chop onion and use
to fill omelet. Fold over and
serve immediately with the
broccoli.

Tuna Scramble on Toast
1 egg, size 3.
50g/2oz tuna in brine.
15ml/1 tablespoon skimmed milk.
salt and pepper.
1 small slice brown or wholemeal
bread (25g/1oz).
Lightly beat together the egg,
flaked tuna and skimmed milk.
Season. Cook in a non-stick pan
over a low heat until creamy.
Toast bread and serve the
scramble on top.

Egg Salad
1 egg, size 3.
15ml/1 tablespoon low-calorie
salad dressing.
1 tomato.
unlimited lettuce, cress,
cucumber, celery, pepper and
spring onions.
1 small slice Slimcea or Nimble.

7g/¼ oz low-fat spread.
Hard boil the egg; cool, shell and halve. Place on a plate and top with salad dressing. Make up a salad and serve with the bread, spread with low-fat spread.

SLIMDAY CHEESE MEALS

Edam Salad
50g/2oz Edam cheese.
1 tomato.
1 spring onion.
unlimited lettuce, cucumber, cress and radishes.
15ml/1 tablespoon oil-free French dressing.

Cheese and Apple
40g/1½ oz Leicester or Gouda cheese.
1 medium apple.

Jacket Potato with Cottage Cheese
175g/6oz potato.
50g/2oz cottage cheese with chives.
Scrub potato and bake in its jacket at 200°C/400°F, gas mark 6, until soft when pinched. Cut it in half and top with cottage cheese.

Cottage Cheese and Fruit Salad (pages 176-7)
113g/4oz carton Eden Vale Cottage Cheese with Pineapple.
1 small orange, peeled and segmented.
1 small pear, cored and diced.
50g/2oz grapes, halved and pipped.

Cottage Cheese with Vegetables and Ham / Salad
170g/6oz carton St Ivel Cottage Cheese with Vegetables and Ham.
lettuce, cucumber, celery, pepper, cress and radishes.
15ml/1 tablespoon oil-free French dressing.

Curd Cheese and Relish Crispbreads
3 Krispen crispbreads.
75g/3oz curd cheese.
25g/1oz cucumber relish.

Cauliflower Cheese
275g/10oz cauliflower.
½ packet Knorr Cheese Sauce Mix.
150ml/¼ pint skimmed milk.
15g/½ oz Edam cheese.
30ml/2 level tablespoons fresh breadcrumbs.
Cook cauliflower in boiling salted water until just tender. Drain and keep warm. Make up cheese sauce mix with the skimmed milk and pour over cauliflower. Grate cheese and mix with breadcrumbs. Sprinkle on top and grill until cheese melts and breadcrumbs start to brown.

SLIMDAY MEAT MEALS

Bacon Steak with Pineapple (pages 176-7)
1 bacon or ham steak (100g/3½ oz raw weight).
1 pineapple ring, canned in natural juice, drained.
125g/4oz Birds Eye Peas, Sweetcorn and Peppers.
15ml/1 tablespoon tomato ketchup.
Grill steak then top with pineapple ring and grill until hot. While the steak is cooking boil the peas, sweetcorn and peppers and serve with the pineapple-topped steak and tomato ketchup.

Chicken Drumsticks with Coleslaw
2 chicken drumsticks, grilled and skin removed.
1 carton Eden Vale Coleslaw in Vinaigrette.

Beefburgers with Grilled Tomatoes
2 Findus Beefburgers, well grilled.
2 tomatoes, grilled without added fat.
15ml/1 level tablespoon Bicks Relish.

Chicken and Mushroom Casserole
1 individual Birds Eye Chicken and Mushroom Casserole.
125g/4oz Birds Eye Peas and Baby Carrots, boiled.

Sausages and Baked Beans
150g/5.3oz can baked beans in tomato sauce.
2 beef chipolata sausages, well grilled.

Roast Beef and Vegetables
1 individual pack Findus Sliced Roast Beef in Gravy.
½ medium packet of Cadbury's Smash.
125g/4oz cauliflower, fresh or frozen.

Kidney and Bacon Grill
2 lamb's kidneys, halved, cored and grilled.
1 rasher streaky bacon, crisply grilled.
1 tomato, grilled.
50g/2oz mushrooms, poached in a little stock.

Beef Casserole with Vegetables
1 individual pack Ross Beef Casserole.
150g/5oz mixed vegetables, frozen.

SLIMDAY FISH MEALS

Cod in Butter Sauce and Peas
1 packet Findus Cod in Butter Sauce.
125g/4oz peas, frozen.

Smoked Haddock with Green Beans
1 pack Findus Buttered Scottish Smoked Haddock.
125g/4oz runner beans.

Prawn Curry with Beansprouts
1 Birds Eye China Dragon Prawn Curry.
125g/4oz beansprouts, boiled.

Salmon Salad
99g/3½oz can salmon.
1 tomato.
unlimited lettuce, cucumber, celery, pepper and spring onions.
15ml/1 tablespoon Waistline Seafood Sauce.

Grilled Cod or Haddock
150g/5oz cod or haddock fillet.
7g/¼oz low-fat spread.
125g/4oz runner beans.
125g/4oz carrots.
15ml/1 tablespoon tomato ketchup.
Dot fish fillet with low-fat spread and grill. Serve with boiled vegetables and ketchup.

Fish Cakes and Peas
2 fish cakes, grilled without added fat.
125g/4oz peas, frozen.
15ml/1 tablespoon tomato ketchup.

Cheesy Grilled Fish
1 Birds Eye Cod, Coley, Haddock or Hake steak.
Limmits Spray & Fry.
15ml/1 level tablespoon Sharwoods Chilli and Tomato Chutney.
15g/½oz Edam cheese.
125g/4oz mixed vegetables, frozen.
Spray fish steak with Limmits Spray & Fry and grill until cooked. Spread chutney over fish and grate cheese on top. Grill until cheese melts. Serve with mixed vegetables.

SLIMDAY RICE, PASTA AND BEAN MEALS

Spaghetti on Toast
1 small slice bread (25g/1oz) toasted.
215g/7.6oz can Heinz Spaghetti in Tomato Sauce.

Spaghetti Bolognese
210g/7.4oz can Heinz Spaghetti Bolognese.
10ml/2 level teaspoons grated Parmesan cheese.

Rice Lunch / Fruit
1 KP Quick Lunch with Rice, any flavour.
1 medium apple or orange.

Beef Risotto
1 Batchelors Beef Risotto Snackpot.

Baked Beans on Toast / Fruit
150g/5.3oz can baked beans in tomato sauce.
1 small slice bread (25g/1oz) toasted.
50g/2oz grapes or 1 mandarin or tangerine.

Prawn and Rice Salad
25g/1oz long-grain rice.
15ml/1 tablespoon oil-free French dressing.
50g/2oz peas, frozen.
50g/2oz cucumber.
1 stick celery.
50g/2oz peeled prawns.
salt and pepper.
Boil rice. Drain, rinse under cold water and drain again. Mix with French dressing and leave to cool. Boil peas. Drain and mix with rice. Dice cucumber and celery. Stir into rice with prawns. Season.

Beans, Ham and Mushrooms
50g/2oz button mushrooms.
40g/1½oz lean cooked ham.
150g/5.3oz can baked beans in tomato sauce.
dash Worcestershire sauce.
Slice mushrooms and poach in salted water for 4 minutes. Drain. Discard all visible fat from ham then dice lean. Mix with mushrooms and baked beans. Add Worcestershire sauce and heat through gently.

SLIMDAY SOUP MEALS

Minestrone
283g/10oz can Crosse & Blackwell Minestrone Soup.
15ml/1 level tablespoon grated Parmesan cheese.
2 bread sticks.

Tomato Soup with Toasted Cheese
295g/10.4oz can Heinz Low Calorie Tomato Soup.
1 small slice Nimble or Slimcea, toasted.
25g/1oz Edam cheese, sliced.

Soup / Chipsticks and Apple
1 sachet Batchelors Slim-s-Soup or Carnation Slim Soup.
1 small packet Smiths Chipsticks.
1 medium apple.

Soup with French Bread
283g/10oz can Waistline Low Calorie Golden Vegetable Soup.
50g/2oz piece French bread.
7g/¼oz low-fat spread.

Soup and Sandwich
283g/10oz can Crosse & Blackwell Oxtail and Vegetable Soup.
2 small slices Nimble or Slimcea bread.
half a 35g/1.23oz pot Shippams Country Pot Beef & Pickle or Pork & Herb Paste.
few slices cucumber.

Vegetable Soup with Cheesy Crispbread
300g/10.6oz can Heinz Farmhouse Thick Vegetable Soup.

1 Energen or Ryvita crispbread.
1 triangle cheese spread.

Tomato Soup with Prawns and Crispbread
425g/15oz can Frank Cooper Tomato Soup with Prawns.
1 Energen or Ryvita crispbread.

Main Course Soup
425g/15oz can Campbell's Steak and Kidney and Vegetable Soup.

SLIMDAY FRUIT MEALS

Berries with Sugar and Cream
225g/8oz fresh or frozen raspberries or strawberries.
15ml/1 level tablespoon sugar.
45ml/3 tablespoons single cream.

Fresh Fruit Salad with Yogurt
1 small orange.
75g/3oz grapes.
1 small pear.
75g/3fl oz apple juice.
half a 142g/5oz carton St Ivel natural yogurt.
Peel and segment orange. Halve and pip grapes. Core and cube pear. Mix all fruit with the apple juice and serve with the yogurt.

Banana / Milk
1 large banana (200g/7oz).
175ml/6fl oz Silver Top Milk or 275ml/½ pint skimmed milk.

Orange and Kiwi Fruit with Yogurt *(page 129)*
1 medium orange.
2 kiwi fruits.
142g/5oz carton St Ivel natural yogurt.
Peel and segment orange. Slice kiwi fruits. Mix all fruit with the yogurt.

Fruit Medley
1 medium apple.
1 medium pear.
1 small banana.
75g/3oz grapes.

Banana with Yogurt and Walnuts
1 medium banana.
142g/5oz carton St Ivel natural yogurt.
2 walnut halves.

SINDAY 50 CALORIE TREATS

Fruit
200g/7oz apricots, fresh.
1 medium apple (150g/5oz).
125g/4oz cherries, fresh.
75g/3oz grapes.
2 mandarins or tangerine oranges, fresh.
1 medium orange (225g/8oz).
1 large pear (175g/6oz).
150g/5oz plums, fresh.
1 large peach (175g/6oz).
200g/7oz raspberries or strawberries, fresh or frozen.
30ml/2 level tablespoons raisins or sultanas.
220g/7.8oz can Boots Fruit Cocktail, Peaches, Pears or Pineapple in Low Calorie Syrup.
198g/7oz can Weight Watchers Blackberries, Fruit Cocktail or Fruit Salad, Grapefruit, Peaches, Pears, Raspberries or Strawberries in Low Calorie Syrup.

Biscuits
2 Rich Tea Finger or Morning Coffee biscuits.
2 sponge fingers.
1 medium digestive.
1 Huntley & Palmer Cornish Wafer.
2 chocolate finger biscuits.
1 McVitie's Abbey Crunch or Fruit Shortcake.
1 McVitie's or Sainsbury's Jaffa Cake.
5 Hotel biscuits.
1 Peak Frean Shortcake.
1 St. Michael Chocolate Chip Cookie or Rich Tea Finger Cream.

Bread and Crispbreads

1 slice French toast.
3 bread sticks.
1 slice Family Nimble.
1 slice Sunblest HiBran.
2 Ryvita crispbreads.
2 Energen Brancrisp.
3 Krispen crispbreads.
2 Crackerbread crispbreads.

Soups

1 sachet Batchelors Slim-a-Soup, any flavour.
1 sachet Carnation Slim Soup, any flavour.
1 can Waistline Golden Vegetable Soup.
1 can Boots Low Calorie Beef & Vegetable Soup.

Milk

150ml/¼ pint skimmed milk.

Alcoholic Drinks (all normal pub measures)

25ml/¹⁄₆ gill Brandy, Whisky (Scotch, Irish or Bourbon), Gin, Rum or Vodka.
25ml/¹⁄₆ gill Kirsch or Tequila.
25ml/¹⁄₆ gill Brandy with Low Calorie American Ginger Ale.
25ml/¹⁄₆ gill Rum or Vodka with Diet Pepsi or Tab.
25ml/¹⁄₆ gill Whisky with Low Calorie American Ginger Ale.
25ml/¹⁄₆ gill Gin with Low Calorie Bitter Lemon or Tonic Water.
50ml/⅓ gill Dubonnet Dry.
50ml/⅓ gill Martini Extra Dry.
50ml/⅓ gill Noilly Dry French.
50ml/⅓ gill (small schooner) Dry Sherry.

100 CALORIE TREATS

Fruit

1 large banana (200g/7oz).
50g/2oz dried apricots.
227g/8oz can Dietade Apricot, Pears or Pineapple in Fruit Sugar Syrup.
227g/8oz can Koo Fruit Cocktail,

Peach Slices or Pear Halves in Apple Juice.

Biscuits

1 Huntley & Palmer Elevenses.
1 Jacob's Club Wafer.
1 MacDonald's Yo Yo.
1 McVitie's Bandit.
1 Rowntree Mackintosh Breakaway or Bue Riband.

Bread and Crispbreads

2 small slices Slimcea spread with 10ml/2 level teaspons low-fat spread.
2 slices Family Nimble, unbuttered.
1 large, medium thick slice bread – brown, white or wholemeal (40g/1½oz).
3 Ryvita crispbreads spread with 7g/¼oz low-fat spread.

Cheese

25g/1oz Cotswold, Danish Blue, Dolcellata, Double Gloucester, Gouda or Leicester.
113g/4oz carton Eden Vale Cottage Cheese, any flavour.
113g/4oz carton St Ivel Cottage Cheese with Onion & Chives or with Pineapple.

Rice and Pasta

25g/1oz macaroni, spaghetti or pasta shapes, raw weight.
25g/1oz rice, raw weight.

Vegetables

150g/5.3oz can baked beans in tomato sauce.
115g/4oz boiled or canned butter, cannellini, haricot or red kidney beans.
125g/4oz boiled potatoes.
125g/4oz sweetcorn, frozen or canned, drained.
½ medium packet Cadbury's Smash.

Small Yogurts

1 Eden Vale or St Michael Natural Yogurt.
1 St Ivel natural yogurt with

50g/2oz raspberries or straw-berries, fresh or frozen.
1 St Ivel Natural Yogurt with 50g/2oz raspberries or straw-berries, fresh or frozen.
1 St. Ivel Prize Fruit Yogurt, any flavour.
1 Safeway Fruit Yogurt, any flavour.

Ice Cream
1 Lyons Maid Chocolate Nut Sundae or Cornish Raspberry Sundae.
1 Lyons Maid Cornish Vanilla Kup.
1 Wall's Blue Ribbon Golden Vanilla Ice Cream Bar.
1 Wall's Soft Golden Vanilla Tub.
1 medium cone Mr Whippy ice cream.
¼ Birds Eye Arctic Roll.

Desserts
1 Birds Eye Mousse, any flavour.
1 Chambourcy Flanby Caramel.
1 Ross Mousse Cup, any flavour.

Milk
275ml/½ pint skimmed milk.
200ml/7fl oz semi-skimmed milk.
150ml/¼ pint Silver Top milk.

Cakes
1 Cadbury's Mini Roll.
1 Lyons Chocolate Caprice.
1 Lyons individual Chocolate Covered Roll.
1 Marco & Carlo Strawberry Cream Puff.
1 British Home Stores Genoese Fancy.
1 Mr Kipling French Fancy.

Alcoholic Drinks (normal pub measures)
25ml/¹⁄₆ gill Tia Maria.
125ml/4fl oz wine.
25ml/¹⁄₆ gill Grand Marnier or Southern Comfort.
25ml/¹⁄₆ gill Bailey's Original Irish Cream.
25ml/¹⁄₆ gill Cointreau or Drambuie.
50ml/⅓ gill Cinzano Rosso or Martini Bianco with Low Calorie Lemonade.
25ml/¹⁄₆ gill Benedictine.
275ml/½ pint Carlsberg Pilsner Lager.
275ml/½ pint Bulmer's Woodpecker Cider.
275ml/½ pint Harp Lager or Arctic Lite Lager.
275ml/½ pint Brown Ale.
275ml/½ pint Heineken Lager.
50ml/⅓ gill (double pub measure) brandy, whisky, gin, rum or vodka.

150 CALORIE TREATS

Cakes
1 Mr Kipling Bakewell Slice.
1 Lyons Viennese Whirl.
1 Mr Kipling Jam, Lemon Curd or Treacle Tart.
1 Mr Kipling Cherry Slice.
1 Sainsbury's Coconut Crunch Cake.

Small Yogurts
1 Chambourcy Black Cherry Curd.
1 Chambourcy Lemon Curd.
1 Eden Vale Banana, Raspberry or Strawberry.
1 Eden Vale Chocolate.
1 Eden Vale Vanilla.
1 Ski, any flavour.
1 St Ivel Country Prize Muesli, Grapefruit or Walnut.
1 St Ivel Countess, any flavour.
1 St Michael Black Cherry, Peach Melba or Raspberry.

Desserts
1 Eden Vale Chocolate or Fresh Fruit Cream Dessert.
1 Findus Raspberry Ripple or Strawberry Ripple Mousse.
1 Ross Devonshire Trifle, any flavour.
1 Sainsbury's Fruit Dessert, any flavour.
1 St Ivel Creme Caramel.

1 St Ivel Trifle, Raspberry or
Strawberry.
1 St Michael Strawberry Delight.
1 St Michael Mandarin or
Raspberry Royale.

Cheese
123g/4oz curd cheese.
50g/2oz Austrian Smoked.
75g/3oz Riccotta.
50g/2oz Tome au Raisin.
2 Kerrygold Processed Cheese
Slices.

Vegetables
175g/6oz potato, baked in its
jacket.
175g/6oz new potatoes, boiled.
223g/7.9oz can Batchelors Butter
or Cannellini Beans.
3 patties Birds Eye Bubble 'n'
Squeak, cooked without added
fat.
5 Birds Eye Potato Croquettes,
cooked without added fat.
225g/7.9oz can baked beans in
tomato sauce.

Savoury Snacks
1 packet Golden Wonder Wotsits
(25g/1oz).
1 packet Record Wholewheat
Crunchies.
1 packet Rileys Wheat
Crunchies.
1 packet Sainsbury's Beef &
Onion Flavour Potato Snacks.
1 packet Sainsbury's Cheese
Flavoured Puffs.
1 small packet crisps, any
flavour.

Milk
425ml/¾ pint skimmed milk.
275ml/½ pint semi-skimmed
milk.
225ml/8fl oz Silver Top milk.

Sweet Treats
1 Jordan's Original Crunchy
Bar.
1 Cadbury's Dipped Flake.
1 pack Cadbury's Buttons (30g).
1 Mars Ripple.
2 Fun Size Milky Ways.

1 Prewett's Date & Fig Bar.
1 Caramac (28g).

Alcoholic Drinks (all normal pub measures)
275ml/½ pint Bulmer's Dry
Pomagne or Dry Special
Reserve.
275ml/½ pint Gaymer's Festival
Vat.
275ml/½ pint Taunton Special
Vat.
275ml/½ pint Stella Artois.
1 bottle Cherry B.

200 CALORIE TREATS

Cakes
1 Lyons Apple Puff Pastry.
1 Lyons or Mr Kipling Mince
Pie.
1 Marco & Carlo Rum Baba.
1 Mr Kipling Apple Sundae.
1 Mr Kipling Redcurrant &
Raspberry Pie.
1 St Michael Blackcurrant or
Chocolate Sponge Curl.
1 St Michael Custard Slice.

Desserts
½ 439g/15½oz can Ambrosia
Creamed Rice, Ground Rice,
Sago, Semolina or Tapioca.
1 Birds Eye Star Turn.
1 Findus Chocolate Ripple
Mousse.
1 Sainsbury's Chocolate Dessert.
1 St Ivel Chocolate Cream
Dessert.
1 Eden Vale Strawberry Fool.
1 St Ivel Lemon or Orange
Soufflé.

Ice Cream
1 Lyons Maid King Cone,
Cornish Dairy, Mint Chocolate,
Strawberry or Vanilla.
1 Wall's Cornetto, Mint Choc
Chip, Rum & Raisin or Strawberry.

Vegetables
150g/5oz roast potatoes, cut in
large chunks.

150g/5oz Birds Eye Crispy
Potato Fritters.
150g/5oz Findus Grill Chips.
115g/4oz Ross Oven Crunches.
142g/5oz pack Birds Eye Small
Onions in White Sauce.
213g/7½oz can Chesswood
Sliced Mushrooms in Creamed
Sauce.
225g/7.9oz can Heinz Curried
Beans with Sultanas.
160g/5.6oz carton Eden Vale
Caribbean Salad.
206g/7¼oz can Heinz Celery
Salad with Potatoes.
198g/7oz carton St Ivel
Vinaigrette Salad.
227g/8oz carton Sainsbury's
Beetroot Salad.

Sweet Treats
1 Boots Fruit Muesli Bar
1 Cadbury's Double Decker.
1 Cadbury's Picnic.
1 Frys Chocolate Cream or
Peppermint Cream or Plain
Centre.
1 Frys Turkish Delight.
1 Aero, any flavour.
1 Rowntree Mackintosh Prize.
1 Terry's Coffee or Tangerine
Cream Bar.

THE BIG BROTHER DIET

1,000 calories

You are in for some surprises as you read on. As the days go by, you may well feel that Big Brother himself has stepped out of the pages of '1984' and is infiltrating your kitchen, your living room and your place of work. Breathing down your neck, keeping his eye on you. Watching . . . waiting for you to dare try a little cheating. If you are one of those slimmers who find it easier to follow a strictly regimented diet then the Big Brother Diet is tailor-made for you. For the whole two-week dieting period, you are told exactly what to eat and how to eat it.

To begin with we insist that you forget everything your mother taught you about eating. There is only room for one boss on this diet. Mums believe that you need to eat to keep up your energy even if you weigh 20st and they tend to believe that you need a lot of energy – even more than other people need. Simply appreciate that energy means the same thing as calories. Calories are units of energy and surplus fat is stored energy. Slim people, who don't carry any surplus fat, certainly need to eat sufficient food to keep going but if overweight people always eat enough to keep up their energy they'll never lose a single surplus pound. It is only by consuming less food than is wanted to fuel your body's daily energy needs that you can make it 'eat' its own surplus fat. If you are overweight, face a very energetic day and don't eat enough food to keep you going, that is a good thing. You can congratulate yourself on it because you will be burning up surplus fat to supply the energy you require.

Another famous maternal saying is that it's wicked to waste food. You can throw that idea out too, along with all those leftovers in the fridge which you've been saving to 'use up'. One of the biggest differences between the slim and the overweight is that the former have a 'stop mechanism' and the latter don't. Slim people will eat as much as they really need and then stop, while fat people don't stop eating until they have cleared their plates, however piled up with food they are. If you are overweight you must develop this stop mechanism in order to reduce and control your weight. You will only achieve this if you can bear to throw away leftovers from your plate. Food fallacies die hard. The things that were drummed into us during our childhood still subconsciously influence us. Carrying on eating like your mother taught you, however, is the sure way to stay fat. That's why Big Brother is going to make sure she stays out of your kitchen during the next two weeks.

DIET RULES

1 You are allowed three meals a day. You may eat them in any order and at any times that suit you.

2 In addition to your three meals, you may have one sweet snack or piece of fruit to eat as a pudding or a between-meal filler. You will find your snack or pudding for each day listed after the meals.

3 You may not have one bite more than is stated in each day's menu. You are, however, permitted to drink as much as you wish of any of the following: black sugarless coffee; black or lemon tea; soft drinks labelled 'low-calorie'; and water. Milk for drinks may be taken from your daily allowance (see page 161).

4 This diet is carefully balanced nutritionally. You must follow each day's menus exactly, in consecutive order, for the whole 14-day period.

Daily Allowance:

275ml/½ pint skimmed milk to use in tea and coffee throughout the day.

Don't be tempted to tip your milk straight into your cup of tea or coffee. Measure your milk allowance into a jug and use this amount throughout the day. And put down that bottle of Silver Top – it's almost twice the calories of skimmed.

DAY 1

Breakfast
Toast and Marmalade

2 small slices bread (25g/1oz each) toasted.
15g/½oz low-fat spread.
15ml/1 level tablespoon marmalade or jam.

We saw that . . . you dipped into that tub of low-fat spread and didn't bother to weigh it. OK so your scales aren't that accurate under 25g/1oz. So weigh out 25g/1oz and divide it into two (you can use the other half tomorrow). Simple, isn't it?

Light Meal
Cottage Cheese Salad

113g/4oz carton Eden Vale or St Ivel Cottage Cheese, natural or with chives, onion or pineapple.
1 tomato.
unlimited lettuce, cucumber, cress, spring onions, celery, radishes.
15ml/1 tablespoon low-calorie salad dressing.

Main Meal
Grilled Ham Steak with Pineapple, Chips, Mushrooms and Green Beans

1 ham or bacon steak (100g/3½oz raw weight).
1 ring pineapple, canned in natural juice, drained.
150g/5oz Findus Grill Chips.
125g/4oz mushrooms.

125g/4oz runner beans.

Serve the grilled steak topped with pineapple. Accompany with Findus Grill Chips, cooked as instructed, mushrooms poached in a little stock or salted water and boiled runner beans.

It doesn't look like a dieting meal does it? So why not cook something similar for your family? Research has shown that people eat more if they eat alone, so be sociable. But, go easy on those chips . . . don't just tip them onto a tray. Weigh out your portion before you cook and keep them separate.

Snack or Pudding
Yogurt

1 Ski Black Cherry, Peach Melba, Pineapple, Plum or Orange Yogurt OR
1 St Ivel Country Prize Grapefruit, Muesli or Walnut Yogurt.

DAY 2

Breakfast
Boiled Egg / Crispbreads and Marmite

1 egg, size 3.
2 Energen Brancrisp or Ryvita crispbreads.
15g/½oz low-fat spread.
5ml/1 level teaspoon Marmite.

Light Meal
Ham and Tomato Sandwich

2 small slices bread (25g/1oz each).
15g/½oz low-fat spread.
25g/1oz lean cooked ham, trimmed of all visible fat.
1 tomato, sliced.

When we say trim off all the visible fat, that's exactly what we mean. Did you know that every 25g/1oz fat that you pop into your mouth costs you over 150 calories? Don't snatch this sandwich meal in a hurry. Prepare it carefully; cut it into four and arrange on a plate. Now take it to the dining table, sit down and eat it slowly. Did you enjoy that? Good . . . so now you will feel mentally satisfied as well as phsyically.

Main Meal
Grilled Fish, Peas and Jacket Potato
1 potato (175g/6oz raw weight).
175g/6oz cod or haddock fillet.
15g/½ oz low-fat spread.
125g/4oz peas, frozen.
15ml/1 tablespoon tomato ketchup.
Bake the potato at 200°C/400°F, gas mark 6, for about 45 minutes, until soft when pinched. Dot the fish fillet with low-fat spread and grill. Serve with baked potato, boiled peas and tomato ketchup.
We bet the first potato you weighed was more than 175g/6oz. It takes a little while to get your calorie-eye trained, but soon you'll be picking out the right sizes automatically.

Snack or Pudding
Fruit
1 small banana (150g/5oz) or 125g/4oz black grapes.

DAY 3

Breakfast
Cereal
25g/1oz Cornflakes, 30% Bran Flakes, Rice Krispies, Special K or Puffed Wheat.
5ml/1 level teaspoon sugar.
150ml/¼ pint skimmed milk, extra to allowance.
We know you don't feel at your brightest first-thing in the morning, but do get those weighing scales and focus on your 25g/1oz cereal portion. Cereals vary enormously in the amount you get in your dish. You'll appear to get twice as much Puffed Wheat as

Cornflakes for your 25g/1oz. So don't guess.

Light Meal
Cheese and Pickle on Toast
1 small slice bread (25g/1oz), toasted.
50g/2oz Edam cheese.
15ml/1 level tablespoon Branston or Ploughman's type pickle.

Main Meal
Sausages and Mash
2 large pork sausages, well grilled.
175g/6oz potatoes.
45ml/3 tablespoons skimmed milk.
50ml/2fl oz fat-less gravy made with Birds, Bisto, Boots or Sainsbury's Gravy Powder.
Grill the sausages and serve with boiled potatoes, mashed with skimmed milk. Make gravy and pour over.

It's true that your sausages will shrink more if you really well grill them, but the calorie saving is worthwhile. Mash your boiled potatoes with skimmed milk. Hold on . . . did we see you use that old silver tablespoon that you inherited from your mother? Tomorrow go out and buy a proper set of measuring spoons. You'll need 5ml/1 teaspoon and 15ml/1 tablespoon measures throughout this diet, and it's useful to have a 2.5ml/½ teaspoon measure too.

Snack or Pudding
Fruit
1 medium apple or pear.

DAY 4
Breakfast
Bacon and Tomatoes
2 rashers back bacon, well grilled.
2 tomatoes, grilled without added fat.
You've finished your breakfast and are sitting having a cup of

tea or coffee. Now is the time to get out a pen and paper and make a list of the foods you need to buy for the next few days dieting. Always make lists of foods when you are feeling full and naughty fancies won't find their way into your shopping basket. Make sure you stick to the list when you're out shopping.

Light Meal
Sardine and Cheese Toast
1 small slice bread (25g/1oz).
2 sardines in tomato sauce (50g/2oz) including sauce.
1 Kraft Processed Cheese Cheddar Single.
Toast bread and top with sardines and Cheese Single. Grill until cheese melts and starts to brown.
By now you've probably discovered a loaf which comes in 25g/1oz slices. If you haven't, try a small brown loaf or a thinly sliced long white loaf. If bread is one of your passions, take out your slices for the day and freeze the remainder.

Main Meal
Lamb Chop and Vegetables
1 lamb chump chop (150g/5oz raw weight).
15ml/1 tablespoon mint sauce.
125g/4oz mixed vegetables, frozen.
175g/6oz potatoes.
Grill lamb chop well. Serve with mint sauce, boiled vegetables and boiled potatoes.

Snack or Pudding
Fruit
1 large orange or 125g/4oz grapes.

DAY 5

Breakfast
Scrambled Egg with Ham on Toast
1 egg, size 3, scrambled with 15ml/1 tablespoon skimmed milk, extra to allowance.
25g/1oz lean cooked ham, trimmed of all visible fat and chopped.
1 small slice bread (25g/1oz), toasted.

Light Meal
Beef with Coleslaw
50g/2oz roast topside of beef, trimmed of all visible fat.
227g/8oz carton Eden Vale Coleslaw in Vinaigrette. Remember that the fattier the slices of beef you buy at the delicatessen or supermarket, the less meat you'll get on your plate. And we did say Eden Vale Coleslaw in Vinaigrette. Other makes simply won't do.

Main Meal
Fish Casserole with Rice
175g/6oz cod, coley or haddock fillet.
227g/8oz can tomatoes.
50g/2oz mushrooms.
25g/1oz onion.
good pinch mixed dried herbs.
salt and pepper.
50g/2oz long-grain rice.
Place fish in an ovenproof dish with tomatoes and their juice. Slice mushrooms, finely chop onion and add to the dish with herbs. Season, cover dish and bake at 180°C/350°F, gas mark 4, for 25-30 minutes. Boil rice and serve with fish.
While your casserole and rice are cooking, lay a place at the dining table. Instead of piling all your food onto your plate, put the casserole and rice on the table in separate dishes. Then take a small portion of each onto your plate. Eat slowly savouring every mouthful. Then serve yourself another small portion. Ask yourself after each portion if you've had enough. If you can answer 'yes', then stop there.

Snack or Pudding
Carton Dessert and Fruit
1 Birds Eye Melba or Mousse, any flavour.
1 medium orange.

DAY 6

Breakfast
Cereal with Banana
25g/1oz Cornflakes, 30% Bran Flakes, Puffed Wheat, Special K or Rice Krispies.
1 small banana (150g/5oz).
150ml/¼ pint skimmed milk, extra to allowance.
Is your measuring jug not too accurate on small quantities? If so use your measuring spoons for milk or other liquids. Ten 15ml tablespoons are equal to 150ml/¼ pint; two 15ml tablespoons are equal to 1fl oz.

Light Meal
Cheese and Crispbreads
50g/2oz Edam, Camembert or Brie.
3 Energen or Ryvita crispbreads.
15ml/1 level tablespoon Branston or Ploughman's pickle.

Main Meal
Ham Omelet with Broccoli
125g/4oz broccoli, fresh or frozen.
2 eggs, size 3.
10ml/2 teaspoons water.
salt and pepper.
50g/2oz lean ham.
5ml/1 level teaspoon butter.
Boil broccoli and keep warm. Lightly beat together eggs, water and seasoning. Trim off and discard all visible fat from ham; chop lean. Brush the surface of a small non-stick omelet pan with the butter. Heat and add eggs. Cook until just set; place ham in the centre and fold over. Serve with broccoli.
We did say a 'level teaspoon of butter'. That means you scoop up the butter (easier if it's a little soft) and level the teaspoon off across the top with a knife. A rounded teaspoon costs twice the calories of a level one.

Snack or Pudding
Ice Cream
1 Lyons Maid Vanilla Kup or Wall's Blue Ribbon Golden Vanilla Ice Cream Bar.

DAY 7
Breakfast
Toast and Marmalade
2 small slices bread (25g/1oz each) toasted.
15g/½oz low-fat spread.
15ml/1 level tablespoon marmalade or jam.

Light Meal
Corned Beef with Coleslaw
(pages 176-7)
50g/2oz corned beef.
50g/2oz white cabbage.
25g/1oz carrot.
1 stick celery.
1 spring onion.
30ml/2 tablespoons low-calorie salad dressing.
salt and pepper.
Shred cabbage, grate carrot and chop celery and spring onion. Mix all vegetables with low-calorie salad dressing and season. Serve with corned beef.
Did you weigh that portion of corned beef? If not take it off your plate and weigh it immediately. If you're not serving the rest of the tin or packet to someone else, slice it and freeze it in 50g/2oz portions so that it is ready to use if you repeat this recipe again.

Main Meal
Liver and Bacon Grill
75g/3oz lamb's or pig's liver.
8 sprays Limmits Spray & Fry.
1 rasher streaky bacon, well grilled.
2 tomatoes, grilled without added fat.

125g/4oz button mushrooms, poached in a little stock or salted water.

115g/4oz Birds Eye or Ross Potato Fritter, grilled without added fat. Spray your liver with a little Spray & Fry before grilling; all the other foods in this meal will grill without adding fat. We know it's not quite what you've been used to, but we promise that once you have got your taste buds accustomed to low-fat cooking, you won't go back to your old fattening ways.

Snack or Pudding
Fruit
1 medium pear or peach.

DAY 8

Breakfast
Cereal
25g/1oz Cornflakes, 30% Bran Flakes, Puffed Wheat, Special K or Rice Krispies.
150ml/¼ pint skimmed milk, extra to allowance.
5ml/1 level teaspoon sugar, optional.

Did you gobble down your breakfast because you were late for work? Or did you eat it mindlessly while trying to get the kids off to school? Well, don't do that again. When you are dieting it is important to enjoy every mouthful of food you take. So don't eat until you can sit down and relax and really think about what you are eating.

Light Meal
Sausage, Bacon and Baked Beans
1 pork chipolata sausage, well grilled.
1 rasher streaky bacon, well grilled.
150g/5.3oz can baked beans in tomato sauce.

Main Meal
Grilled Chicken with Sweetcorn and Jacket Potato
1 chicken breast (175g/6oz raw weight) grilled and skin removed.
125g/4oz sweetcorn, frozen or canned.
1 potato (175g/6oz raw weight).
7g/¼ oz low-fat spread.

Serve chicken with cooked sweetcorn and potato that's been baked in its jacket (200°C/400°F, gas mark 6) for about 45 minutes. Top potato with low-fat spread.

Now take that chicken skin out of your mouth. When we said remove it, we didn't mean that it should be eaten separately. Feed skin immediately to your dog or cat, or put it into the nearest bin. You'll be discarding about 55 calories from this chicken breast.

Snack or Pudding
Yogurt
1 small carton Chambourcy or St Ivel Natural Yogurt.

DAY 9

Breakfast
Poached Egg on Toast
1 egg, size 3, poached.
1 small slice bread (25g/1oz).
Who told you to put that knob of butter into your poacher? Not us. If you have a non-stick poacher your egg will cook just as well without adding any extra calories. Otherwise poach your eggs in water with a little vinegar.

Light Meal
Jacket Potato with Cottage Cheese
1 potato (225g/8oz raw weight).
113g/4oz carton Eden Vale Cottage Cheese with Chives or St Ivel Cottage Cheese with Onion and Chives.
Scrub potato and bake in its jacket. Scoop out centre and mix

with cottage cheese. Pile back into potato case and serve.

Main Meal
Double Decker Beefburger
1 bap (50g/1 ¾ oz).
2 Findus Beefburgers, well grilled.
15ml/1 tablespoon Bick's Relish, any flavour.
1 tomato.
Split the bap horizontally in two places and toast the cut surfaces. Fill with two well-grilled beef-burgers, relish and sliced tomato. Did you grill those two beefbur-gers on a wire rack, letting all the fat drip away and make sure they were really well grilled on both sides? No, no, no . . . you may not dip your bap into the fat before you make up your double decker.

Snack or Pudding
Ice Cream and Berries
1 Lyons Maid Vanilla Kup or Wall's Blue Ribbon Golden Vanilla Ice Cream Bar.
125g/4oz raspberries or straw-berries, fresh or frozen.

DAY 10
Breakfast
Savoury Cheese Toast
1 small slice bread (25g/1oz) toasted.
5ml/1 level teaspoon Marmite or Bovril.
50g/2oz curd cheese.

Light Meal
Spaghetti and Cheese on Toast
1 small slice bread (25g/1oz) toasted.
215g/7.6oz can spaghetti in tomato sauce.
1 Kraft Processed Cheese Cheddar Single.
Heat the spaghetti and pile on top of toast. Cover with cheese slice and grill until melted. So who forgot to buy the packet

of Kraft Singles and decided to stick a lump of Cheddar on top of the spaghetti instead? Well we hope you cut your cheese very thinly. A Kraft Singles slice is equal to 15g/½oz ordinary Cheddar.

Main Meal
Liver Casserole with Potato
125g/4oz lamb's or pig's liver.
50g/2oz mushrooms.
1 tomato.
25g/1oz onion.
pinch mixed herbs.
125ml/4fl oz water.
½ beef stock cube.
5ml/1 level teaspoon cornflour.
½ medium packet Cadbury's Smash.
Slice liver and place in a small casserole dish with sliced mushrooms, chopped tomato, onion and mixed herbs. Boil 75ml/3fl oz water and use to dissolve stock cube. Blend remaining cold water with corn-flour, then add to stock. Pour over liver and vegetables. Cover dish and bake at 180°C/350°F, gas mark 4, for 45 minutes. Make up Smash and serve with casserole.
When you have put your casserole into the oven to cook, do a few relaxation exercises before you eat. Tensions often lead to fast and excessive eating. Set the table, then pour yourself a glass of mineral water or a low-calorie mixer. Sit and sip your drink slowly. Feel the day's tensions and stresses slipping away.

Snack or Pudding
Fruit Yogurt
1 St Ivel Prize Fruit Yogurt.

DAY 11
Breakfast
Grapefruit / Muesli Yogurt
½ grapefruit, sprinkled with

5ml/1 level teaspoon sugar.
1 small carton St. Ivel natural yogurt, mixed with 25g/1oz muesli.

We know we've been nagging you for ten days to weigh and measure everything, but it really is important if you want to lose weight fast. Failed slimmers who swear they can't lose weight on 1,000 calories a day are usually found to be careless over weighing and suffer from eating 'amnesia' about certain foods – particularly drinks. You are still keeping to your 275ml/½ pint skimmed milk allowance aren't you? Do remember to weigh that muesli – it is a very heavy cereal because of the fruit and nuts it contains.

Light Meal
Prawn Salad
125g/4oz shelled prawns.
30ml/2 tablespoons Waistline Seafood Sauce.
1 tomato.
lettuce, cucumber, celery and cress.

There's nothing worse than sitting around thinking about the next meal. If you find this happening to you, try to find something interesting to concentrate your thoughts on. If possible get out of the house and away from the kitchen. At the very least, do something if it's only a task you've been putting off. You may not actually enjoy it, but you'll feel wonderful when it's finished. You just need to pop this evening's meal into the oven and to boil the vegetables so there is no reason to think about it until about half an hour before you eat.

Main Meal
Shepherd's Pie with Mixed Vegetables
1 individual Birds Eye Shepherd's Pie.
125g/4oz mixed vegetables, frozen.
15ml/1 tablespoon tomato ketchup or brown sauce.
Heat Shepherd's Pie as instructed. Serve with boiled mixed vegetables and ketchup or brown sauce.

Snack or Pudding
Carton Dessert
1 Birds Eye Trifle, any flavour or 1 St Michael Royale, any flavour.

DAY 12

Breakfast
Sausages and Baked Beans
2 pork chipolata sausages, well grilled.
150g/5.3oz can baked beans in tomato sauce.

Light Meal
Salmon and Cucumber Sandwich
2 small slices bread (25g/1oz each).
50g/2oz canned salmon.
15ml/1 tablespoon Waistline Seafood Sauce.
few slices cucumber.

Now remember what we said last week. Don't eat your sandwich standing up or while you're reading a book. Make the most of every meal you eat. Think about what you are eating and really enjoy every mouthful.

Main Meal
Pork Chop and Vegetables
1 pork chop (185g/6½oz raw weight), well grilled.
15ml/1 tablespoon unsweetened apple sauce.
125g/4oz cauliflower.
125g/4oz carrots.
Well grill the chop. Serve with apple sauce and boiled vegetables.

Snack or Pudding

1 Lyons Maid Cornish Vanilla or Dark Satin Choc Ice or 1 Wall's Blue Ribbon Golden Vanilla or Dark and Golden Choc Ice.

Did you eat your choc ice at midday and now wish you'd saved it for later? Well tomorrow you'll know better. Always save your snacks and treats for your most vulnerable moments. And it's a good tactic to postpone eating your treat until as late in the day as you can. So if you feel like nibbling at 4.00, say to yourself, 'I'll just wait until 5.00 and see how I feel then.' and so on. You may find you don't bother to eat it at all in the end, and that's an extra treat you can save for a difficult day.

DAY 13

Breakfast
Grapefruit / Boiled Egg and Crispbread

½ grapefruit.
5ml/1 level teaspoon sugar.
1 egg, size 3.
1 Energen or Ryvita crispbread.
Turn off that radio while you're eating. Anything that takes your attention away from what you are eating is bad for your diet. You may not even taste the food and it's easy to grab an extra crispbread if you're not really thinking what you are doing.

Light Meal
Chicken Drumsticks with Apple and Celery Salad

2 chicken drumsticks.
1 small apple (75g/3oz).
2 sticks celery.
2 walnut halves
30ml/2 tablespoons low-calorie salad dressing.
salt and pepper.
Grill chicken drumsticks and remove skin. Core and dice apple, roughly chop celery and walnuts and mix with apple and low-calorie dressing. Season and serve with drumsticks.

Main Meal
Fish Fingers with Peas and Chips

4 fish fingers, grilled without added fat.
125g/4oz peas, frozen.
125g/4oz Findus Grill Chips.
15ml/1 tablespoon tomato ketchup.
So there are six fish fingers in a packet, but that doesn't stop you from putting the remaining two back in the freezer. They'll still be alright when you want to repeat this meal. The only thing that should top your boiled peas is the tomato ketchup allowed. We know you usually serve them with a knob of butter, but that can add over 100 calories.

Snack or Pudding
Fruit

1 small banana or 125g/4oz grapes.

DAY 14

Breakfast
Bacon Sandwich

2 small slices bread (25g/1oz each).
2 rashers streaky bacon, well grilled.
15ml/1 tablespoon tomato ketchup.
As this is Day 14 we'll assume no one dipped their bread into the bacon fat. You'll find spreading your bread slices with the tomato ketchup a much tastier way to sandwich up your bacon. You can tell if your bacon is really well grilled if you can crumble it.

Light Meal
Smoked Haddock with Bread

1 packet Findus Buttered Scottish Smoked Haddock.
1 small slice bread (25g/1oz).
7g/¼oz low-fat spread.

Main Meal
Savoury Mince with Potato
125g/4oz minced beef.

5ml/1 level teaspoon flour.

25g/1oz onion.

50g/2oz mushrooms.

15ml/1 level tablespoon tomato
purée.

pinch mixed herbs.

½ Red Oxo cube.

150ml/¼ pint water.

125g/4oz runner beans.

Brown mince in a non-stick pan
then drain off all fat. Place in a
saucepan and stir in flour. Chop
onion and mushrooms and add
to pan with all other ingredients
except beans. Cover pan and
simmer for 30 minutes. Boil
beans and serve with mince.
Did you add your flour to the
frying pan rather than use a fresh
saucepan? We realise that it's
more washing up the other way
but the chances are that you
won't have got rid of all the fat
from the mince. In a recent
experiment we found that 100
calories' worth of raw mince lost
30 calories of fat when cooked.
Please don't fry the onions and
mushrooms with the mince; they
will absorb all those calories
you're trying to discard.

Snack or Pudding
1 medium pear.

THE MARVELLOUS
MOODY DIET   1,000 calories

Some mornings you wake up all sunshine and smiles, ready to take on the world. When you feel like this it's easy to keep to a strict diet. On days like this you could walk past a million bars of chocolate quite unnerved. Pity it isn't like that every morning. Some days you wake up feeling distinctly grey and grumpy. You snap at everybody, trip over the cat, and slam the front door on the way out . . . All you want is a comforting arm around your shoulder, but you settle instead for an extra three pieces of toast, then a large piece of chocolate gateau and then you're onto the cheesecake . . . and all because you started the day feeling rotten.

Sticking to a diet, keeping yourself motivated, is extra hard when you're a woman and naturally prone to fluctuating moods. Of course, there are those lovely days when you feel really good, totally in control and dieting is relatively easy. But then something happens – you get a ghastly statement from the bank, have a row with your man/woman, suffer dreary pre-menstrual tension, get caught in a cloudburst and you suddenly feel sad and gloomy. Even though you're determined not to give in, you can feel your willpower slithering perilously close to what feels like the edge of a precipice. You know it's going to need only a tiny nudge to make it keel over and carry your entire self-control with it.

To win through and lose weight it helps to accept that female moods do vary from day to day and that, for many of us, the safest thing is to be flexible. 'Good' moods mean you can be strict with yourself, but 'bad' moods call for comforting. Psychiatrists don't really understand why some foods are comforting and others aren't – yet nearly every woman knows this to be true. There's little comfort in a carrot or a piece of cold meat but a great deal in the warming stodgy dishes which most of us had as children – shepherd's pie, steak and kidney, bananas and custard, rice pudding . . . We have designed a diet which caters marvellously for moods. Our 'bad' mood menus provide a generous allowance of 1,500 calories a day and include comforting carbohydrates and delicious treats. The 'good' mood menus are organised around a strict daily 750 calories intake and only include those foods which slide with maximum ease into the minimum calorie allowance.

To lose surplus weight at maximum speed, aim over each week or fortnight to average 1,000 calories a day. There are 7 1,500 calorie Bad Mood menus and 14 Good Mood menus at 750 calories to choose from. Obviously the more good mood menus you follow, the faster you will lose weight; but even if you have three bad mood days in one week, you will – so long as you stick to your 750-calorie menus on good days – still be averaging a fast-losing 1,000 calories a day overall. Even if you had seven bad mood days in a row, you'd still probably lose a little weight and you certainly wouldn't gain any.

You're bound to begin your diet in a good mood, so choose your first menus from these lists after reading the diet rules which follow.

DIET RULES

1 Your Good Mood menus allow for three meals a day, plus 275ml/½ pint skimmed milk for use in drinks. You may eat your meals at any time that suits you. Many people prefer to skip breakfast and eat later on. In this case, your breakfast meal may be used as a snack meal whenever you like.

2 Your Bad Mood menus allow three main meals, plus a pudding and a snack. You may eat the meals and snack whenever you wish.

3 Bad Mood milk allowance gives you a choice of 425ml/¾ pint skimmed milk, or 275ml/½ pint semi-skimmed or 225ml/⅓ pint Silver Top milk for use in drinks.

4 Sugar is not allowed in drinks in either Good or Bad Mood menus. Use a sugar substitute like saccharin if you must.

5 Both Good and Bad Mood menus have been carefully arranged to give you maximum nutritional benefit for your calories. So please choose your complete menu for the day and do not try to substitute a meal from one day to another. You may, however, omit any complete day's menu if you don't happen to care for the foods in it and substitute another complete day's menu instead.

6 Black coffee, black or lemon tea, water and drinks labelled 'low calorie' are permitted throughout this diet in unlimited amounts.

GOOD MOOD DAYS

Daily Milk Allowance
275ml/½ pint skimmed milk

DAY 1
Breakfast
Grapefruit / Boiled Egg and Crispbread
½ grapefruit.
1 egg, size 3.
1 Energen or Ryvita crispbread.

Light Meal
Chicken Salad
1 chicken breast (175g/6oz raw weight) grilled and skin removed.
227g/8oz carton Eden Vale Coleslaw in Vinaigrette.

Main Meal
Cod in Sauce with Peas / Yogurt
1 pack Findus Cod in Butter Sauce.
125g/4oz peas, frozen.
1 small carton Eden Vale or St Michael natural yogurt.

DAY 2
Breakfast
Cereal
25g/1oz Cornflakes, 30% Bran Flakes, Frosties, Rice Krispies, Special K or Puffed Wheat.
150ml/¼ pint skimmed milk, extra to allowance.
5ml/1 level teaspoon sugar.

Light Meal
Crispbreads with Cottage Cheese
113g/4oz carton St Ivel Cottage Cheese with Onion and Cheddar.
3 Energen or Ryvita crispbreads.
few slices cucumber.

Main Meal
Fish Fingers with Runner Beans / Orange
3 fish fingers, grilled without added fat.
15ml/1 tablespoon tomato ketchup.

125g/4oz runner beans.
1 large orange.

DAY 3
Breakfast
Bacon Sandwich
2 rashers streaky bacon, well grilled.
2 small slices Slimcea or Nimble.
15ml/1 tablespoon tomato ketchup.

Light Meal
Cottage Cheese Salad
113g/4oz carton Eden Vale Cottage Cheese with Pineapple.
1 tomato.
unlimited lettuce, cucumber, cress, celery, pepper and spring onions.
15ml/1 tablespoon low-calorie salad dressing.

Main Meal
Grilled Liver and Vegetables/ Banana
125g/4oz lamb's liver, grilled.
8 sprays Limmits Spray & Fry.
125g/4oz broccoli.
125g/4oz mushrooms, poached in a little salted water or stock.
1 small banana.

DAY 4
Breakfast
Cereal
25g/1oz Cornflakes, 30% Bran Flakes, Rice Krispies, Frosties, Special K or Puffed Wheat.
150ml/¼ pint skimmed milk, extra to allowance.
5ml/1 level teaspoon sugar.

Light Meal
Cheese Spread and Pickle Sandwich
2 small pieces Nimble or Slimcea.
1 triangle cheese spread (15g/½oz).
15ml/1 level tablespoon Branston or Ploughman's pickle.

Main Meal
Shepherd's Pie and Vegetables / Apple
1 individual Findus Shepherd's Pie (227g/8oz).
15ml/1 tablespoon brown sauce or tomato ketchup.
125g/4oz mixed vegetables, frozen.
1 medium apple.

DAY 5
Breakfast
Toast and Marmalade
2 small slices Nimble or Slimcea.
15g/½ oz low-fat spread.
10ml/2 level teaspoons jam or marmalade.

Light Meal
Salmon Salad
99g/3½ oz can salmon.
1 tomato.
unlimited lettuce, cucumber, celery, cress, pepper and spring onions.
15ml/1 tablespoon Waistline Seafood Sauce.

Main Meal
Grilled Ham Steak and Pineapple / Apple
1 ham or bacon steak (100g/3½ oz raw weight).
1 ring pineapple, canned in natural juice, drained.
125g/4oz sweetcorn, canned or frozen.
125g/4oz mushrooms, poached in a little salted water or stock.
1 medium apple.

DAY 6
Breakfast
Poached Egg on Toast
1 egg, size 3.
1 small slice Nimble or Slimcea.

Light Meal
Fish Cakes with Tomatoes
2 fish cakes, grilled without added fat.
2 tomatoes, grilled without added fat.

Main Meal
Chicken and Mushroom Casserole with Vegetables / Banana
1 individual Birds Eye Chicken & Mushroom Casserole.
125g/4oz peas, frozen.
½ medium packet Cadbury's Smash made up as instructed without fat.
1 medium banana.

DAY 7
Breakfast
Bacon and Tomatoes
2 rashers streaky bacon, well grilled.
2 tomatoes, grilled without added fat.

Light Meal
Liver Sausage and Tomato Sandwich
2 small slices Nimble or Slimcea.
10ml/2 level teaspoons low-fat spread.
50g/2oz liver sausage.
1 tomato.

Main Meal
Grilled Fish and Vegetables / Pear
175g/6oz cod or haddock fillet, grilled.
7g/¼ oz low-fat spread.
125g/4oz mixed vegetables, frozen.
1 medium pear.

DAY 8
Breakfast
Scrambled Egg on Toast
1 egg, size 3.
15ml/1 tablespoon skimmed milk.
1 small slice Nimble or Slimcea.

Light Meal
Beefburger Sandwich
1 Findus Beefburger, well grilled.
15ml/1 level tablespoon Bicks Relish, any flavour.
2 small slices Nimble or Slimcea.

Main Meal
Grilled Chicken and Vegetables / Yogurt
1 chicken breast (175g/6oz raw weight) grilled and skin removed.
125g/4oz sweetcorn, canned or frozen.
125g/4oz runner beans.
1 small carton St Ivel natural yogurt.

DAY 9
Breakfast
Toast and Marmalade
2 small slices Nimble or Slimcea.
15g/½oz low-fat spread.
10ml/2 level teaspoons jam or marmalade.

Light Meal
Soup / Crispbreads with Cheese Spread
1 can Boots, Waistline or Heinz Low Calorie Oxtail, Tomato or Vegetable Soup.
4 Energen or Ryvita crispbreads.
2 triangles cheese spread (15g/½oz each).
1 tomato, sliced.

Main Meal
Mixed Grill with Vegetables
2 lamb's kidneys, grilled.
1 pork chipolata sausage, well grilled.
1 rasher streaky bacon, well grilled.
5ml/1 level teaspoon mustard or 15ml/1 tablespoon tomato ketchup.
125g/4oz mushrooms, poached in a little salted water or stock.

DAY 10
Breakfast
Baked Beans on Toast
150g/5.3oz can baked beans in tomato sauce.
1 small slice Nimble or Slimcea.

Light Meal
Corned Beef Salad
50g/2oz corned beef.
1 tomato.

142g/5oz carton St Ivel Coleslaw in Low Calorie Dressing.

Main Meal
Prawn Curry with Rice
1 pack Birds Eye China Dragon Prawn Curry.
25g/1oz long-grain rice, raw weight.

DAY 11
Breakfast
Cereal
25g/1oz Cornflakes, 30% Bran Flakes, Frosties, Rice Krispies, Special K or Puffed Wheat.
5ml/1 level teaspoon sugar.
150ml/¼ pint skimmed milk, extra to allowance.

Light Meal
Sardine and Cucumber Sandwich
2 small slices Nimble or Slimcea.
2 sardines in tomato sauce, mashed.
few slices cucumber.

Main Meal
Roast Beef with Vegetables / Apple or Orange
1 pack Ross Gravy with Roast Beef (113g/4oz).
½ medium packet Cadbury's Smash.
125g/4oz Brussels sprouts.
125g/4oz carrots.
1 medium apple or orange.

DAY 12
Breakfast
Grapefruit / Boiled Egg with Bread
½ medium grapefruit.
1 egg, size 3.
1 small slice Nimble or Slimcea.
5ml/1 level teaspoon low-fat spread.

Light Meal
Savoury Rice / Pear
1 pot Golden Wonder Pot Rice, Savoury Beef or Spicy Tomato Flavour.
1 medium pear.

Main Meal
Grilled Lamb Chop with Mushrooms and Tomatoes
1 lamb loin chop (150g/5oz raw weight) well grilled.
15ml/1 tablespoon mint sauce.
125g/4oz mushrooms, poached in a little salted water or stock.
2 tomatoes, grilled without fat.

DAY 13
Breakfast
Banana and Yogurt
1 small banana.
1 small carton St Ivel natural yogurt.
15ml/1 level tablespoon muesli.

Light Meal
Cheese and Onion Crispbreads
3 Energen or Ryvita crispbreads.
45ml/3 level tablespoons Waistline Onion Spread.
25g/1oz Edam cheese.

Main Meal
Casserole / Pear
1 Findus Broad Oak Casserole.
125g/4oz runner beans, boiled.
1 medium pear.

DAY 14
Breakfast
Sausages and Baked Beans
2 pork chipolatas, well grilled.
150g/5.3oz can baked beans.

Light Meal
Cheese and Tomato on Toast
2 small slices Nimble or Slimcea.
1 tomato, sliced.
25g/1oz Edam cheese.

Main Meal
Smoked Haddock Pancakes and Runner Beans / Fruit
2 Findus Smoked Haddock Pancakes, cooked without fat.
15ml/1 tablespoon ketchup.
125g/4oz runner beans.
1 medium apple or pear.

BAD MOOD DAYS

Daily Milk Allowance:
425ml/¾ pint skimmed milk or
275ml/½ pint semi-skimmed milk or
225ml/⅓ pint Silver Top milk to use in drinks.

The menus are given first, then the recipes. All recipes serve 1.

DAY 1
Breakfast
Muesli with Apricots
50g/2oz muesli.
2 dried apricots, chopped.
125ml/4fl oz skimmed milk, extra to allowance.

Light Meal
Baked Beans on Toast
225g/7.9oz can baked beans in tomato sauce.
1 small slice bread (25g/1oz).

Main Meal
Salmon and Macaroni Cheese.*
125g/4oz runner beans.

Pudding
Mousse or Caramel Dessert
1 Ross Mousse Cup, any flavour, or 1 Chambourcy Chamby Caramel.

Snack
Crispbreads with Cheese Spread and Pickle
2 Energen or Krispen crispbreads.
1 triangle cheese spread (15g/½oz).
15ml/1 level tablespoon Branston or Ploughman's pickle.

Salmon and Macaroni Cheese*
50g/2oz macaroni.
99g/3½oz can John West Pink Salmon.
water.
15ml/1 level tablespoon cornflour.
45ml/3 level tablespoons

HIGH-FIBRE DIET. Minestrone Soup;
Kidney and Mushroom Jacket Potato with
Salad; Prunes and Yogurt; Crispy Topped
Fish with Pasta and Broccoli.

SLIM AND SIN DIET. SlimDay – Bran Flakes with Dried Apricots; Cottage Cheese and Fruit Salad; Bacon Steak with Pineapple; Orange and Kiwi Fruit with Yogurt. On a SinDay you could have those meals plus the wine, chocolate, cake and biscuit.

BIG BROTHER DIET tells you exactly what to eat and how to eat it. You'll need that jug, scale, and measuring spoons.

EASY FREEZER DIET. The basic Pork Casserole is combined with additional ingredients to make three quite different dieting meals.

Italian Pork

Pork & Corn Pie

Oriental Pork

powdered skimmed milk.
50g/2oz Edam cheese.
salt and pepper.
30ml/2 level tablespoons fresh
breadcrumbs.

Cook macaroni in boiling, salted
water until just tender. Drain
and set aside. Drain salmon and
make the liquid up to 150ml/¼
pint with water. Blend cornflour
and powdered skimmed milk
with a little of this liquid until
smooth. Add remaining liquid
and pour into a small pan. Bring
to the boil, stirring continuously
and simmer for 1-2 minutes.
Flake salmon and add to the
sauce with most of the cheese
and macaroni. Season and turn
into an ovenproof dish. Sprinkle
on remaining cheese and
breadcrumbs and bake at
190°C/375°F, gas mark 5, for 15
minutes.

DAY 2
Breakfast
Toast and Marmalade
2 small slices bread (25g/1oz
each) toasted.
15g/½oz low-fat spread.
20ml/4 level teaspoons
marmalade.

Light Meal
Pâté with French Bread
75g/2.6oz can Princes Pâté de
Canard a l'Orange.
50g/2oz piece French bread.
15g/½oz low-fat spread.

Main Meal
Lasagne with Salad
250g/9oz Birds Eye Lasagne.
green salad made with lettuce,
cucumber, green pepper, cress
and spring onions.
15ml/1 tablespoon oil-free French
dressing.

Pudding
Rich Chocolate Mousse.*

Snack
Chocolate Biscuit / Pear
1 Jacob's Club Biscuit or 1
McVitie's Milk Chocolate Sport.
1 medium pear.

Rich Chocolate Mousse*
25g/1oz plain chocolate.
5ml/1 teaspoon black coffee.
1 egg, size 3.
2 walnut halves.

Place chocolate and black coffee
in a basin over a pan of gently
simmering water. The bottom of
the basin should not touch the
water. Leave until chocolate has
melted. Remove from heat.
Separate the egg and stir yolk
into chocolate. Whisk the white
until stiff but not dry and fold
gently into the chocolate mixture.
Turn into a small dish and chill
for at least 30 minutes. Chop
walnuts and sprinkle on top.

DAY 3
Breakfast
Porridge
50g/2oz instant porridge oats.
150ml/¼ pint skimmed milk,
extra to allowance.
10ml/2 level teaspoons sugar.

Light Meal
Cottage Cheese and Bacon
Stuffed Potato.*

Main Meal
Pizza
1 Marco & Carlo Pizza Pie.

Pudding
Yogurt with Banana
1 small banana.
1 small carton St Ivel Prize Fruit
Yogurt, any flavour.

Snack
1 medium pear.

Cottage Cheese and Bacon
Stuffed Potato*
1 potato (225g/8oz).
1 rasher back bacon.
113g/4oz carton St Ivel Cottage

Cheese with Onion and Cheddar.
30ml/2 tablespoons skimmed
milk, extra to allowance.
salt and pepper.
Bake the potato in its jacket at
200°C/400°F, gas mark 6, for 45
minutes or until soft when
pinched. Cut in half lengthways
and carefully scoop out flesh,
leaving shell intact. Grill bacon
until crisp and chop. Mix potato
flesh with bacon, cottage cheese
and skimmed milk. Season. Pile
back into potato cases and reheat
in the oven for 10-15 minutes.

DAY 4
Breakfast
Bacon Roll
1 crusty roll, brown or white.
2 rashers streaky bacon, well
grilled.

Light Meal
Egg and Chips
2 eggs, size 3, fried.
125g/4oz Findus Grill Chips.
15ml/1 tablespoon tomato
ketchup or brown sauce.

Main Meal
Fishy Crumpet Pizza.*

Pudding
Mousse or Creme Caramel
1 Birds Eye Supermousse, any
flavour or
1 Ross Creme Caramel

Snacks
Crisps and Fruit
1 small packet Golden Wonder,
KP, Sainsbury's, Smiths or.
Tesco's crisps.
1 medium apple or orange.

Fishy Crumpet Pizza*
2 crumpets.
1 tomato.
106g/3¾oz can John West Sild
in Tomato Sauce.
2 pinches dried mixed herbs.
1 spring onion.
25g/1oz Edam cheese.
Toast crumpets. Slice tomato and
arrange on top with the sild.
Sprinkle with herbs. Discard
roots and tough green leaves of
spring onion. Chop bulb. Grate
Edam cheese. Sprinkle chopped
onion and cheese on top of
crumpets and grill slowly until
the cheese melts and the topping
is heated through.

DAY 5
Breakfast
Scrambled Eggs on Toast
2 eggs, size 3.
30ml/2 tablespoons skimmed
milk.
salt and pepper.
1 small slice bread (25g/1oz).

Light Meal
Pancakes with Baked Beans
2 Birds Eye or Findus Savoury
Pancakes with Minced Beef.
150g/5.3oz can baked beans in
tomato sauce.

Main Meal
Captain's Pie with Broccoli
1 Birds Eye Captain's Pie.
125g/4oz broccoli.

Pudding
Banana with Hot Chocolate
Sauce.*

Snack
Fruit
1 large orange or 150g/5oz black
grapes.

Banana with Hot Chocolate Sauce*
7.5ml/1½ level teaspoons cocoa.
7.5ml/1½ level teaspoons
cornflour.
150ml/¼ pint skimmed milk,
extra to allowance.
5ml/1 level teaspoon sugar.
1 large banana.
Blend cornflour and cocoa with
30ml/2 tablespoons of the milk
until smooth. Add sugar. Heat
remaining milk to boiling point
then pour onto the blended
mixture, stirring all the time.

Return to pan and bring to the boil, stirring continuously. Simmer for 1-2 minutes. Peel and slice banana and place in a serving dish. Pour on the hot chocolate sauce and serve immediately.

DAY 6

Breakfast
Cereal with Banana
25g/1oz Cornflakes, 30% Bran Flakes, Frosties, Puffed Wheat, Rice Krispies or Special K.
1 small banana.
5ml/1 level teaspoon sugar.
150ml/¼ pint skimmed milk, extra to allowance.

Light Meal
Creamed Mushrooms on Toast
213g/7½oz can Chesswood Sliced Mushrooms in Creamed Sauce.
1 small slice bread (25g/1oz) toasted.

Main Meal
Minced Beef and Baked Bean Pie.*

Pudding
Trifle
1 Ross Devonshire Trifle or St Ivel Trifle.

Snacks
Chocolate Bar and Fruit
1 large Cadbury's Flake or Cadbury's Creme Egg or Fry's Turkish Delight or Rowntree Mackintosh Toffee Crisp or Terry's Coffee or Tangerine Cream Bar.
1 medium apple or orange.

Minced Beef and Baked Bean Pie*
125g/4oz minced beef.
25g/1oz onion.
1 tomato.
225g/7.9oz can baked beans in tomato sauce.
dash Worcestershire sauce.

salt and pepper.
½ medium packet Cadbury's Smash.
Brown minced beef in a non-stick pan then drain off all the fat. Finely chop the onion. Peel and roughly chop the tomato. Stir onion, tomato, baked beans and Worcestershire sauce into the minced beef. Season and place in a small ovenproof dish. Cover and bake at 190°C/375°F, gas mark 5, for 30 minutes. Make up Smash and spread over mince and beans. Return to the oven for another 15 minutes, uncovered.

DAY 7

Breakfast
Pineapple and Muesli Yogurt* / Pineapple Juice
Juice from a 227g/8oz can pineapple in natural juice (see recipes for use of pineapple).

Light Meal
Cheese and Pickle Toast
1 small slice bread (25g/1oz).
15ml/1 level tablespoon Branston or Ploughman's pickle.
50g/2oz Edam cheese.

Main Meal
Grilled Chicken with Sweetcorn and Jacket Potato
1 chicken breast (175g/6oz raw weight) grilled.
125g/4oz sweetcorn, frozen or canned, drained.
1 potato (200g/7oz raw weight).
7g/¼oz low-fat spread.

Pudding
Pineapple Rice.*

Snack
Chocolate Biscuit or Flake Bar
1 Penguin biscuit or Cadbury's Dipped Flake or Mars Ripple.

Pineapple and Muesli Yogurt*

2 rings pineapple, canned in
natural juice, drained.
30ml/2 level tablespoons muesli.
1 small carton Eden Vale or St
Michael natural yogurt.
Roughly chop pineapple rings
and stir into yogurt with muesli.

Pineapple Rice*

30ml/2 level tablespoons round-
grain or pudding rice.
150ml/¼ pint skimmed milk,
extra to allowance.
15ml/1 level tablespoon powdered
milk.
5ml/1 level teaspoon honey.
2 rings pineapple, canned in
natural juice, drained.
Place the rice, skimmed milk,
powdered milk and honey in a
basin and cover with a piece of
foil. Place basin over a pan of
simmering water and cook for 45
minutes, stirring occasionally.
Remove foil and cook for another
15-30 minutes until creamy.
Roughly chop pineapple and stir
into the creamed rice. Serve hot
or cold.

THE EASY FREEZER DIET

1,000 calories

Next weekend could change your shape forever. That is if you take the time to stock up your freezer with all the foods in the Easy Freezer Diet. Over the weekend we will be asking you to do a lot of shopping, a lot of cooking, some freezing and a lot of planning in many areas of your life. Does that sound like much trouble? Are you too busy? Do you have other plans in mind? Well, that's up to you – but maybe, in future, you shouldn't tell people that you'd do *anything* to be slim. Anybody who really would do anything to be slim will find a detailed plan of action below. This time, it really can be different.

To begin with we would like you to write down answers to these six questions:

1 What went wrong last time you broke your diet?
2 What's in the kitchen now that could prove irresistible?
3 What have you planned for next weekend?
4 Are you likely to get bored?
5 Who is likely to sabotage your diet?
6 Just how important is it to you to get slim?

Now let's look at some of those answers. Was it a discouraging remark, a miserable day, the sight of a cake-shop window, a craving for a particular food which broke your slimming resolve last time? It could have been any one of a hundred things. Try to reconstruct each disaster and work at avoiding the situations which trapped you before. Where most slimmers make their biggest mistake is in

181

concentrating their resolution on stoically resisting all temptations – rather than mustering their ingenuity to work out how to avoid coming face to face with them.

Have you any irresistibles sitting in your kitchen now? If you don't know, go and have a look. Admitting it to yourself is what counts – simply accepting the unsurprising fact that if you can't resist a certain type of biscuit and if it's at hand, there is going to be some moment during the next day or week when you will end up eating it. If you live alone, the solution is simple. Collect your 'irresistibles' and either give them away or throw them away immediately. If you have a cooperative family, enlist their aid in eating these danger foods up for you now, so that you are not tempted next weekend.

What will you be doing each evening during your diet? If you haven't really thought about it, or aren't sure, then do think about it this weekend. Plan your leisure programme for the week ahead every bit as carefully as you plan your diet menus as it is just as important in determining whether you will weigh less by the end of your two-week diet. Generally, unless you are moving into another food-filled environment, such as a restaurant, the further you are away from your kitchen, the safer you are. So, unless you are tied indoors with small children, get on the telephone and arrange evening walks, visits to the cinema and to friends. If you experience a boring week, a boring day, even just a very boring few hours, you are not going to get through without resorting to extra eating to cheer yourself up. Boredom is the greatest food-inducing mood of all. Plan to beat it if you plan to shed weight. Do this deliberately, even making a contingency list this weekend of things to do if you get bored.

If you live with other people, the chances that someone will put temptation right in front of your nose during your diet is dangerously high. So put a family pow-wow on the agenda for this weekend. Be honest and tell them what they usually do to sabotage your diet. If you explain what they can do to help (like not eating snacks in your sight or not expecting you to bake) you will often find everyone surprisingly helpful.

Is getting slim at the present time one of the most important things in your life? Unless it has that major priority, you won't succeed at dieting. Ask yourself who you are trying to please by losing weight. If it's someone close to you – particularly your husband – then you are setting out on an impossible mission. Sooner or later an apparent ingratitude or lack of understanding will infuriate you off your diet. You can only diet to please yourself.

What's the basic secret of successful dieting? Plan as much as you can; anticipate and work at avoiding all probable difficulties as carefully as you can. But expect the unexpected. It almost always happens but loses at least half its danger if it is anticipated. Armed with this advice you should now be ready to prepare your diet.

DIET RULES

1 The weekend you buy and prepare your Easy Freezer Diet menus is *most important*. Do not be tempted to do some of it now, and some of it next weekend. The value of this diet is that you are spending time now to save time later. If you don't do *all* your food preparation in one go, the chances are that you'll never get round to doing the rest later anyway. You'll be 'too busy'! Think of the weekend you spend on planning as the weekend that really gets you slim . . .

2 Each day you are allowed breakfast, one light meal, one main meal and a pudding. You may eat these meals at any time of the day you wish. If you do not eat all your four meals, then you can save one for another day. We give calories on the recipes, but there is no need to keep count of what you eat. Just take a parcel from the freezer each mealtime and your total calories for the two weeks will average out at a fast-losing 1,000 calories a day.

3 You are allowed 425ml/¾ pint skimmed milk each day for use in drinks and on your cereal. If you use long-life skimmed milk you can order enough to last you the fortnight (6 litres/10½ pints). If your milk comes in 500ml/18fl oz cartons, that means you'll need 12 for the two weeks. You won't have to measure this milk as you use it; but remember that if you finish your allowance before the end of the two weeks, that's your lot.

4 You may drink unlimited amounts of any of the following: black coffee or lemon tea (with artificial sweeteners); soft drinks labelled 'low calorie' and water.

Shopping list
Meat
675g/1½lb minced beef.
675g/1½lb pork fillets.
225g/8oz chicken livers.
75g/3oz lean cooked ham.

Fish (frozen)
4 Findus Cod Steaks
(340g/12oz).

Milk, Cheese, Yogurt, Eggs
6 litres/10½ pints long-life
skimmed milk or order from
milkman to give 425ml/¾
pint per day.
40g/1½oz mature Cheddar
cheese.
113g/4oz carton natural cottage
cheese.
71g/2½oz tub Primula Cheese
Spread, Natural or with Celery
or Green Pepper or Pineapple.
3 individual cartons British
Home Stores, Raines, Safeway,
Sainsbury's, St Ivel or Waitrose
natural yogurts.
1 egg, size 3.

Bread
1 large, long medium-sliced loaf,
brown or white.

Fresh Fruit and Vegetables
1 carrot.
2 courgettes.
1 green or red pepper.
4 tomatoes.
575g/1¼lb potatoes.
sprig parsley.
350g/12oz onions.
225g/8oz mushrooms.
2 large oranges.
1 apple.
3 kiwi fruits.
175g/6oz grapes.
450g/1lb melon.

Fruit and Vegetables
225g/8oz packet carrots, frozen.
350g/12oz mixed vegetables,
frozen.
225g/8oz French beans or
haricots verts, frozen.
75g/3oz sweetcorn kernels, frozen

or canned, drained.
175g/6oz raspberries, frozen or
fresh.

Canned Foods
198g/7oz can salmon.
439g/15½oz can red kidney
beans.
227g/8oz can tomatoes.
283g/10oz can peaches in natural
juice.

Cereals, Rice and Pasta
250g/9oz packet Special K.
12 biscuit box Weetabix.
75g/3oz pasta shapes.
150g/5oz long-grain rice.

Ice Creams and Carton Desserts
Choose any three:
Birds Eye Melba or Mousse, any
flavour.
Lyons Maid Chocolate Nut
Sundae or Gold Seal Mint
Choc Sundae or Vanilla Kup.
Ross Mousse Cup, any flavour.
Wall's Blue Ribbon Golden
Vanilla Ice Cream Bar or
Blue Ribbon Golden Vanilla
Tub.

Store Cupboard
3 chicken stock cubes.
1 beef stock cube.
cornflour (45g/1⅔oz).
powdered skimmed milk
(40g/1½oz).
sugar (approximately 70g/2½oz).
sultanas (30ml/2 level
tablespoons).
Hermesetas Sprinkle Sweet.
Waistline Seafood Sauce.
tomato purée.
mango chutney.
curry powder.
3 small gherkins.
dried basil or mixed herbs.
chilli powder.
garlic salt.
ground cumin, optional.
vinegar.
soy sauce.
low-fat spread.

BREAKFASTS

For the two weeks you need to buy a 12-biscuit box of Weetabix and a 250g/9oz packet Special K. Each day you can have either 2 Weetabix or 25g/1oz Special K with milk from your allowance. You may also have 5ml/1 level teaspoon sugar on your cereal if you wish. If you do not want to eat your cereal for breakfast, then you may eat this meal at any other time during the day when you feel like a snack.

LIGHT MEALS

Chicken Liver Pâté and Toast

Make up the recipe given below and when cool, pack in four individual tubs. Small cottage cheese or yogurt cartons are ideal. Wrap two slices of bread in foil or freezer film and freeze with the pâté. The pâté can be thawed in the refrigerator overnight. Toast the bread to serve with it.

(4 portions: 110 calories each.)
225g/8oz chicken livers.
50g/2oz onion.
60ml/4 tablespoons water.
5ml/1 level teaspoon tomato purée.
salt and pepper.
113g/4oz carton natural cottage cheese.

Cut chicken livers into small pieces and place in a small saucepan. Chop onion and add to pan with the water and tomato purée. Season with salt and pepper. Cover pan and simmer gently for 8-10 minutes. Drain off excess liquid. Leave until cold then purée in an electric blender with the cottage cheese. Or rub cottage cheese through a sieve then mash with chicken livers using a fork. Pack and freeze.

Salmon and Gherkin Sandwiches

(3 portions: 250 calories each.)
6 slices bread (35g/1¼oz each).
198g/7oz can salmon.
3 small gherkins.
15ml/1 tablespoon Waistline Seafood Sauce.

Drain salmon and mash with a fork. Chop gherkins. Mix with salmon and seafood sauce and make into sandwiches. Wrap, freeze and use as for Ham and Cheese Sandwiches.

Ham and Cheese Sandwiches

(3 portions: 250 calories each.)
6 slices bread (35g/1¼ oz each).
71g/2½ oz pack Primula Cheese

Spread, Plain or with Pineapple
or Celery or Green Pepper.
75g/3oz lean cooked ham.

Spread the bread with cheese spread. Discard all visible fat from the ham and sandwich lean between the bread slices. Cut each sandwich in half, wrap in foil or freezer film and freeze. Thaw overnight in the refrigerator or for about four hours at room temperature. The sandwiches could be toasted before serving.

Mushroom Soup with Cheese / Bread

Make up the recipe given below and when cold pack in four individual containers. Grate 50g/2oz Cheddar cheese and divide into four. Wrap each portion in a piece of freezer film or foil. Spread four slices of bread (35g/1¼ oz each) with 25g/1oz low-fat spread. Cut each slice in half and sandwich the two halves together. Wrap in foil or freezer film. For each meal keep a container of soup, a portion of cheese and a slice of bread in a polythene bag. To use, thaw overnight in the refrigerator or for about three hours at room temperature. Heat the soup in a small saucepan, stirring all the time and sprinkle the cheese on top. Serve with the bread

(4 portions: 85 calories each.)
225g/8oz mushrooms.
50g/2oz onion.
850ml/1½ pints water.
2 chicken stock cubes.

salt and pepper.
25g/1oz cornflour.
40g/1½ oz powdered skimmed milk.

Finely chop mushrooms and onion and place in a saucepan with water and stock cubes. Season with salt and pepper and bring to the boil. Cover pan and simmer for 15 minutes. Blend the cornflour and powdered skimmed milk with a little cold water until smooth. Add to pan and bring back to the boil, stirring continuously. Simmer for 2 minutes; cool, pack and freeze as above.

MAIN MEALS

Minced Beef Meals

For these meals you need to buy 675g/1½lbs minced beef and use it to make the basic mince mixture given in the following recipe. When cooked divide into three and use for Curried Mince, Chilli Con Carne and Shepherd's Pie. Divide each completed dish into two and freeze individually with the given accompaniments.

Basic Cooked Minced Beef

675g/1½lbs minced beef.
20ml/4 level teaspoons flour.
125g/4oz onion.
275ml/½ pint boiling water.

1 beef stock cube.
30ml/2 level tablespoons tomato purée.
salt and pepper.

Brown the mince in a large non-stick frying pan then drain off all the fat that cooks out. Place mince in a casserole dish and stir in flour. Chop onion and add to the casserole with boiling water, crumbled stock cube and tomato purée. Season and stir well. Cover and cook at 180°C/350°F, gas mark 4, for 40 minutes. Divide into three and use in the recipes below.

Curried Mince with Rice

(2 portions: 375 calories each.)
⅓ basic beef mixture.
1 medium eating apple.
5ml/1 level teaspoon curry powder.

15ml/1 level tablespoon mango chutney.
30ml/2 level tablespoons sultanas.
50g/2oz long-grain rice.

Place mince in a saucepan. Peel, core and roughly chop apple and add to pan with curry powder, mango chutney and sultanas. Stir well then cover the pan and simmer for 5 minutes. Divide between two freezer containers and cool quickly. Freeze. Either boil the rice as instructed, drain, cool and divide between two freezer containers or polythene bags; or simply weigh it out and label it, then boil it when you are ready to eat the curried mince.
To serve, thaw the mince overnight in refrigerator or for about 4 hours at room temperature, then heat in a small saucepan. Or heat from frozen in a small saucepan over a low heat, stirring frequently. If using rice from frozen, place in a small pan with 6mm/¼-inch water and heat until boiling. Drain and use.

Shepherd's Pie with Carrots

(2 portions: 375 calories each.)
⅓ basic mince mixture.
275g/10oz peeled potatoes.*
½ egg, size 3 (see Pork Meals

for other half).
salt and pepper.
227g/8oz packet carrots, frozen.

Divide the mince between two ovenproof freezer containers. Boil potatoes until tender. Drain and mash. Beat the egg, then beat it into the potato. Spread over the mince and leave to cool. Wrap and freeze. Divide carrots into two 125g/4oz portions and place in freezer bags. Keep one portion near each Shepherd's Pie.
To serve, either thaw pie overnight in the refrigerator then cook at 190°C/375°F, gas mark 5, for 20-35 minutes. Or cook from frozen at 200°C/400°F, gas mark 6, for 30-45 minutes or until heated through. Boil the carrots and serve with pie.

* An identical portion of mashed potato is needed for the Pork and Corn Pie, so make double quantities (575g/1¼ lb potatoes and 1 size 3 egg) and then divide.

Chilli Mince

(2 portions: 375 calories each.)
⅓ basic mince mixture.
2.5ml/½ level teaspoon chilli powder.
pinch ground cumin, optional.

2.5ml/½ level teaspoon sugar.
2 tomatoes.
439g/15½oz can Batchelors Red Kidney Beans.

Stir the chilli powder, cumin and sugar into the mince. Peel and chop tomatoes. Drain kidney beans. Add tomatoes and beans to mince and leave to cool. Place in two freezer containers and freeze. To serve, either thaw in the refrigerator overnight or at room temperature for about 4 hours. Heat in a small pan. Or heat from frozen, stirring frequently to prevent sticking.

Pork Meals (page 193)

Make up this basic pork casserole and divide into three. Make each third into two freezer meals by following the recipes below.

Basic Pork Casserole

675g/1 ½ lbs pork fillet.
125g/4oz onion.
425ml/¾ pint water.
1 chicken stock cube.

salt and pepper.
30ml/2 level tablespoons
cornflour.

Discard all visible fat and any sinews from the pork and cut lean into bite-size pieces. Place in a casserole dish. Chop onion and add to dish with most of the water and the crumbled stock cube. Cover and cook at 170°C/325°F, gas mark 3, for 1 hour. Blend remaining water with cornflour until smooth then stir into the casserole. Season. Cook for a further 15 minutes. Divide into three and use in the recipes below.

Oriental Pork

(2 portions: 375 calories each.)
⅓ basic pork casserole.
1 carrot.
½ green pepper.
15ml/1 tablespoon Soy sauce.
5ml/1 level teaspoon sugar.

5ml/1 teaspoon vinegar.
2 rings pineapple, canned in natural juice, drained (see Fruit Salad for use of rest of can).
75g/3oz long-grain rice.

Cut carrot into matchstick-shaped pieces and cook in boiling, salted water for 5 minutes. Discard white pith and seeds from pepper and dice flesh. Add to carrot, cook for another 3 minutes and drain. Drain the liquid from the pork casserole into a small pan and heat to boiling point. Add Soy sauce, sugar and vinegar and stir until the sugar has dissolved. Pour back over the pork. Cut pineapple into small pieces and add to meat with carrot and pepper. Cool quickly, divide between two freezer containers and freeze. Either boil the rice, drain, pack in two containers and freeze; or divide the raw rice into two parcels and keep in the cupboard to use when you eat the pork.

To serve, thaw pork in the refrigerator overnight then heat through in a saucepan. Or heat from frozen over a low heat, stirring frequently.

Italian Pork

(2 portions: 375 calories each.)
⅓ basic pork casserole.
½ green pepper.
2 medium courgettes.
227g/8oz can tomatoes.

1.25ml/¼ level teaspoon dried basil or mixed herbs.
pinch garlic salt.
75g/3oz pasta shapes.

Discard white pith and seeds from pepper and dice flesh. Slice courgettes and place in a saucepan with the pepper, tomatoes and their juice, basil and garlic salt. Simmer uncovered for 10 minutes. At the end of the cooking time most of the tomato juice should have evaporated. Stir occasionally while cooking and add a little water if necessary to prevent sticking. Boil pasta shapes as instructed. Drain and stir into the pork casserole with vegetable mixture. Cool quickly, divide between two freezer containers and freeze.
To serve, thaw overnight in the refrigerator then heat through in a small saucepan or heat from frozen over a low heat, stirring frequently to prevent sticking.

Pork and Corn Pie with Green Beans

(2 portions: 375 calories each.)
⅓ basic pork casserole.
75g/3oz sweetcorn, frozen, cooked or drained, canned.
275g/10oz potatoes, peeled.

½ egg, size 3.
salt and pepper.
227g/8oz packet French beans or haricots verts, frozen.

Mix pork casserole with the sweetcorn and divide between two ovenproof freezer dishes. Cook potatoes in boiling salted water until tender. Drain and mash. Beat in the egg and season with salt and pepper. Spread over the pork and cool quickly. Wrap and freeze.
Divide beans into two and wrap in freezer bags. Keep in the freezer next to the pies. To use, thaw overnight in the refrigerator then cook at 190°C/375°F, gas mark 5, for 20-25 minutes. Or cook from frozen at 200°C/400°F, gas mark 6, for 35 minutes or until heated through. Boil the beans and serve with the pie.

Cheesy Fish Crumble with Vegetables

(2 portions: 375 calories each.)
15g/½oz low-fat spread.
4 Findus Cod Steaks (340g/12oz)
frozen.
1 slice bread (see Light Meals
section).
40g/1½oz mature Cheddar
cheese.
2 tomatoes.
10ml/1 rounded teaspoon
chopped parsley.
salt and pepper.
350g/12oz mixed vegetables,
frozen.

Melt low-fat spread and brush some on the base of two foil freezer containers. Place two frozen cod steaks in a single layer in each dish and brush with remaining low-fat spread. Make bread into crumbs. Grate cheese. Peel and roughly chop tomatoes. Mix together breadcrumbs, cheese, tomatoes and parsley and season with salt and pepper. Place mixture on top of the fish, taking care to completely cover the surface. Cover dish with foil, wrap and freeze. Divide the mixed vegetables into two parcels and store with the fish. To use, bake fish crumble from frozen with foil cover on for 20 minutes at 190°C/375°F, gas mark 5. Remove foil cover and cook for 15 minutes longer to crisp top. Boil mixed vegetables and serve with the fish.

PUDDINGS

You are allowed one pudding each day. Make up the recipe for fruit salad below and this will give you eight of your puddings. The raspberry yogurt dessert makes another three portions. For the remaining three days buy in three of the individual ice cream products listed on page 184.

Raspberry Yogurt Dessert

(3 portions: 100 calories each.)
3 individual cartons British Home Stores, Raines, Safeway, Sainsbury's, St Ivel or Waitrose natural yogurt.

175g/6oz raspberries, fresh or frozen.
10ml/2 level teaspoons Hermesetas Sprinkle Sweet.

Mix together yogurt, raspberries and Sprinkle Sweet. Divide between three individual containers and freeze. If frozen raspberries are used do not thaw before mixing. To serve, thaw overnight in the refrigerator and serve chilled.

Fruit Salad

(8 portions: 100 calories each.)
2 large oranges.
175g/6oz grapes.
450g/1lb melon.
3 kiwi fruits.

283g/10oz can peach slices in natural juice.
2 cans pineapple in natural juice (227g/8oz each).

Peel and segment oranges; cut each segment in half. Do this on a plate to catch any juice and squeeze all the juice from the skins before you discard them. Halve and pip grapes. Cut skin away from melon and discard pips. Cut flesh into bite-size pieces. Peel and slice kiwi fruit; cut each slice in half. Mix all fresh fruit together and add juice from the oranges, canned peaches and pineapple. Reserve two slices of pineapple for the Oriental Pork recipe and cut the remaining slices into small pieces. Add to fresh fruit with peaches. Mix well, divide between eight individual freezer containers and freeze.

To use, thaw overnight in the refrigerator or for about four hours at room temperature.

Oops, you've done it again!

You are doing very well on your diet, then one night you are feeling extra tired and the fish-and-chip shop you pass on the way home from work sends out a particularly delicious aroma. Before you know exactly what you are doing you have ordered a large battered cod, double chips and a portion of mushy peas. You can't let your family know you've cheated so you devour the lot on the way home. Then, to keep up the pretence, you have to eat your diet meal on top of that so they will think you're still being saintly. Later you are so overwhelmed with feelings of guilt that you decide you are a total failure and just don't have the willpower to get slim. Was it an incident like this that stopped you dieting last time? Well, it could happen again, but if you read on you will be better able to cope with those binges that seem to appear out of the blue.

Willpower is a quality that everyone thinks everyone else has got much more of. But you have got more than you think – we'd bet on it – because it is typical for most of us to dwell on our lapses in willpower and to dismiss our triumphs. So you ate an extra slab of fruit cake on your second day of dieting? Bad mark. Don't forget to award yourself some good marks, though, for that first day when you didn't succumb to cake of any kind. If you can get through one day of dieting with a clean sheet, you can get through another day. You only have to diet for a day at a time. So don't depress your willpower by thinking of all those days ahead and don't dwell on your lapses.

Willpower is self-generating. After a strong-willed day of strict dieting, you are right in the mood to repeat your success next day. After a bad day of binge eating, your willpower is at its lowest ebb. Willpower feeds and grows on that 'pleased and proud of yourself' feeling, and withers and dies at the slightest hint of self-disgust. Be aware on that dismal morning after the diet-breaking day before that you are at your most vulnerable and then see it as a challenge and a new start and not an old despair. If you can wipe the slate clean and diet steadily through today (without trying to 'starve' yourself) you have shown all the willpower you need to get slim. You must stem that masochistic urge to punish yourself immediately if you have the occasional slip. Learn to believe that you will be able to compensate for a lapse if you use a little patience and wait for the right mood. It may not hit you tomorrow or the next day. So on those days don't try anything more difficult than keeping to your ordinary diet. But if you wait and watch confidently for it, the right mood will arrive – and that's the day when you can be very strict with yourself and make complete amends.

Probably the most helpful fact about slimming is that if you eat a lot one day and a little on another day, you will lose just as much weight as you would by eating a moderate amount on both days. Most people know this. Most people, however, use this knowledge in the wrong way. So many slimming efforts are sunk by an over-optimistic 'today I'll stuff down food, tomorrow I'll absolutely starve' approach. What goes wrong is that when tomorrow comes you are often in a worse dieting mood than today, because you feel so guilty about all the food you ate yesterday. Yet, used correctly, the fact that you can eat a fairly large amount on some days and get away with it by compensating on others can be the saving of your figure.

Willpower is frequently over-estimated. It crumples simply because you are asking it to do the impossible. Buying yourself a fruity-topped cheesecake (your favourite food) and telling yourself that you will only have one tiny slice and not one crumb more is to attempt the impossible. In most cases this is sheer, foolhardy optimism. It would be much better to apply your willpower to not buying a fruity-topped cheesecake in the first place – that will probably only take up to 30 minutes of willpower while you are walking round the shops. Not eating all the cheesecake you have purchased is going to take you hours, and hours, worth of willpower. And do not think you can hide that goodie away in a tin or behind a cupboard door. Like some gorgeous daydream, that fruity-topped cheesecake will penetrate all physical barriers and be with you in spirit all day.

Another mistake many slimmers make is to opt for the fastest and strictest diet they can find. It is natural, usual and almost inevitable that you should experience this instinct. In the light of previous experience, though, consider whether you really can follow a diet which offers no sweet food, for instance. If a sugar craving killed off your last diet, do be realistic and admit that it is more than likely to strike again. In this book you'll find plenty of strict diets that will allow you to indulge in the foods you really crave.

Many would-be slimmers experience an almost masochistic tendency when they decide to diet; maybe it's a deep-down drive to punish themselves for having put on weight. They feel a positive urge to cut out all alcohol, sweet and starchy foods, anything that doesn't provide the pure and worthy aura of a carrot. If they can keep to this resolve, fine! But many people can't; in which case it is much better to include a small ration of 'indulgence' foods.

Willpower seems to wane with each passing hour of the day. We're not quite sure why. Maybe you get more tired. Maybe you get less busy. Whatever the reason, the later the hour the stronger the urge to break the slimming rules. Even the most ardent sweet-tooth slimmer is unlikely to eat an illicit chocolate bar for breakfast! So bear in mind that willpower which rises shining bright with the morning sun often sinks slowly in the west in the evening. If your willpower allows you to miss breakfast with no strain at all but decreases to such an extent that you are screaming for food in the evening, have your breakfast for supper. It makes no great difference when you eat, as long as you don't eat more than your total allowance for the day. Eat as little as you can during the day if you are an evening food yearner. Save your sweet goodies for the evening if you have a sweet tooth. Why work against your willpower when timing and rationing food for the day?

Willpower is often misdirected. There's the classic example of the housewife suffering from the blues who settles in with the chores on a wet Monday, all alone at home, and tells herself she will be strong-willed and avoid the biscuit tin. What a hope! It's much better to direct your willpower towards doing something to lift and alter the course of the day. You may not feel like telephoning a friend and getting out; doing that takes willpower when you're in a 'poor old me' mood. Think again. It takes only a short burst of willpower to step out of the front door or pick up the telephone – and from then on your spirits start on an upward trend. Staying in and not eating takes sixteen hours of solid willpower (assuming you sleep eight hours at night). That's an awful strain. If you simply can't get out, try writing down five dreary jobs that you ought to do and haven't done and will do today. Now work through them and tick them off methodically. Sounds totally depressing? Just wait until that feeling of virtue envelops you as you get under way. Wearing a halo is a sure way to boost your willpower.

Willpower is fortified by the truth and wanes under the weight of guilty secrets. Privately facing up to any weakness does wonders and confession is good for the willpower as well as the soul. If you are riddled with guilt about what you've eaten today, tell somebody, anybody – even though that sometimes takes a little willpower, too. Willpower is inclined to be deceitful. Other people are generally less than honest and tend to tell you when they have been strong-willed about their eating but evade telling you when they have just eaten half a fruit cake, three pork pies and a bowl of muesli with sugar and the top of the milk. That's one of the reasons why you think you lack willpower. You don't. You have got just as much willpower potential as anyone else.

Now use it to get back on that diet.

More power to your elbow
Here are ten tips to keep a slimmer's will strong and her/his arm in the anti-grab position.

1 Cook and shop on a satisfied stomach. If you are hungry it takes almost superhuman strength of will not to pick when preparing food. In the same way high-calorie goodies in the supermarket seem doubly attractive and more difficult to resist just before lunch.

2 Go shopping with a list. It's the impulse buy that can do a lot of damage to your diet, so decide what you need as far in advance as you can and don't deviate.

3 Plan all your meals ahead. Do this at least one day in advance; some super-organised slimmers can work out a whole week's menus ahead.

4 Cut down the time you spend in the kitchen. In other words don't linger longer than strictly necessary in the danger area. If you have a

freezer you can often manage with one or two weekly cook-ups for the family, rather than one or two a day.

5 Keep some low-calorie items prepared. If you always have radishes, celery and similar nibbles to hand, you won't meet a sudden irresistible eating urge with an instant biscuit.

6 Remember that many drinks are unrestricted. Tea with lemon and coffee without milk and cream (both unsugared) can give you a lift without adding a calorie. So can the many low-calorie soft drinks now sold specially for slimmers.

7 Save ahead for special dates. Enjoy a party or meal out occasionally by cutting your calorie consumption in advance so that you can afford to be a bit less strict. Yes, you can 'pay back' any extra calories consumed by being sterner afterwards, but you'll feel more relaxed if you do it in advance.

8 Be artful over party drinks. A Slimline tonic with ice and lemon appears indistinguishable from a gin and tonic with ice and lemon. If you can't avoid one initial gin, then top it up all evening with low-calorie tonic or bitter lemon.

9 Avoid tempting sights and scents. If the whiff from the baker's shop drives you wild, allow time for a lengthy detour; the extra exercise will do you nothing but good. Run past unavoidable sweet shop displays.

10 Remember your ultimate goal. Don't dwell solely on reaching your target weight but keep thinking about all the dreams that can come true when you are slim. Set against the thrill of becoming a bikini belle or being able to buy clothes in your ideal size without any difficulty at all, of stunning your family and friends with your new shape, a cream bun can suddenly seem quite unimportant.

KNOW YOUR ENEMIES

W hich single edible item can put your diet in most danger? Well, taking a look at the biggest temptations around, it's hard to point a finger at just one food as The Most Fattening Of All. Here, however, we pick out the top six fatteners, starting with an almost universal diet destroyer.

CHOCOLATE

It isn't simply a matter of chocolate being high in calories – though, at 150 calories an ounce, it is extremely high. To make a champion fattener there have to be additional factors. First, chocolate's calories are very concentrated: it doesn't, alas, take a large quantity of chocolate to make a nasty dent in a dieter's calorie allowance. Perhaps the most important factor is that all these calories are crammed into a very palatable form of food. Chocolate is so more-ish that most of us would have no trouble at all in getting through an average 50g/2oz bar within minutes – even seconds! And there are few people who, if common politeness or public shame didn't dictate otherwise, would not go on to eat considerably more if there were any more going. In fact, the sheer physical ease with which we can polish off a lot of chocolate in one go is another key factor in making it so fattening. It comes ready to eat and takes no chewing. Given the chance, it literally melts in the mouth. Nobody is inclined to eat nearly so much of foods that take a bit of work. It's not unusual to hear of a woman having a chocolate binge, but we've yet to hear of anyone bingeing on half a dozen steaks!

To a dieter, chocolate has yet another built-in danger. As it slips down so easily, it tends to be eaten between meals – in addition to all the other foods we eat. Most people can eat quite a lot of chocolate mid-morning or mid-afternoon and still go on to enjoy meat pies and steak and chips for lunch or supper.

When we asked 100 slimmers to tell us about their chocolate-eating habits, we were not at all surprised to find that the majority had often eaten three or four thick bars or a whole box of chocolates at a sitting. But who, a slimmer or not, has ever been known to stop at just one little square of a chocolate bar? It seems that just a taste of the stuff is liable to trigger off a desire for more. Indeed, so many people say they can't stop once they've started, and that they even have cravings for chocolate 'out of the blue' from time to time, that it raises the question of whether chocolate contains some special substance to give it an almost addictive quality.

Besides fat, sugar and cocoa, it does contain the stimulant caffeine. There is nearly as much caffeine in a 100g/3½oz bar of plain chocolate as there is in a cup of instant coffee. There is less caffeine, about half as much, in a bar of milk chocolate. In our nutritionists' view, though, there really isn't enough caffeine in chocolate to have any significant effect on the central nervous system. Caffeine, however, is known to be mildly addictive, and it just could be that its presence even in small quantities contributes to chocolate's 'kick'.

Whatever the reasons for chocolate's almost irresistible powers of temptation, there is no doubt that many people face extreme difficulty in curbing their cravings after the first taste; and for many a slimmer, a chocolate binge spells the demise of a diet. If chocolate happens to be your slimming downfall, the best way to learn to cope with it and bring it under control is to recognise what is normal behaviour in relation to chocolate and what is abnormal. You have probably, without knowing it, been trying to behave abnormally! For instance, it is abnormal for a slimmer to be able to keep a bar of chocolate in the house and go through an entire day without finishing it off. In fact, few people can do this. So if you ever find yourself tempted to buy chocolate 'to last me through the week' – don't. Unless you have abnormal self-control, that chocolate will be eaten before the next sun has set. It is just as difficult to be able to resist chocolate kept in the house by other people or for other people. So guard against this 'for other people' factor, too. We have found that the normal woman who feels guilty about eating chocolate because she is trying to lose weight will find all sorts of reasons for buying it for somebody else in the house.

Chocolate cravings are often most intense in the evening when you are tired and your will-power is at its lowest ebb. This is when the chances are very high that you will help yourself to some of the chocolate you bought for everybody else. Cravings can be triggered off by the sight of somebody else eating it or merely the smell of it; so a family ban on eating chocolate right in front of your eyes and nose makes the best kind of sense. Even if they kindly keep their chocolate out of sight, you'll have times when you feel compelled to hunt it out.

Chocolate cravings are not confined to those with a weight problem. Practically everybody who likes chocolate experiences cravings from time to time. The difference is one of degree. A slim person may well say he or she experiences a craving for chocolate very occasionally and that just one chocolate bar is enough to satisfy it. Those who are overweight tend to experience cravings much more often and eat much more chocolate before they are satisfied.

The other trigger that makes most people buy chocolate without thinking is seeing it in front of them in the shops. How often, for example, have you gone in to pay the newspaper bill – and come out with chocolate along with the receipt? Consciously cut down the number of times you are presented with a close-up of chocolates on sale. Get somebody else to pay your newspaper bill, if necessary! The vital thing to remember is that if you have chocolate around, you will eat it. If you see it, you will probably buy it. The answer is to cut it out of your life as much as possible.

PASTRY

At first sight pastry does appear to be a fairly controllable danger. It certainly lacks the magnetism and charisma of chocolate. Neither does it possess the mouth-watering appeal of cakes smothered in fresh cream or the sheer more-ishness of peanuts and crisps. In fact, pastry lacks the star, tantalising quality shared by some of the other major threats to your figure. Well, would you relish an egg-and-bacon flan with the same enthusiasm that you could fancy a box of chocolates? But please, please be warned. What it lacks in obvious appeal, it makes up for in fattening power. At 160 calories per 25g/1oz of flaky pastry and 150 calories for the same amount of shortcrust, this particular threat has a danger rating to rival chocolate (150 calories an ounce). A fruit pie can be much higher in calories than a cream-filled cake. All things considered, pastry is explosive stuff and needs to be handled warily.

What makes it so insidious is its ability to appear everywhere. It is used to line, contain or support hosts of other foods in a variety of guises. Unless you train yourself to recognise and dodge the enemy, the calorie cost can add up alarmingly. We are sure you can remember occasions when you went into a pub for lunch or met a friend in a self-service restaurant. We bet you grudgingly sloped past the banks of sausages and mash, lasagne and other creamy fattening dishes to arrive at the salad counter. There, probably sitting among a mound of lettuce, was the noble quiche. You probably saw this as your best slimming option. But an average slice of quiche can easily top 500 calories.

Another peculiar quirk of pastry is the way in which it pops up in tempting bite-size savouries at buffet parties. Beware. That luscious-looking little vol-au-vent is at least 100 calories – and how many of us can stop at one? A single tasty cheese straw is 15 calories – and we know that one straw can lead to 20. Ten minutes of haphazard feasting off a buffet tray, and you could easily consume 700 to 800 calories . . .

Perhaps one of the worst features of pastry is the terrible post-baking deeds it encourages. How many of us who set out to make one apple pie or quiche ever stop there? All those pastry left-overs are such a challenge. So, naturally enough, they are rolled into intricate combinations with jam, honey, currants – or whatever is lurking in your larder. They're tucked into the oven alongside the main event and emerge as tantalising bun-men, mini jam roly-polies or maxi cheese turnovers. If you have to bake at all (and, harsh though it sounds, we suggest you don't if at all possible), throw away your scraps. Save your creative powers for a lesser evil.

So how do you cope with this particular enemy? The best way, of course, is to be totally ruthless and cut pastry out altogether. If you can't – and we appreciate that mothers with young children find pastry-topped dishes easy, filling and economical – you can, at least, compromise. Working on the simple logic that the more pastry you use the more calories you have, a sensible compromise is to make the least amount of pastry go the furthest distance. For instance, an average portion of apple pie with pastry top and bottom is 450 calories; make that same pie with just one layer of pastry on top and none on the bottom and the calorie content of a portion works out at around 290. So: keep your pies bottomless and your tarts topless. It goes without saying, of course, that we expect you to tear up any recipe which suggests you wrap food in pastry.

CHEESE

Cheese is *not* a saintly food for slimmers. We can recall two slimmers completely fooled by this cheese myth. Both wailed that they had been 'dieting' for months and yet nothing had happened. After closer questioning, one slimmer revealed that she always chose cheese instead of dessert in a restaurant because it was 'more slimming' than the great fattening pud her friends were tucking into . . . while the other slimmer said that, instead of an evening meal, she had switched to just a few assorted chunks of cheese and a handful of biscuits because she thought this was less fattening than meat-and-two-veg. Both women recoiled in shock when we totted up the calories they were consuming. Our restaurant-eater was tucking into around 440 calories of cheese, butter and biscuits, more than is found in many restaurant desserts. And our evening 'saint' was innocently getting through 600-700 calories a night – all the time under the mistaken impression she was only indulging in a slimming snack. So, first, while cottage or curd cheese is every slimmer's friend, cheese in general is definitely not a safe slimming food to be eaten freely. Just 25g/1oz of Cheddar is 120 calories; and while some hard cheeses, like Edam, are lower at 88, most come in the 100-calories-plus category.

Like all high-calorie foods, cheese needs to be handled with supreme caution. We know another girl who has a lovely figure but struggles hard to keep surplus pounds at bay. 'It isn't as if I even have lunch every day,' she complained. 'All I have is a chunk of cheese and an apple.' We pointed out that her 'no-lunch lunch' added up to around 300 calories, the amount you would expect to spend on a complete low-calorie meal. Her reaction? 'But I've always thought I was safe with cheese. It's full of protein and so good for you, isn't it?' Well, we hate to shatter even more illusions but we have to knock myth number two on the head. Cheese does contain protein and we need some protein in our daily diet, but current nutritional thinking is that we don't need as much as was previously thought. Nor does 'lots of protein' do us more good than 'just enough'. Nutritionists today advise us to eat just a moderate amount, along with cereal foods, fruit and vegetables, as part of a mixed diet. And here's another attitude that might surprise you. In the view of some eminent nutritionists, including Derek Miller, *Slimming Magazine*'s Consultant Editor at Queen Elizabeth College, London, cheese doesn't really deserve that loose title of a protein food. He considers that it is more deserving of the description 'a fatty food'. There is more fat than protein in many hard cheeses – 33% fat to 26% protein in Cheddar, for instance; and many other cheeses, like Brie and Camembert, contain at least as much fat as protein. As nutritionists are encouraging us more and more to reduce the fat content in our diets, we should really treat cheese as gingerly as we would cream or pastry.

Cheese is a particularly subtle enemy in that it attacks when you're at your weakest . . . Its most persuasive quality is its availability. You perhaps wouldn't yearn for Cheddar in the same way you might hanker after a cream cake or a bar of chocolate. But if you felt a hunger pang right now in the middle of reading this and opened the fridge, what would jump up to greet you would be a lovely chunk of cheese! As one nibble often leads to ten or many many more, you are likely to consume quantities of calories thoughtlessly. The fact that most people buy it by the half-pound (at least) and keep it readily available in the house is what makes cheese such a threat. Many slimmers still see cheese dishes as light snacks, rather than the substantial meals their calorie contents proclaim them to be. The humble cheese sandwich can be a staggering 545 calories. Even the noble cheese salad – many a slimmer's staple – will be around 390 calories (much better to have lean ham or prawns with your salad instead).

So accept that cheese – with the exception of cottage cheese (27 calories per ounce) and curd cheese (40 calories an ounce) – is a highly fattening food. You need not eliminate it entirely from your diet but you should treat most kinds of cheese with the utmost respect. The golden rule is: never, never leave cheese lying footloose and free in your fridge. Plan your cheese meals carefully and buy exactly what you need as near to the event as you can. Hard cheese like Stilton and Cheddar will freeze well, so you could buy in bulk, freeze it and keep it out of sight, which removes the instant-nibble temptation. Incidentally, if cheesecake is a passion, buy it only in individual portions (around 260 calories). We don't know anyone who has ever bought a whole cheesecake and stopped after the first portion! One final word of warning. Never, never go anywhere near cheese if you're ravenously hungry. With this particularly powerful temptation, it is wise to avoid any contact at all unless you feel really strong. So have your favourite cheese meal or snack once, twice or even three times a week – but plan well, be prepared so that this enemy won't get the better of you.

BUTTER

If you are particularly partial to butter and tempted to be lavish in its use, you should put it right at the top of your own individual danger list. Of all the fattening foods, butter can easily be the one that makes the biggest difference to your weight. Nearly all butter's weight-gain dangers apply equally to margarine which has exactly the same calorie value. The only real difference between the two is that people tend to be rather less lavish with margarine. The inimitable combination of flavour and texture tempts butter fans to use generous quantities and margarine's easier 'spreadability' tends towards the use of more sparing quantities.

The first factor that makes butter such a danger is its calorie content. At 210 calories for one ounce it's twice as high as sugar, over three times as high as bread and nearly ten times as high as potatoes. The real menace about butter is that it insinuates its sky-high calorie count into and onto so many foods. A bit of butter on a slice of bread here and a pat of butter on a potato there can add up to a lot of calories in a day. The effect that cumulative tiny amounts can have was illustrated recently by one of *Slimming Magazine*'s readers who seemed to be eating in a careful and controlled way, but complained that she couldn't lose an ounce. Her usual breakfast was a couple of slices of toast. For lunch she had crispbreads and boiled eggs. Dinner seemed to be the ultimate in saintly restraint – fish and low-calorie vegetables with water biscuits and cottage cheese to follow. The typical menus she listed averaged out at 1,200 calories a day – a figure that should certainly result in weight loss. But surely she used some butter? Indeed she did: on toast, on crispbreads and on vegetables. Just to find out how much butter she got through in a typical day, we asked her to start with a fresh half-pound pack and give us what was left at bedtime. She had used 65g/2½oz – that's 525 calories. Her daily total now came to around 1,700 calories. Most people, we suspect, just don't realise how much butter they eat. *Slimming Magazine*'s home economists held a series of tea and dinner parties to get some clues. At each, they put a measured amount of butter on the table, then weighed what remained after the unsuspecting guests had helped themselves. They found that guests consistently ate at least 150 calories' worth of butter with sweetcorn and a minimum of half an ounce (105 calories) with a jacket potato. A crumpet saturated with butter takes a full half-ounce; and muffins and teacakes ought to come with horns and a tail because each one easily absorbs over 150 calories. Even a slice of bread buttered with a reasonably generous hand accounts for 70 calories in butter alone. It pays to be aware of how much we use in cooking, too. Most people use far too much butter in preparing dishes. If you make a white sauce with a roux of butter and flour, for example, it is impossible to use less than 105 calories' worth of butter to every quarter-pint of sauce. Following the average recipe for a rich casserole means pre-frying meat and vegetables in two or more ounces (420 or more calories) of butter. Most of us dot butter over breadcrumb-topped dishes, too, easily adding 100 extra calories. Our kitchen tests showed that an average portion of traditional mashed potatoes contains 55 calories of butter; and that a butter-dotted, grilled 175g/6oz fillet of plaice turns from 156 calories to 210 calories. Fresh fish absorbs less than frozen, but if you add the buttery juice from the pan you put on at least an extra 100 calories to this good dieting food.

Is there any substitute for butter? Yes, there is: but this leads us into an area of great confusion. Don't be fooled into thinking that margarines labelled 'high in polyunsaturates' or 'low cholesterol' are low-calorie. They are not. Labels like these are based on the claim that polyunsaturate fats help lower the body's cholesterol. Cholesterol is a health factor and not a calorie one, however, and margarines such as Flora have exactly the same calorie value as ordinary margarines and butter. The only kind of butter-substitute spreads which genuinely contain fewer calories are those labelled 'low fat', such as Outline or St Ivel Gold, which contain exactly half the calories of butter at 105 calories an ounce. Low-fat spreads do have the additional advantage of a soft texture which allows them to be spread very thinly. So you tend to spread less as well as halving the calories in what you spread. If you prefer to keep to butter you must be super strict and super accurate in the quantity you use each day if you want to lose weight. Reflect on the fact that the modest half-pound pack contains 1,680 calories. For speedy weight loss, you can't allow yourself more than half an ounce of butter a day, because even that uses up more than a tenth of a strict dieting allowance. If you do allow yourself more you'll have to cut down so much on plate and stomach filling food that hunger will get the better of your resolve. Half an ounce is such a small quantity that the only way to ensure accuracy is to measure it out each morning – and when you've finished your little pat, that's it for the day! Dipping into the family pack is a sure recipe for dieting disaster. Next time you reach for your butter knife, reflect that a half ounce, an amount easily lost on a thick slice of toast, contains as many calories as two scoops of ice cream or a small can of baked beans.

CREAM

Some years ago *Slimming Magazine*'s consultant editor, Derek Miller, set up a unique scientific experiment: to investigate the extent to which slim people could be made to put on weight by over-feeding. A major problem was to get his volunteers to find the time and tenacity to take in enough calories for the experiment's purposes – up to 9,000 a day! – before jaw fatigue and totally full-up feelings took over. He discovered that the best way to cram as many calories as possible into people was to use cream. Of all the high-calorie, tantalising foods at his disposal for the experiment, cream got the star prize because it played a sneaky double role. Not only did it slip down very easily on its own, but it also helped many other foods slip down more easily, too. Derek's overriding conclusion was: if you are prone to putting on weight and you want to get fat fast, then eat cream! It is its semi-liquid consistency which makes cream such a hazard. You can get through a lot very quickly – one gulp, a quick swallow and it's gone. Combine this with the fact that it is so high in calories and you'll appreciate why we feel that even a tablespoon of cream deserves to have danger written over it.

Our research suggests that, as far as cream is concerned, the world divides sharply into two. There are those who love it with reckless passion and the others who can't really see what the fuss is all about. May we suggest that, if you have a weight problem and feel indifferent about cream, then you gain from this by being able to cut cream completely out of your life? It makes sense when you are slimming to conserve calories for the foods you really can't live without. If, on the other hand, cream isn't a take-it-or-leave-it affair with you but a major craving, we do sympathise. Stay calm, though. There are ways of dealing with this particular addiction. Before we put forward our defence strategies, we would like to clear up some common creamy misunderstandings.

The biggest fallacy is that there is 'goodness' in cream, which obviously harks back to the old-fashioned notion that dairy produce is 'virtuous'. With modern nutritionists urging us to eat a low-fat, high-fibre diet with more fruit and vegetables, dairy produce has to some extent fallen from grace, especially with slimmers. While cheese, milk, eggs and meat do have important nutrients as well as fats, and moderate amounts of all these foods are still advisable, there is nothing to be said for cream. The bare fact is this: cream has very little nutritional value. It does contain a certain amount of the important fat-soluble vitamins A and D but the likelihood that going without cream will lead to vitamin deficiency is downright impossible. Another nutritional point: cream is virtually all saturated fat which means raised cholesterol levels in the bloodstream, and science seems to indicate at present that people with high cholesterol levels run a greater risk of heart disease.

Calorie-wise, cream is the iron fist in a velvet glove; it packs an enormous punch without your realising it. For this reason, it is important to know exactly where the enemy lurks. If you adopt an attitude whereby you don't accept anything which contains cream you will be half-way to conquering the enemy. Beware in particular of cream cheese, which contains 50 per cent cream. You needn't be so severe when it comes to soups and ice cream. While labelling regulations insist on a minimum of cream in any soup or ice cream product which says it contains cream, amounts could be quite small. For example, a 10.6oz tin of Heinz Cream of Tomato Soup contains only one per cent of cream and totals 235 calories. A plain tomato soup can be as high as 285 calories or as low as 65 calories. While all dairy ice creams contain at least five per cent butter or cream, an average 50g/2oz portion is still only 100 calories. Generally, the more expensive the ice cream, the more cream it contains. One golden rule in the game of compromise is: never cook with cream. It's so easy to add a spoonful (or two or three) to this and a great big blob to that. Before you know where you are, you have stirred about 300 or 400 calories into your sauce. When nothing but cream will do – with strawberries, say – then we suggest you buy 'half cream'. It's widely on sale now, and fools most people who haven't seen the carton that it's single cream. In fact, at 35 calories an ounce or 20 calories per tablespoon, it's the best cream option there is.

SUGAR

You may well feel that sugar is one major enemy that a slimmer hardly needs to be warned about. Out of all the everyday things we eat, sugar has just about the worst reputation. Indeed, we have lost count of the slimmers who swear that they don't take it in tea or coffee and never touch sweets, and if there were any justice in the world they'd be rewarded with a visibly shrinking shape. So why aren't they? The answer may surprise you. Sugar in itself isn't all that much of a calorie baddy. At 112 calories an ounce it is not nearly as high as many other much less wicked-looking foods. What can make sugar such a big fattener is that it keeps bad company. Once teamed with fat – in chocolates, toffees, cakes, pastry and cream gateaux – it becomes a diet-wrecking monster. A fruit gum made of sugar plus flavouring costs just 5 calories. A chocolate – with sugar and fat as partners in crime – will cost about 35. Don't, however, waste calories on sugary drinks. The amount of sugar that finds its way into cola-type and soft drinks like fizzy lemonades, tonics and bitter lemons amounts to a horror story. There's over an ounce in the average can – and quenching your thirst is a sure way to zoom up your calorie count. Seeing that all your drinks are labelled low-calorie makes slimming sense. As for sugar in tea and coffee, that's a terrible waste of calories too. Most people are likely to stir in two rounded teaspoons and drink around 60 calories that could be better enjoyed another way. If you still sugar your drinks, please stop! After a few sugarless weeks, if you're given a sweetened cuppa, you will wonder how you could ever have stood the stuff!

This is a habit that once broken stays broken. If you don't feel strong-minded enough to foreswear sweetened tea and coffee yet, you can switch to artificial no-calorie sweeteners.

There is no doubt that, on health grounds, too much sugar is bad. The scientific evidence gathered in research laboratories and from human guinea pigs shows that high sugar consumption can raise the blood's cholesterol level and lead to a number of bodily disorders including diabetes-associated changes. From a slimming point of view, an interesting idea to come out of all this research is that refined sugar isn't nearly as sustaining and satisfying as sugar that occurs in fruits with a high-fibre content. It has been proved that people who habitually eat vast quantities of refined sugar and sugary foods often develop 'backlash' hunger within an hour or two of a sugary meal. There is a good physiological reason for this. When you eat a lot of refined sugar, the sudden rush of sugar increases the sugar (glucose) level in the blood. So your body produces a rush of insulin to reduce this very high blood sugar level to normal. However, in restoring the status quo, it may reduce the blood sugar levels too much – and your temporarily lowered levels make you feel hungry again. If, however, you eat sugar in a high-fibre 'pack' – in dried or fresh fruits – the digestive process is slower. Sugar is gradually released and the body gradually produces insulin to cope with it. Your energy levels are maintained and you go on ticking over nicely without feeling any 'backlash' hunger. When you crave something sweet, the best thing is a piece of sweet fruit. Apples and pears are full of sugar and have a good fibre content as well. For something more chewy, dried fruits such as raisins, figs and dates give you sugar in a form that is full of fibre. These are highish in calories, though, so count them carefully.

If you really *can't* resist the sweet shop, avoid confectionery with fat in it. Go for wine gums, mints or fruit chews. They're mostly sugar and your dentist certainly won't be happy, but they won't do your shape as much harm as toffees or chocolate.

A–Z CALORIE CHART

Exact metric conversions have been given in the chart below. In the recipes in the main part of the book, as with the portions below, the metric equivalents have been rounded off for convenience. Average sizes of fruit and vegetables have been given.

A

Almonds
shelled,
per 28g/1oz — 160
ground, per
15ml/1
level tablespoon — 30
per almond,
whole — 10
per sugared
almond — 15

Anchovies
per 28g/1oz — 40
per anchovy fillet — 5

Anchovy Essence
per 5ml/1 level
teaspoon — 5

Angelica
per 28g/1oz — 90
per average stick — 10

Apples
eating, per
28g/1oz — 10
cooking, per
28g/1oz — 10
medium whole
eating, 150g/5oz — 50
medium whole
cooking, 225g/8oz — 80
apple sauce,
sweetened, per
15ml/1 level
tablespoon — 20
apple sauce,
unsweetened, per
15ml/1 level
tablespoon — 10
apple pie, average
slice with pastry

top and bottom,
125g/4oz — 420

Apricots
canned in natural
juice, per 28g/1oz — 13
canned in syrup,
per 28g/1oz — 30
dried, per
28g/1oz — 52
fresh with stone,
per 28g/1oz — 7
per dried apricot
half — 10
per apricot half,
canned in syrup — 15
per whole fruit — 7

Arrowroot
per 28g/1oz — 101
5ml/1 level
teaspoon — 10

Artichokes
globe, boiled, per
28g/1oz — 4
Jerusalem, boiled,
per 28g/1oz — 5

Asparagus
raw or boiled, per
28g/1oz — 5
per asparagus
spear — 4

**Aubergines
(Eggplants)**
raw, per 28g/1oz — 4
sliced, fried,
28g/1oz raw
weight — 60
whole aubergine,
200g/7oz — 28

whole aubergine,
sliced, fried,
200g/7oz raw
weight — 405

Avocado
flesh only, per
28g/1oz — 63
per half avocado,
105g/3¾oz — 235

B

Bacon
per 28g/1oz
back rasher, raw — 122
collar joint, raw,
lean and fat — 91
collar joint,
boiled, lean only — 54
collar joint,
boiled, lean and
fat — 92
streaky rashers,
raw — 118
1 streaky rasher,
well grilled or
fried, 20g/¾oz
raw weight — 50
1 back rasher,
well grilled or
fried, 35g/1¼oz
raw weight — 80
1 bacon steak,
well grilled,
100g/3½oz
average raw
weight — 105

Baking Powder
per 28g/1oz — 46

per 5ml/1 level
teaspoon 7

Bamboo Shoots
per 28g/1oz 10

Bananas
dried, per
28g/1oz 123
flesh only, per
28g/1oz 22
flesh and skin,
per 28g/1oz 13
small whole fruit,
150g/5oz 65
medium whole
fruit, 175g/6oz 80
large whole fruit,
200g/7oz 95
whole fruit,
peeled and fried
in batter,
175g/6oz raw
weight 170

Barcelona nuts
shelled, per
28g/1oz 181

Barley
pearl, raw, per
28g/1oz 102
pearl, boiled, per
28g/1oz 34
per 15ml/1 level
tablespoon, raw 45

Bass
fillet, steamed,
per 28g/1oz 35

Bean Sprouts
canned, per
28g/1oz 3
raw, per 28g/1oz 5

Beans
per 28g/1oz:
aduki, raw weight 92
baked, canned in
tomato sauce 20
black-eye, raw
weight 93
broad, boiled 14
butter, boiled 27

butter, raw
weight 78
cannellini, canned 38
French, frozen 10
haricot, boiled 26
haricot, raw
weight 77
Lima, raw weight 93
mung, raw weight 92
red kidney,
canned 25
red kidney, raw
weight 77
runner, boiled 5
runner, raw 7
snap, raw, green 10
soya, dry weight 115

Beech nuts
shelled, per
28g/1oz 160

Beef
per 28g/1oz:
brisket, boiled,
lean and fat 92
brisket, raw, lean
and fat 71
fillet steak,
medium grilled,
per 175g/6oz raw
weight 305
ground, lean, raw 45
ground, lean,
fried and drained
of fat 55
ground, lean,
fried and drained
of fat, per
28g/1oz raw
weight 40
minced, raw 63
minced, well fried
and drained of fat 55
minced, well fried
and drained of
fat, per 28g/1oz
raw weight 45
rump steak, fried,
lean only 54

rump steak, well
grilled, 175g/6oz
raw 260
rump steak,
medium grilled,
175g/6oz raw 290
rump steak, rare
grilled, 175g/6oz
raw 310
rump steak, raw,
lean and fat 56
silverside, salted,
boiled, lean and
fat 69
silverside, salted,
boiled, lean only 49
sirloin, roast, lean
and fat 80
sirloin, roast, lean
only 55
stewing steak,
raw, lean only 35
stewing steak,
raw, lean and fat 50
stewing steak,
stewed, lean and
fat 63
topside, raw, lean
only 35
topside, raw, lean
and fat 51
topside, roast,
lean and fat 61
topside, roast,
lean only 44

Beefburgers
fresh or frozen,
well grilled,
50g/2oz raw
weight 90
fresh or frozen,
grilled, 125g/4oz
raw weight 245

Beetroot
raw, per 28g/1oz 8
boiled, per
28g/1oz 12
per baby beet,

boiled	5	**Brains**		long sliced loaf	60
Bilberries		per 28g/1oz		medium slice,	
raw, per 28g/1oz	16	calves' and		from large sliced	
Biscuits		lamb's, raw	31	loaf	85
per average biscuit:		calves' boiled	43	medium slice	
Chocolate chip		lamb's boiled	36	from large long	
cookie	60	**Bran**		loaf	75
Digestive, large	70	per 28g/1oz	58	thick slice from	
Digestive,		per 15ml/1 level		large sliced loaf	100
medium	55	tablespoon	10	thick slice from	
Digestive, small	45	**Brandy butter**		long sliced loaf	90
Fig roll	65	per 28g/1oz	170	**Rolls, buns, etc.**	
Garibaldi, per		**Brawn**		baby bridge roll,	
finger	30	per 28g/1oz	43	15g/½oz	35
Ginger nut	40	**Brazil nuts**		bagel, 40g/1½oz	150
Ginger snap	35	shelled, per		bap, 40g/1½oz	130
Jaffa cake	50	28g/1oz	176	Bath bun,	
Lincoln	40	per nut	20	40g/1½oz	120
Malted milk	40	per buttered brazil	40	bread stick	15
Marie	30	per chocolate		brioche roll,	
Morning coffee	25	brazil	55	45g/1¾oz	215
Nice	45	**Bread**		Chelsea bun,	
Osborne	35	per 28g/1oz slice:		90g/3¼oz	255
Petit Beurre	30	black rye	90	croissant,	
Rich tea finger	25	bran	65	40g/1½oz	165
Rich tea, round	45	brown or		65g/2½oz	280
Sponge finger	20	wheatmeal	63	crumpet,	
Blackberries		currant	70	40g/1½oz	75
raw, per 28g/1oz	8	enriched, eg		crusty roll, brown	
stewed, without		cholla	110	or white,	
sugar, per 28g/1oz	7	French	65	45g/1¾oz	145
Blackcurrants		fried, 28g/1oz,		currant bun,	
fresh, per 28g/1oz	8	unfried weight	160	45g/1¾oz	150
stewed without		fruit sesame	120	Devonshire split,	
sugar, per		granary	70	65g/2½oz	195
28g/1oz	7	light rye	70	dinner roll, soft,	
Black pudding		malt	70	40g/1½oz	130
raw, per 28g/1oz	78	milk	80	French toast,	
sliced, fried, per		soda	75	average slice	50
28g/1oz raw		Vogel	65	hot cross bun,	
weight	85	wheatgerm	65	50g/2oz	180
Bloaters		white	66	Hovis roll,	
fillet, grilled, per		wholemeal		45g/1¾oz	115
28g/1oz	71	(100%)	61	muffin, 60g/2¼oz	125
on the bone,		per slice, white bread:		pitta, 65g/2½oz	205
grilled, per		thin slice from		scone, plain,	
28g/1oz	53	large sliced loaf	75	50g/2oz	210
		thin slice from		soft brown roll,	

45g/1¾oz — 140
soft white roll,
45g/1¾oz — 155
tea cake, 50g/2oz — 155
wholemeal roll,
45g/1¾oz — 125
per 15ml/1 level tablespoon:
breadcrumbs, dried — 30
breadcrumbs, fresh — 8
bread sauce — 15

Breakfast cereals
per 28g/1oz:
All Bran — 70
Cornflakes — 100
Muesli or Swiss style — 105
Porridge oats — 115
Puffed wheat — 100
Sultana bran — 90
Weetabix or whole wheat biscuits, per biscuit — 55

Broccoli
raw, per 28g/1oz — 7
boiled, per 28g/1oz — 5

Brussels sprouts
raw, per 28g/1oz — 7
boiled, per 28g/1oz — 5

Butter
all brands, per 28g/1oz — 210

C

Cabbage
per 28g/1oz:
raw — 6
boiled — 4
pickled red — 3

Cakes
Home-made, per average slice or small cake:
butterfly cake, 35g/1¼oz — 202
cherry cake, 75g/3oz slice — 335
chocolate cake, filled with butter icing and topped with chocolate glacé icing, 125g/4oz — 525
Christmas cake, or wedding, with marzipan and royal icing, 100g/3½oz — 350
Eccles cake, 50g/2oz — 290
flapjack, 40g/1½oz piece — 300
fruitcake, plain, 75g/3oz slice — 300
jam tart, 28g/1oz — 110
Madeira cake, 75g/3oz — 335
mince pie, 40g/1½oz — 185
scone, plain, 50g/2oz — 210
sponge sandwich, jam filled, whisked fatless method, 40g/1½oz slice — 130
Victoria sandwich, jam filled, 50g/2oz slice — 260
Fresh cream cakes:
Per average cake:
chocolate eclair, 71g/2½oz — 275
cream doughnut, 71g/2½oz — 260
cream slice, with puff pastry and glacé icing, 100g/3½oz — 420
meringue, 71g/2½oz — 195
strawberry tart, 75g/3oz — 200

Candied peel
per 28g/1oz — 90
per 15ml/1 level tablespoon — 45

Candy floss
per 28g/1oz — 80
per medium stick — 60

Capers
per 28g/1oz — 5

Carrots
raw, per 28g/1oz — 6
boiled, per 28g/1oz — 5
per average carrot, 50g/2oz — 12
sliced, fried, 28g/1oz raw weight — 30

Cashew nuts
shelled, per 28g/1oz — 160
per nut — 15

Cassava
fresh, per 28g/1oz — 45

Cauliflower
raw, per 28g/1oz — 4
boiled, per 28g/1oz — 3

Caviar
per 28g/1oz — 75

Celeriac
boiled, per 28g/1oz — 4

Celery
raw, per 28g/1oz — 2
boiled, per 28g/1oz — 1
per stick of celery — 5

Cheese
per 28g/1oz:
Austrian smoked — 78
Babybel — 97
Bavarian smoked — 80
Blue Stilton — 131
Bonbel — 102

Boursin 116
Bresse bleu 80
Brie 88
Caerphilly 120
Caithness full fat soft 110
Caithness Morven 110
Camembert 88
Cheddar 120
Cheese spread 80
Cheshire 110
Cheviot 120
Cotswold 105
Cottage cheese, plain, or with chives, onion, peppers or pineapple 27
cream cheese 125
curd cheese 40
Danbo 98
Danish blue 103
Danish Elbo 98
Danish Esrom 98
Danish Fynbo 100
Danish Havarti 117
Danish Maribo 100
Danish Molbo 100
Danish Mozzarella 98
Danish Mycella 99
Danish Samsoe 98
Derby 110
Dolcellata 100
Double Gloucester 105
Edam 88
Emmenthal 113
Fetta 54
Gorgonzola 112
Gouda 100
Gruyère 132
Ilchester cheddar and beer 112
Jarlsberg 95
Lancashire 109
Leicester 105
Norwegian blue 100

Norwegian Gjeost 133
Orangerulle 92
Orkney Claymore 111
Parmesan 118
Philadelphia 90
Port Salut 94
processed 88
Rambol, with walnuts 117
Red Windsor 119
Riccotta 55
Roquefort 88
Sage Derby 112
skimmed milk soft cheese (Quark) 25
St Paulin 98
Tôme au raisin 74
Wensleydale 115
White Stilton 96

per 15ml/1 level tablespoon:
cheese spread 50
cottage cheese 15
cream cheese 60
curd cheese 20
Parmesan cheese, grated 30

Cherries
fresh, with stones, per 28g/1oz 12
per cocktail cherry 10
glacé, per 28g/1oz 60
per glacé cherry 10

Chestnuts
per 28g/1oz
shelled 48
with shells 40
unsweetened chestnut purée 30

Chick peas
per 28g/1oz, raw 91

Chicken
per 28g/1oz:
on bone, raw, no skin 25
meat only, raw 34
meat only, boiled 52

meat only, roast 42
meat and skin, roast 61
chicken breast, fried, 170g/6oz, average raw weight 215
chicken breast, fried and skin removed, 170g/6oz, average raw weight 150
chicken breast, grilled, 170g/6oz, average raw weight 200
chicken drumstick, raw, 100g/3½oz average raw weight 90
chicken drumstick, fried, 100g/3½oz average raw weight 105
chicken drumstick, fried in egg and breadcrumbs, 100g/3½oz average raw weight 130
chicken drumstick, grilled and skin removed, 100g/3½oz average raw weight 65
chicken drumstick, grilled, 100g/3½oz average raw weight 85
chicken leg joint, raw, 225g/8oz

average weight 410
chicken leg joint,
grilled and skin
removed, 225/8oz
average raw
weight 165
chicken leg joint,
grilled, 225g/8oz 250
chicken leg joint,
fried, 225g/8oz
average raw
weight 285

Chicory
raw, per 28g/1oz 3
essence, per
28g/1oz 60

Chillies
dried, per
28g/1oz 85

Chinese leaves
raw, per 28g/1oz 3

Chives
per 28g/1oz 10

Chocolate
per 28g/1oz:
milk or plain 150
cooking 155
filled chocolates 130
Vermicelli 135
per 5ml/1 level
teaspoon:
chocolate spread 20
drinking chocolate 10
Vermicelli 20

Clams
with shells, raw,
per 28g/1oz 15
without shells,
raw, per 28g/1oz 25

Cob nuts
with shells, per
28g/1oz 39
shelled, per
28g/1oz 108
per nut 5

Cockles
without shells,
boiled, per 28g/1oz 14

Cocoa powder
per 28g/1oz 89
per 5ml/1 level
teaspoon 10

Coconut
per 28g/1oz
fresh 100
desiccated 172
coconut ice 110
coconut milk, per
28ml/1fl oz 6
creamed coconut 218
desiccated, per
15ml/1 level
tablespoon 30

Cod
per 28g/1oz:
fillet, raw 22
fillet, baked or
grilled with a
little fat 27
fillet, poached in
water or steamed 24
frozen steaks, raw 19
on the bone, raw 15
fillet in batter,
deep fried,
175g/6oz raw
weight 460

Cod Liver Oil
per 5ml/1 level
teaspoon 40

Cod roe
raw, hard roe,
per 28g/1oz 32
fried in egg and
breadcrumbs, per
28g/1oz 55

Coffee
per 28g/1oz:
coffee and chicory
essence 60
instant 28
instant coffee, per
10ml/1 rounded
teaspoon 0

Coley
per 28g/1oz:

raw 21
on the bone,
steamed 24
fillet, steamed 28

Cooking or salad oil
per 28g/1oz 255
per 15ml/1 level
tablespoon 120

Corned beef, canned
per 28g/1oz 62

Cornflour
per 28g/1oz 100
per 15ml/1 level
tablespoon 33

Cornish pasty
per average pasty,
150g/5oz 470

Corn oil
per 28g/1oz 255
per 15ml/1 level
tablespoon 120

Corn on the cob
fresh, boiled,
kernels only, per
28g/1oz 35
average whole cob 85

Cough syrup
thick, per 5ml/1
teaspoon 15
thin, per 5ml/1
teaspoon 5

Courgettes
raw, per 28g/1oz 4
per courgette,
70g/2½oz 10
sliced, fried, per
28g/1oz 15

Crab
with shell, per
28g/1oz, boiled 7
meat only, per
28g/1oz, boiled 36
average crab with
shell 95

Cranberries
raw per 28g/1oz 4

Cranberry sauce
per 28g/1oz 65

per 15ml/1 level
tablespoon 45

Cream

per 28g/1oz:

clotted	165
double	127
half cream	35
imitation	85
single	60
soured	60
sterilised, canned	65
whipping	94

per 15ml/1 level
tablespoon:

clotted	105
double	60
half cream	20
imitation	55
single	30
soured	30
sterilised, canned	35
whipping	45

Crispbreads

per average crispbread	30

Crisps (potato)

all flavours, per 28g/1oz	150

Cucumber

raw, per 28g/1oz	3

Currants

per 28g/1oz	69
per 15ml/1 level tablespoon	21

Curry paste or concentrate

per 28g/1oz	40

Curry powder

per 28g/1oz	66
per 5ml/1 level teaspoon	12

Custard

per 150ml/¼ pint
serving, made
with custard
powder, sugar
and skimmed
milk 135

per 150ml/¼ pint
serving, made
with custard
powder, sugar
and whole milk 175

Custard apple

flesh only, per
28g/1oz 25

Custard powder

per 28g/1oz	100
per 15ml/1 level tablespoon	33

D

Damsons

fresh, with stones,
per 28g/1oz 10
stewed, no sugar,
per 28g/1oz 8

Dates

per 28g/1oz:

dried, with stones	60
dried, without stones	70
fresh, with stones	30
per date, fresh	15

Delicatessen sausages

per 28g/1oz:

Belgian liver sausage	90
Bierwurst	75
Bockwurst	180
Cervelat	140
Chorizo	140
Continental liver sausage	85
Frankfurter	78
French garlic sausage	90
garlic sausage	70
ham sausage	50
Kabanos	115
Krakowska	80
liver sausage	88
Mettwurst	120
Mortadella, Italian	105
Pastrami	65
Polish country sausage	60
Polony	80
pork boiling ring, coarse	110
salami, Belgian	130
salami, Danish	160
salami, Hungarian	130
salami, German	120
Saveloy	74
smoked Dutch sausage	105
smoked ham sausage	65
smoked pork sausage	130

Dripping

per 28g/1oz	253
per 15ml/1 level tablespoon	125

Duck

per 28g/1oz:

raw, meat only	35
raw, meat, fat and skin	122
roast, meat only	54
roast, meat, fat and skin	96

Duck eggs

100g/3½oz egg	170

E

Eel

meat only, raw,
per 28g/1oz 48
meat only,
stewed, per
28g/1oz 57
jellied eels, plus
some jelly,
75g/3oz 180

Eggs (each)	**raw**	**fried**
size 1	95	115
size 2	90	110
size 3	80	100
size 4	75	95
size 5	70	90

raw fried

	raw	fried
size 6	60	80
size 3 yolk		65
size 3 white		15
scrambled eggs, made with two (size 3) eggs, 7g/¼oz butter and 15ml/1 tablespoon milk		225
omelet, plain, made with two (size 3) eggs, and 7g/¼oz butter		215

Endive
raw, per 28g/1oz 3

F

Faggots
per 28g/1oz 75

Fennel
raw, per 28g/1oz 6
boiled, per 28g/1oz 8

Figs
dried, per 28g/1oz 60
fresh, green, per 28g/1oz 12
per dried fig 30

Fish cakes
per average fish cake, grilled or baked without added fat 60

Fish fingers
per average fish finger, grilled without added fat 50

Flounder
on the bone, raw, per 28g/1oz 20
on the bone, steamed, per 28g/1oz 15

Flour
per 28g/1oz:
wheatmeal 93
white, plain 99
white, self-raising 96
white, strong 96
wholemeal 90
buckwheat 99
cassava 97
granary 99
maizemeal (96%) 103
maizemeal (60%) 101
rice 100
rye (100%) 95
soya, low fat 100
soya, full fat 127
yam 90
per 15ml/1 level tablespoon:
white 32
wholemeal 29

French dressing
per 15ml/1 tablespoon 75

Fruit
crystallised, per 28g/1oz 75

G

Gammon
per 28g/1oz:
joint, raw, lean and fat 67
joint, boiled, lean and fat 76
joint, boiled, lean only 47
rashers, grilled, lean and fat 67
rashers, grilled, lean only 49
rashers, per 175g/6oz raw weight 260

Garlic
one clove 0

Gelatine, powdered
per 15ml/1 level tablespoon 30
per 28g/1oz 96
per 10g/½oz

envelope 35

Ghee
per 28g/1oz 235

Gherkins
per 28g/1oz 5

Ginger
ground, per 28g/1oz 73
ground, 5ml/1 level teaspoon 8
stem, drained, per 28g/1oz 60

Goose
roast, on bone, per 28g/1oz 55
roast, meat only, without skin, per 28g/1oz 90

Gooseberries
fresh, ripe dessert, per 28g/1oz 10
fresh, cooking, per 28g/1oz 5

Grapefruit
per 28g/1oz:
canned in syrup 17
canned in natural juice 11
flesh only 6
flesh and skin 3
juice, unsweetened, per 28ml/1 fl oz 9
medium whole fruit, 350g/12oz 36
sweetened canned juice, 125ml/4fl oz 45
unsweetened juice, 125ml/4fl oz 35

Grapes
black, per 28g/1oz 14
white, per 28g/1oz 17
per grape 4

Gravy
per 30ml/2 tablespoons, thick, made with meat

dripping 30
thick, no fat 10
thin, no fat 5
Greengages
fresh, with stones,
per 28g/1oz 13
stewed, with
stones, no sugar,
per 28g/1oz 11
Grenadine syrup
per 28g/1oz 72
Ground rice
per 28g/1oz 100
per 15ml/1 level
tablespoon 33
Grouse
roast, meat only,
per 28g/1oz 50
Guavas
canned, per
28g/1oz 17
medium whole
fruit, with seeds 16
Guinea fowl
roast, on bone,
per 28g/1oz 30
roast, meat only,
per 28g/1oz 60

H
Haddock
per 28g/1oz:
fillet, raw 21
fillet in bread-
crumbs, fried 50
on the bone, raw 15
on the bone, in
breadcrumbs,
fried 45
smoked fillet,
steamed or
poached in water 29
fillet in bread-
crumbs, fried,
175g/6oz raw
weight 435
fillet in batter,
deep-fried,

175g/6oz raw
weight 460
Haggis
cooked, per
28g/1oz 89
Hake
per 28g/1oz:
fillet, raw 20
fillet, steamed 30
fillet, fried 60
on the bone, raw 10
Halibut
per 28g/1oz:
fillet, steamed 37
on the bone, raw 26
on the bone,
steamed 26
steak, 175g/6oz 155
Ham
per 28g/1oz:
chopped ham roll
or loaf 75
boiled, lean 47
boiled, fatty 90
honey roast 50
old smokey 65
Maryland 55
Virginia 40
steak, well grilled,
100g/3½oz
average raw
weight 105
Hare
stewed, meat
only, per 28g/1oz 55
stewed, on bone,
per 28g/1oz 39
Haslet
per 28g/1oz 80
Hazelnuts
shelled, per
28g/1oz 108
per nut 5
chocolate hazelnut
whirl, each 40
Heart
per 28g/1oz:
lamb's, raw 34

ox, raw 31
pig's, raw 26
whole lamb's
heart, roasted,
125g/4oz average
raw weight 270
Herring
per 28g/1oz:
fillet, raw 66
fillet, grilled 56
fillet in oatmeal,
fried 66
on the bone,
grilled 38
on the bone in
oatmeal, fried 66
Herring roe
fried, per 28g/1oz 69
raw, soft roe 23
Rollmop herring 47
rollmop, herring,
70g/2½oz
average weight 120
whole herring,
grilled,
128g/4½oz
average raw
weight 170
Honey
per 28g/1oz 82
per 5ml/1
teaspoon 18
Horseradish
fresh root, per
28g/1oz 17
horseradish sauce,
per 15ml/1 level
tablespoon 13
Humus
per 28g/1oz 50
**Hundreds and
Thousands**
per 5ml/1 level
teaspoon 15

I
Ice cream
per 28g/1oz:

215

chocolate	55	**Kiwi fruit**		grilled, 150g/5oz			
coffee	50	medium whole		raw weight	205		
Cornish dairy	52	fruit	30	leg steak,			
raspberry ripple	50			boneless, well			
soft ice cream	43	**L**		grilled, 225g/8oz			
strawberry	52	**Lamb**		raw weight	370		
vanilla	47	per 28g/1oz:		loin chop, well			
Icing		breast, boned,		grilled, 150g/5oz			
butter, per		raw, lean and fat	107	raw weight	175		
28g/1oz	145	breast, boned,		**Lard**			
royal, per 28g/1oz	85	roast, lean and fat	116	per 28g/1oz	253		
		breast, boned,		**Laverbread**			

chocolate 55
coffee 50
Cornish dairy 52
raspberry ripple 50
soft ice cream 43
strawberry 52
vanilla 47
Icing
butter, per
28g/1oz 145
royal, per 28g/1oz 85

J
Jam
per 28g/1oz 74
per 5ml/1 level
teaspoon 17
Jelly
cubes, as sold,
per 28g/1oz 73
made up with
water, per
150ml/¼ pint 85
per cube 29

K
Kidney
all types, raw, per
28g/1oz 25
lamb's kidney,
grilled, 50g/2oz
average raw
weight 50
lamb's kidney,
fried, 50g/2oz
average raw
weight 65
Kippers
fillet, baked or
grilled, per
28g/1oz 58
on the bone,
baked, per
28g/1oz 32
whole kipper,
grilled, 175g/6oz
raw weight 280

Kiwi fruit
medium whole
fruit 30

L
Lamb
per 28g/1oz:
breast, boned,
raw, lean and fat 107
breast, boned,
roast, lean and fat 116
breast, boned,
roast, lean only 72
leg, raw, lean
only without bone 46
leg, raw, lean and
fat without bone 68
leg, roast, lean
and fat, without
bone 76
leg, roast, lean
only, without
bone 54
scrag and neck,
raw, lean and fat,
weighed with
bone 54
scrag and neck,
raw, lean and fat,
weighed without
bone 90
scrag and neck,
stewed, lean only,
weighed with
bone 38
scrag and neck,
stewed, lean only,
weighed without
bone 72
scrag and neck,
stewed, lean and
fat, weighed
without bone 83
shoulder, boned,
roast, lean and fat 89
shoulder, boned,
roast, lean only 56
chump chop, well

grilled, 150g/5oz
raw weight 205
leg steak,
boneless, well
grilled, 225g/8oz
raw weight 370
loin chop, well
grilled, 150g/5oz
raw weight 175
Lard
per 28g/1oz 253
Laverbread
per 28g/1oz 15
Leeks
raw, per 28g/1oz 9
average whole
leek, raw 25
Lemon
flesh and skin,
per 28g/1oz 4
whole lemon,
150g/5oz 20
lemon juice, per
15-20ml/1
tablespoon 0
Lemon curd
per 28g/1oz 80
per 5ml/1 level
teaspoon 13
Lemon sole
per 28g/1oz:
fillet, steamed or
poached 26
on the bone, raw 23
on the bone,
steamed or
poached 18
Lentils
raw, per 28g/1oz 86
boiled, per
28g/1oz 28
Lettuce
fresh, per 28g/1oz 3
Liver
per 28g/1oz:
chicken's, raw 38
chicken's, fried 55
lamb's, raw 51

lamb's, fried	66	per 206g/7¼oz		**Marrow**	
ox, raw	46	can	255	raw, per 28g/1oz	5

lamb's, fried 66
ox, raw 46
ox, stewed 56
pig's, raw 44
pig's, stewed 54
lamb's, fried,
125g/4oz raw
weight 235
lamb's, grilled
without fat,
125g/4oz raw
weight 205
Lobster
with shell, boiled,
per 28g/1oz 12
meat only, boiled,
per 28g/1oz 34
Loganberries
fresh, per 28g/1oz 5
canned in syrup,
per 28g/1oz 28
Low-fat spread
all brands, per
28g/1oz 105
per 5ml/1 level
teaspoon 15
Luncheon meat
per 28g/1oz 89
Lychees
per 28g/1oz:
fresh, flesh only 18
canned 19
per lychee 8

M
Macadamia nuts
per 28g/1oz 188
Macaroni
white or whole-
wheat, raw, per
28g/1oz 105
boiled, per
28g/1oz 33
macaroni cheese,
per average
serving, 225g/8oz 395
macaroni cheese,

per 206g/7¼oz
can 255
Mackerel
per 28g/1oz:
fillet, raw 63
fillet, fried 53
on the bone, fried 39
kippered 62
smoked 70
whole raw
mackerel,
225g/8oz 318
Maize
whole grain, per
28g/1oz 103
Mandarins
canned, per
28g/1oz 16
fresh, with skin,
per 28g/1oz 7
medium whole
fruit, 70g/2½oz 20
Mango
raw, per 28g/1oz 17
canned, per
28g/1oz 22
medium, whole
fruit, 275g/10oz 100
mango chutney,
per 15ml/1 level
tablespoon 35
Maple Syrup
per 28g/1oz 70
per 5ml/1 level
teaspoon 17
Margarine
all brands except
those labelled
low-fat, per
28g/1oz 210
Marmalade
per 28g/1oz 74
per 5ml/1 level
teaspoon 17
Marron glacé
per medium
marron glacé 45

Marrow
raw, per 28g/1oz 5
boiled, per
28g/1oz 2
**Marzipan (Almond
Paste)**
per 28g/1oz 126
petit fours 126
Mayonnaise
per 28g/1oz 205
per 15ml/1 level
tablespoon 95
Medlars
flesh only, per
28g/1oz 12
Melon
per 28g/1oz:
Cantaloupe, with
skin 4
Honeydew or
Yellow, with skin 4
Ogen, with skin 5
watermelon, with
skin 3
slice of
Cantaloupe,
Honeydew or
Yellow, with skin,
225g/8oz 32
Milk
per 568ml/1 pint:
buttermilk 232
Channel Island or
gold top 432
evaporated, full
cream,
reconstituted 360
goat's 400
homogenised or
red top 370
semi-skimmed 300
instant dried
skimmed milk
with vegetable
fat, reconstituted 280
longlife or UHT 370
pasteurised or

silver top 370
pasteurised or
silver top with
cream removed,
500ml/18fl oz 240
skimmed or
separated 200
soya milk, diluted
as directed 370
sterilised 370
untreated farm
milk or green top 370
per 15ml/1 level
tablespoon:
Channel Island or
gold top 15
condensed full
cream, sweetened 50
condensed,
skimmed,
sweetened 40
evaporated, full
cream 23
homogenised,
pasteurised, green
top, silver top
and sterilised 10
instant low fat
milk, dry 18
instant low fat
milk,
reconstituted 5
skimmed or
separated 5
canned milk, per
28g/1oz:
evaporated full fat
milk 45
condensed,
skimmed,
sweetened 76
condensed, full
fat, sweetened 91
condensed,
unsweetened 40
Mincemeat
per 28g/1oz 67
per 15ml/1 level

tablespoon 40
per medium
mince pie 50g/2oz 250
Mint
fresh, per 28g/1oz 3
Mint Sauce
per 15ml/1 level
tablespoon 5
Molasses
per 28g/1oz 78
per 15ml/1 level
tablespoon 45
Muesli
per 28g/1oz 105
per 15ml/1 level
tablespoon 30
Mulberries
raw, per 28g/1oz 10
Mullet
raw, per 28g/1oz 40
Mushrooms
raw, per 28g/1oz 4
button, fried
whole, 50g/2oz
raw weight 80
button, sliced and
fried, 50g/2oz raw
weight 100
flat, fried whole,
50g/2oz raw
weight 120
flat, sliced and
fried, 50g/2oz raw
weight 150
Mussels
with shells,
boiled, per
28g/1oz 7
without shells,
boiled, per
28g/1oz 25
per mussel 10
Mustard
dry, per 28g/1oz 128
made English or
French mustard,
per 5ml/1 level
teaspoon 10

Mustard and cress
raw, per 28g/1oz 3
per carton 5

N
Nectarines
with or without
stones, per
28g/1oz 14
Noodles
cooked, per
28g/1oz 33
Nutmeg
powdered, per
2.5ml/½ teaspoon 0

O
Oatmeal
raw, per 28g/1oz 114
per 15ml/1 level
tablespoon, raw 38
Octopus
raw, per 28g/1oz 20
**Okra (ladies'
fingers)**
raw, per 28g/1oz 5
Olive oil
per 28ml/1fl oz 255
per 15ml/1 level
tablespoon 120
Olives
stoned, in brine,
per 28g/1oz 29
with stones, in
brine, per
28g/1oz 23
per stuffed olive 5
Onions
per 28g/1oz:
raw 7
boiled 4
fried 98
onion rings in
batter, fried 145
dried, per 15ml/1
level tablespoon 10
fried, per 15ml/1
level tablespoon 25

whole onion, raw, 75g/3oz	20
pickled onion, each	5
spring onion, each	5
cocktail onion, each	1

Oranges

flesh only, per 28g/1oz	10
flesh with skin, per 28g/1oz	7
whole fruit, small, 150g/5oz	37
whole fruit, medium, 225g/8oz	56
whole fruit, large, 275g/10oz	75

Orange juice

per 28ml/1fl oz:

sweetened	15
unsweetened	11

Oxtail

stewed, without bone, per 28g/1oz	69
on the bone, stewed and skimmed of fat, per 28g/1oz	26

Oysters

with shells, raw, per 28g/1oz	2
without shells, raw, per 28g/1oz	14
per oyster	5

P

Parsley

fresh, per 28g/1oz	6
parsley sauce, per 15ml/1 level tablespoon	45

Parsnips

per 28g/1oz:

raw	14
boiled	16

roast	30

Partridge

roast, on bone, per 28g/1oz	36
roast, meat only, per 28g/1oz	60

Passion fruit

flesh only, per 28g/1oz	10
with skin, per 28g/1oz	4

Pasta

all shapes, per 28g/1oz:

white, raw	105
white, boiled	33
wholewheat, raw	95
wholewheat, boiled	34

Pastry

per 28g/1oz:

choux, raw	61
choux, baked	94
flaky, raw	121
flaky, baked	160
shortcrust, raw	129
shortcrust, baked	150
wholemeal, raw	125
wholemeal, baked	145

Paw Paw (Papaya)

canned, per 28g/1oz	18
fresh, flesh only, per 28g/1oz	11
medium whole fruit	100

Peaches

canned in natural juice, per 28g/1oz	13
canned in syrup, per 28g/1oz	25
fresh, with stones, per 28g/1oz	9
whole fruit, 125g/4oz	35

Peanuts

per 28g/1oz:

shelled, fresh	162

dry roasted	160
roasted and salted	168
per peanut	5

Peanut butter

per 28g/1oz	177
per 5ml/1 level teaspoon	35

Pears

per 28g/1oz:

cooking pears, raw, peeled	10
dessert pears	8
canned in natural juice	11
canned in syrup	22
canned in syrup, drained, per half pear	30
whole fruit, medium, 150g/5oz	40

Peas

per 28g/1oz:

fresh, raw	19
frozen, boiled	15
canned, garden	13
canned, processed	23
dried, raw	81
dried, boiled	29
split, raw	88
split, boiled	34

per 15ml/1 level tablespoon:

dried, boiled	30
fresh or frozen, boiled	10

Pease pudding	35

Pecans

per nut	15

Pepper

powdered, per pinch	0

Peppers (Capsicums)

red or green, per 28g/1oz	4
average pepper, 150g/5oz	20

Perch
white, raw, per
28g/1oz   35
yellow, raw, per
28g/1oz   25
Pheasant
meat only, roast,
per 28g/1oz   60
on the bone,
roast, per 28g/1oz   38
Pickles and relishes
per 28g/1oz:
mixed pickles   5
Piccalilli   15
Ploughman's   35
sweet pickle   35
Pigeon
meat only, roast,
per 28g/1oz   65
on the bone,
roast, per 28g/1oz   29
Pike
raw, per 28g/1oz   25
Pilchards
canned in tomato
sauce, per 28g/1oz   36
Pimentos
fresh, per 28g/1oz   4
Pineapples
canned in natural
juice, per 28g/1oz   15
canned in syrup,
per 28g/1oz   22
fresh, per 28g/1oz   13
ring of canned,
drained pineapple
in syrup   35
ring of canned,
drained pineapple
in natural juice   20
ring of canned,
drained pineapple
in syrup, fried in
batter   65
Pistachio nuts
shelled, per
28g/1oz   180
per nut   5

Plaice
per 28g/1oz:
fillet, raw or
steamed   26
fillet, in batter,
fried   79
fillet, in bread-
crumbs, fried   65
whole fillet in
breadcrumbs,
175g/6oz raw
weight   435
Plantain
per 28g/1oz:
green, raw   30
green, boiled   35
ripe, fried   76
Plums
per 28g/1oz:
cooking plums
with stones,
stewed without
sugar   6
fresh dessert
plums, with stones   10
cooking plums,
with stones   7
Victoria dessert
plums, each   15
Pollack
on the bone, raw,
per 28g/1oz   25
Polony
per 28g/1oz   80
Pomegranate
flesh only, per
28g/1oz   20
whole
pomegranate,
205g/7¼oz   65
Popcorn
per 28g/1oz   110
Pork
per 28g/1oz:
belly rashers,
raw, lean and fat   108
belly rashers,
grilled, lean and

fat   113
fillet or
tenderloin, raw,
lean only   42
leg, raw, lean and
fat, weighed
without bone   76
leg, raw, lean
only, weighed
without bone   42
leg, roast, lean
and fat   81
leg, roast, lean
only   53
crackling   190
scratchings   185
crackling, average
portion, 9g/⅓oz   65
pork chop, well
grilled,
185g/6½oz raw
weight   240
pork pie,
individual,
150g/5oz   535
Potatoes
per 28g/1oz:
raw   25
baked, weighed
with skin   24
boiled, old
potatoes   23
boiled, new
potatoes   22
canned, new
potatoes, drained   20
chips (average
thickness)   70
chips (crinkle cut)   80
chips (thick cut)   40
chips (thin cut)   85
oven chips or grill
chips   55
crisps   150
roast, large
chunks   40
roast, medium
chunks   45

roast, small
chunks 50
sauté 40
instant mashed
potato powder,
per 15ml/1
tablespoon, dry 40
jacket-baked
potato, 200g/7oz
raw weight 170
jacket-baked
potato with
15g/½oz knob
butter 275
mashed potato,
150g/5oz raw
weight, mashed
with 45ml/3 table-
spoons skimmed
milk 140
mashed potato,
150g/5oz raw
weight, mashed
with 45ml/3 table-
spoons whole milk
and 7g/¼oz
butter 205
potato salad, per
28g/1oz 50
roast potato,
medium chunk,
45g/1¾oz 75
average portion
chips from fish
and chip shop,
200g/7oz 455
Prawns
with shells, per
28g/1oz 12
without shells, per
28g/1oz 30
per shelled prawn 2
Prunes
per 28g/1oz:
dried 46
stewed, without
sugar 21
prune juice 25

per prune 10
**Puddings and
desserts**
per portion:
apple crumble,
150g/5oz 295
apple pie, pastry
top and bottom,
125g/4oz 420
bread and butter
pudding,
150g/5oz 225
Christmas
pudding, 75g/3oz 260
custard tart,
75g/3oz 245
fruit pie, pastry
top only,
125g/4oz 205
jelly, 150ml/¼
pint 85
lemon meringue
pie, 125g/4oz 370
milk pudding,
home-made rice,
semolina or
tapioca, 175g/6oz 220
rice pudding,
canned, 175g/6oz 155
sponge pudding,
steamed,
150g/5oz 485
suet pudding,
steamed,
150g/5oz 470
treacle tart,
125g/4oz 420
trifle, 150g/5oz 225
Pumpkin
raw, per 28g/1oz 4

Q
Quiche
average slice,
125g/4oz 445
Quinces
raw, per 28g/1oz 7

R
Rabbit
per 28g/1oz:
meat only, raw 35
meat only, stewed 51
on the bone,
stewed 26
Radishes
fresh, per 28g/1oz 4
per radish 2
Raisins
dried, per
28g/1oz 70
per 15ml/1 level
tablespoon 25
Raspberries
fresh or frozen,
per 28g/1oz 7
canned, drained,
per 28g/1oz 25
Redcurrants
fresh, per 28g/1oz 6
redcurrant jelly,
per 5ml/1 level
teaspoon 15
Rhubarb
raw, per 28g/1oz 2
stewed without
sugar, per
28g/1oz 2
Rice
per 28g/1oz:
brown, raw 99
white, raw 103
boiled 35
pudding, home-
made 35
pudding, canned 25
per 15ml/1 level
tablespoon:
boiled 20
fried 35
raw 35
Rock
seaside rock, per
28g/1oz 95

Rock salmon (Dogfish)
fried in batter, per 28g/1oz — 75

S
Sago
raw, per 28g/1oz — 101
Saithe (Coley)
per 28g/1oz:
fillet, raw — 21
fillet, steamed — 28
on the bone, steamed — 24
Salad cream
per 28g/1oz — 110
per 15ml/1 level tablespoon — 50
low-calorie salad cream, per 28g/1oz — 50
low-calorie salad cream, per 15ml/1 level tablespoon — 25
Salmon
per 28g/1oz:
canned — 44
fillet, steamed — 56
on the bone, raw — 52
on the bone, steamed — 45
smoked — 40
Salsify
boiled, per 28g/1oz — 5
Salt
per 28g/1oz — 0
Sardines
canned in oil, drained, per 28g/1oz — 62
canned in tomato sauce, per 28g/1oz — 50
Sausages
per sausage:
beef chipolata,

well grilled — 50
beef, large, well grilled — 120
beef, skinless, well grilled — 65
pork chipolata, well grilled — 65
pork, large, well grilled — 125
pork, skinless, well grilled — 95
pork and beef chipolata, well grilled — 60
pork and beef, large, well grilled — 125
Sausage roll
small, 28g/1oz — 135
Scallops
steamed without shells, per 28g/1oz — 30
Scampi
peeled, raw, per 28g/1oz — 30
fried in breadcrumbs, per 28g/1oz — 90
Seakale
boiled, per 28g/1oz — 2
Semolina
raw, per 28g/1oz — 99
per 15ml/1 level tablespoon — 35
semolina pudding, per 28g/1oz, home-made — 35
semolina pudding, per 28g/1oz, canned — 25
Sesame seeds
per 28g/1oz — 165
Shepherd's pie
per average portion, 225g/8oz — 270

Shrimps
per 28g/1oz:
canned, drained — 27
fresh, with shells — 11
fresh, without shells — 33
Skate
fillet, in batter, fried, per 28g/1oz — 57
Smelts
without bones, fried, per 28g/1oz — 115
Snails
flesh only, per 28g/1oz — 25
Sole
per 28g/1oz:
fillet, raw — 23
fillet, fried — 61
fillet, steamed or poached — 26
on the bone, steamed or poached — 18
Spaghetti
per 28g/1oz:
raw — 105
wholewheat, raw — 95
boiled — 34
canned in tomato sauce — 17
Spinach
raw, per 28g/1oz — 7
boiled, per 28g/1oz — 9
Sprats
fried without heads, per 28g/1oz — 110
Spring greens
boiled, per 28g/1oz — 3
Spring onions
raw, per 28g/1oz — 10
Squid
flesh only, raw, per 28g/1oz — 25

Strawberries
fresh or frozen,
per 28g/1oz 7
canned, drained,
per 28g/1oz 23
per fresh
strawberry 2
Sturgeon
on the bone, raw,
per 28g/1oz 25
Suet
shredded, per
28g/1oz 235
per 15ml/1 level
tablespoon 85
Sugar
white or brown,
caster, Demerara,
granulated, icing,
per 28g/1oz 112
per 5ml/1 level
teaspoon 17
large sugar lump 20
small sugar lump 10
Sultanas
dried, per
28g/1oz 71
per 15ml/1 level
tablespoon 25
Sunflower seed oil
per 28g/1oz 255
per 15ml/1 level
tablespoon 120
Swedes
raw, per 28g/1oz 6
boiled, per
28g/1oz 5
boiled, per
15ml/1 level
tablespoon 5
Sweetbreads
lamb's, raw, per
28g/1oz 37
lamb's, fried, per
28g/1oz 65
Sweetcorn
canned in brine,
per 28g/1oz 22

canned, per
15ml/1 level
tablespoon 10
frozen, per
28g/1oz 25
whole cob 85
Sweets
per 28g/1oz:
barley sugar 100
boiled sweets 93
butterscotch 115
filled chocolates 131
fudge 111
liquorice allsorts 105
marshmallows 90
nougat 110
nut brittle or
crunch 120
peppermints 111
toffee 122
cough sweet,
boiled, each 10
cough pastille,
each 5
Syrups
per 28g/1oz:
golden 85
maple 70
rosehip 66
per 5ml/1 level
teaspoon:
cough syrup,
thick 15
cough syrup, thin 5
per 15ml/1 level
tablespoon:
golden 60
maple 50

T
Tangerines
flesh, only, per
28g/1oz 10
flesh with skin,
per 28g/1oz 7
whole fruit,
75g/3oz 20

Tapioca
dry, per 28g/1oz 102
Taramasalata
per 28g/1oz 135
Tartare sauce
per 15ml/1 level
tablespoon 35
Tea
all brands, per
cup, no milk 0
Tomatoes
per 28g/1oz:
raw 4
canned 3
fried, halved 20
fried, sliced 30
chutney 45
ketchup 28
purée 19
whole medium
tomato, 50g/2oz 8
tomato juice, per
115g/4fl oz 25
per 15ml/1 level
tablespoon:
chutney 45
ketchup 15
purée 10
Tongue
per 28g/1oz:
lamb's, raw 55
lamb's, stewed 82
ox, boiled 83
Treacle
black, per 28g/1oz 73
per 15ml/1 level
tablespoon 50
Treacle tart
per average slice,
125g/4oz 470
Tripe
dressed, per
28g/1oz 17
stewed, per
28g/1oz 28
Trout
fillet, smoked, per
28g/1oz 38

on the bone,
poached or
steamed, per
28g/1oz 25
whole trout,
poached or grilled
without fat,
175g/6oz 150
whole smoked
trout, 156g/5½oz 150

Tuna
per 28g/1oz:
canned in brine,
drained 30
canned in oil 82
canned in oil,
drained 60

Turkey
per 28g/1oz:
meat only, raw 30
meat only, roast 40
meat and skin,
roast 49

Turnips
raw, per 28g/1oz 6
boiled, per
28g/1oz 4
per 15ml/1 level
tablespoon,
mashed 4

V
Veal
per 28g/1oz:
cutlet, fried in
egg and
breadcrumbs 61
fillet, raw 31
fillet, roast 65
jellied veal,
canned 35
escalope, fried in
egg and bread-
crumbs, 75g/3oz
raw uncoated
weight 310
Venison
roast meat only,

per 28g/1oz 56
Vinegar
per 28ml/1fl oz 1

W
Walnuts
shelled, per
28g/1oz 149
per walnut half 15
Waterchestnuts
per 28g/1oz 25
Watercress
per 28g/1oz 4
Watermelon
flesh only, per
28g/1oz 6
flesh with skin,
per 28g/1oz 3
Wheatgerm
per 28g/1oz 100
per 15ml/1 level
tablespoon 18
Whelks
with shells,
boiled, per
28g/1oz 4
without shells,
boiled, per
28g/1oz 26
Whitebait
fried, per 28g/1oz 149
White pudding
as sold, per
28g/1oz 129
Whiting
per 28g/1oz:
fillet, fried 54
fillet, steamed 26
on the bone, fried 49
on the bone,
steamed 18
Winkles
with shells,
boiled, per
28g/1oz 4
without shells,
boiled, per
28g/1oz 21

Worcestershire sauce
per 28ml/1fl oz 20
per 15ml/ 1 level
tablespoon 13

Y
Yams
raw, per 28g/1oz 37
boiled, per
28g/1oz 34
Yeast
fresh, per 28g/1oz 15
dried, per
28g/1oz 48
dried, per 15ml/1
level tablespoon 8
Yogurt
per 28g/1oz:
low fat, natural 15
low fat, flavoured 23
low fat, fruit 27
low fat, hazelnut 30
Yorkshire pudding
cooked, per
28g/1oz 60